Celia's Secret

A Journey towards Reconciliation

Written as a memoir, this story follows the discovery of a secret.
It analyses the emotional impact on family members and searches for understanding and forgiveness.
It seeks reconciliation both for the living and for those beyond the grave.

Martha Ashwell

The majority of names in this story have been changed to preserve confidentiality.

ISBN: 978-1-326-23443-0

For my Family with love

To Sarah,

With best wishes,

Martha Ashwell

x

Acknowledgements

I would like to thank my sister, my brother, my husband, and my children for the support they have given me during the writing of this memoir.

I also thank Sarah Dyer, Maureen Froggatt, Stephanie Donaldson, Deirdre Peden, Sarah Swarbrick, Geraldine Rea, Rita Kecskes, Claire and Tom Jenkins and all friends who commented so kindly on the earlier drafts. I thank them all for their time and thoughtful criticism.

Several family photographs feature in the book and I am grateful to my family for allowing their inclusion.

I thank Anita Lowry, my long-lost second cousin, and her husband and family for welcoming me into their home and I acknowledge Samuel Hanna and Graham McAleer, local historians, for the help and information I received from them during my visit to Bessbrook.

Thanks are also due to Gwen Morrison of Publish Nation for patiently guiding me through the editing and publication process.

Finally, thanks to Robert Rochford robrochford@yahoo.co.uk for his help with my website www.marthaashwell.co.uk

Contents

This book contains several references to musical items which identify and heighten the author's memory of events.

Each item is noted and referenced to enable the reader to play the piece, if they wish, through the YouTube link given in the Catalogue of Music and Song at the end of the book.

Prologue

'The link between Love and Truth shall not be broken.'

Thomas Moore,[1] the contemporary American writer, describes the family as the nest into which soul is born, nurtured and released into life. Looking at the intricate dynamics of family life, he explains that families are complex and paradoxical; containing both good and bad influences and it is the combination of these positive and negative elements which enable children to adapt and grow. Through struggling with these forces the child emerges into adulthood. Children usually survive their experiences of family life but many carry noticeable scars and deficiencies which can remain with them, perhaps forever. The family, he says, is not a sentimental creation; it exists for a purpose and is a rite of passage. It is in coming to terms with these 'battle wounds' that we discover who we are. Undeniably, family life has a profound effect on the formation of the individual and one recognized truth is that the spirit of the child lives on in the adult.

Most families have their imperfections for they are only human. Their stories are an entanglement of secrets, memories and manipulations of the truth which throw light on the everyday workings of family life and how we manage its complexities. This memoir is the story of my family secret and its effect on me and other close family members. Family secrets can have serious long-term consequences. Sometimes, one family member may bear the burden of the secret alone fearing the consequences if the secret is divulged. Often it is not what is said that gives away the secret, but what is not said. Children can be left with a damaged sense of identity and a sense of sadness, loss and grief. They can feel that they have been profoundly betrayed. Pretending to be someone you are not is a waste of the person you are. Did you not love me enough to tell me the truth?

When I embrace the truth I am not always rewarded with a clear conscience and peace of mind? The truth is not always friendly and it is not always simple; it can cause pain and division. The truth can bind a person instead of setting them free. My story follows my own discovery of the family secret, my changed relationship with my mother and the enduring emotional fallout following that discovery. The process of reconciliation is woven, like a pattern, into my life story and has taken many years to achieve. A broken heart and anger will close a heart until honesty and love is found once again. I have put honesty and love at the heart of my search for reconciliation. I hope that these will remain an enduring legacy of this story.

---

[1] Moore, T. 'Care of the Soul' Piatkus (1992)

PART ONE
'The Beginning'

Chapter One

'You don't have a soul. You are a soul. You have a body.'
C. S. Lewis

A secret holds and binds you; it imprisons its victim in a dark cage in solitary confinement. I became the human animal circling my cage, trying to work out how to set myself free. How do I open the door without a handle? How do I break the lock that has no key? Can I escape without outside help? Will I ever be free again?

In the very beginning, I wasn't aware of the secret. War was giving a special intensity to life that had never been experienced before, and perhaps never would be again. In early February, it was snowing. It lay four inches deep on the little road in Withington, a suburb to the south of the city of my birth, Manchester. The blackened buildings of this important inland port and industrial giant were in the grip of war and it would be several decades before they would be blasted of their hundred years of grime. Today, it is a city of cleaner facades, standing upright and proud of its great heritage and industry. In 1942, it was producing the Rolls-Royce Merlin engines to power the

Spitfire, Hurricane and Mosquito Fighters and the Lancaster Bombers. Whilst making history with its constant supply of armaments it was hanging its head in the depression of war.

As far back as I can remember I have been aware of conflict. There are always wars raging somewhere in the world and they were raging at the time of my birth. As a small child, I sensed conflict within the family; there were constant tensions between my mother, Celia and my father, John. At that time anxiety and fear existed in almost every home in England because loved ones were either away fighting or working for the war as fire-fighters, in munitions factories, as ARP wardens, as canteen workers or on the land or in other equally fraught occupations. There must have been a palpable sense of fear and danger. Yet, for some, it was the most exciting time they had ever known, full of uncertainty and snatched romance. For many, the structure of orderly living had been shattered, restraints were removed, barriers extended. There was a feeling of buoyancy; of being anchorless. It was a time when rules and boundaries were set aside; 'Enjoy today, who knows what tomorrow may bring.' 'I would not have missed being in London throughout the war for anything,' the Anglo-Irish author Elizabeth Bowen recalled, 'It was the most interesting period in my life.' Of the blackout, she said, 'Nature tapped out with the heels on the pavement an illicit semaphore.' It seemed that new rules were being written to accommodate the changing social patterns; risks were being taken, opportunities were being grasped. There was an urgency to live life in the here and now for the uncertainties of war were everywhere.

Home births were commonplace then, although my sister, Hannah, had been delivered in a private nursing home, possibly as a precaution because she was the firstborn. On the first of February the doctor and midwife came to my mother at home; the trusted GP, Dr Eccles and the midwife, Brenda Flynn. Nurse Flynn must have been particularly trustworthy that night because Mum asked her to become my godmother. Although I was never to meet her again, Brenda marked her presence at the christening with a brooch, still kept amongst my odd bits of jewellery today. The birth went well and I was a strong and healthy baby.

Snow is nature's way of levelling everything. It covers imperfections. A rubbish heap can look beautiful when covered in snow. When the snow melts, reality is revealed in its actual form whether ugly or beautiful and we can see it and confront it for what it truly is. Snow, soft and white, transforms our world but it is always fleeting and when it's gone, its comforting blanket disappears and leaves us with a starker reality. For the first few years of my life, my world was covered in snow. Lies and deceit were like snowflakes; they covered up unpleasant truths but soon the snow would begin to melt. Soon, I would experience the thaw; I would lose the softness of its blanket and be exposed to feelings of icy rejection.

At six months old my senses were developing but I had no language with which to express my thoughts and feelings. I could hear what I knew later to be music. My mother is listening to the radio. Popular songs drift over me, something about 'bluebirds' and 'Johnny going to sleep' ….. '…… the home fires burning' ….. I'll be seeing you'…... I can hear my mother's voice. I feel her heartbeat. I am warm, secure and comforted. The colours around me are pink and white and clear. There is tenderness and peace in this warm place.

Celia and Martha

'Music has the ability to wrap up the past like a beautiful gift' says Howard Goodall. Music was to be the soft blanket into which I would be absorbed. Music takes you into another world. It tells you of love you have not yet experienced. It describes the heartache of loss and pain. It becomes part of you because it has met your needs by expressing your emotions. It has an extraordinary ability to fill a space in your mind and to hold that place as its own forever. It comes to symbolize your feelings; almost like a seventh sense. Its power to recall moments of intense emotion, whether euphoric or fearful, remains constant and pervading. It encompasses the sensations of individual memory even into old age.

I listened to Vera Lynn singing 'Now is the Hour'♪1 telling me of the pain of separation, the endurance of love and the hope of reconciliation.

~~~~~

I was the second daughter of four children born to Celia and John Barkworth. I had a sister, Hannah, who was a year and a half older and two younger brothers, Daniel and Edward. My mother had given birth four times in five years. My earliest memories were of playing in the house and garden. The little red-brick house stood on a corner plot, the garden was L- shaped with a pear tree against the hedge at the back of the house; a tree that I climbed with my brothers when we were older. Behind the kitchen was a washhouse and coal shed. Later, during summer holidays I, with Daniel and Edward, would climb out of the small bedroom window onto the roof of these low buildings and sit there in the sunshine or jump down onto the small patch of grass. There was an Anderson bomb shelter in the garden. It was very cramped inside but had been used by the family during air raids. In the years after the war, we children played on top of it when weeds covered the shelter like a mound. Eventually, the ground was levelled and grass was able to grow again.

I was too young to recall very much about the war but one of my earliest memories was the street party that was held soon after VE Day. Long tables were set up on the pavement with tablecloths to cover their rough surfaces and bunting and flags decorated the houses and gates and lampposts. Sandwiches, pies, cakes, jelly and blancmange were set out and everyone joined with their neighbours in what was now a peaceful world. I
~~~~~

remember waiting a long time for my mother to get ready; she always loved to be dressed well with carefully applied makeup and perfect hair before she would leave the house. By the time my mother and we children arrived, the celebrations were well under way but she had a good excuse; she had to get four children ready as well as herself. Mum was kept very busy with her young family but she was always at home in those early years and always there when we came home from school. In 1946, Churchill made his famous speech about the serious threat coming from behind the Iron Curtain; the fear of the Soviet Union and its intentions of expansion. The war was over but the world was not at peace.

Hannah *Martha* *Daniel* *Edward*

The Barkworth children were slim, with blue eyes and fair complexions. I was small for my age and had a few freckles on my nose and mousey fine brown hair. I was utterly devoted to my mother but felt little connection with my father. He was my father but, for some reason, I didn't feel close to him. It would be a long time before I discovered the true state of the marriage; there was a secret at the heart of the story they presented to the outside world. There are many truths we cannot know but we can tiptoe to the edge of revealed knowledge and look down into the chasm of the unknown. This is attempted in science, in the arts, in all fields of research and development. Why should we not attempt it in our own personal lives to reveal undiscovered elements which will help us to make sense of the whole?

My mother was a strong, powerful but gentle presence in my life. In those very early days, the family seemed to be housebound most of the time. Mum was going through her pregnancies with my two younger brothers; the youngest was born when I was three. I remember going to the shops or to school with Hannah or to church. We were all raised as Roman Catholics, following Mum's upbringing as the child of an Irish immigrant family. There were no such things as coffee mornings or play groups and mothers didn't meet up with other mothers, except to gossip in the street.

Mothers with sisters and other close family members may have been more integrated but since she was an only child and didn't appear to have any friends, Mum's life was particularly isolated. I don't remember meeting a single child outside my family before I started school. We had no visitors. My mother always regretted that she had no brothers or sisters. In fact, she had no relatives other than a second cousin and an elderly aunt. The only person she was in contact with was her own mother, and Grandma rarely visited. The family seemed confined to the home even though we lived in a heavily populated area. As we got older, we would play with the other children in the street but we weren't in the habit of visiting one another's houses. Week by week, the only people the family saw were the local traders; the bread man in his sweet-smelling van, offering fresh bread and cakes; the man selling drinks from the back of his lorry; beer in pot bottles, lemonades, dandelion and burdock - a penny back on the bottles. There was the sound of the ice cream man, playing nursery songs, and offering the most delicious whipped vanilla ice-cream in a cone or in a block between two large wafers. Later, lollipops and a wider choice of flavours would be available. The local window cleaner would call occasionally and we received a steady flow of door to door salesmen, usually selling shoe polish, shoelaces, dusters and cleaning materials. Finally, the milkman could be heard, with his horse and cart or, later, an electric milk float. The bottles would rattle together as he drove along the cobbled street. In the early days he'd fill your jug with fresh milk from a milk churn. Later, the milk was sold in half-pint and pint bottles and was kept chilled by the latest method of refrigeration. Prior to starting school, these were my contacts with the sights and sounds of the outside world.

Although John, my father, was a presence in my life, he was not a positive presence. Tension levels seemed to rise whenever he entered a room. Sadly, I never developed a loving relationship with him. There was something missing and only my mother's secret would reveal what that was. I remember Dad as a lethargic, brooding, unpleasant figure; part of the furniture and fixtures of our lives; someone, who seemingly had no purpose and therefore commanded little respect. Physically a large man, fat and bald, he gave the impression of being emotionally weak and displayed little empathy or engagement with the family. He shaved every day and had a pale pinkish complexion which made him look smooth and clean. This, however, was contrary to the truth and it was something of a family joke that he took a bath just once a year. Unfortunately, this was not an exaggeration and, consequently, his personal hygiene left much to be desired. He was scruffy in his overall appearance and I remember him sitting, reading the newspaper or pottering about the house, smoking his pipe. My mother did nothing to include him in discussions relating to the family's daily lives and there were no signs of kindness or warmth between them. Any interaction between John and Celia was strained and marked by sharp or negative responses; dialogue was kept to a minimum. There was no conversation in the normally understood definition of that word.

Dad looked after himself; he cooked his own meals, washed his own clothes. He did not sit down for family meals although he would sometimes cook for the children at breakfast or lunch. He lost his temper regularly and these outbursts became worse and worse as the years went by. Mum would put them down to his mental state saying that the moon affected his moods. The rows between them were loud and highly charged. Dad used language rather than fists to score points. Although my mother tried not to engage with him, the ranting and raving which ensued was enough for both of them as he became more and more frustrated. There was no physical violence but the dynamics of the emotional abuse were very damaging and I would often cover my ears to shut out the verbal violence showering around us like shrapnel from an explosion. Many silent tears were shed in an attempt to deal with the stress of these outbursts.

How different this was from Mum's own happy childhood. My mother was a strong character; a product of her own happy upbringing. She was a much-loved only child whose beloved father had died when she was just seventeen. The devastation of this loss was evident. Mum was completely devoted to her father. She had her differences with her mother; the age-old generation gap, and longed to be independent and free. She inherited a substantial sum of money from her father when she became twenty-one. At this point she met and married John despite her mother's objection to the marriage. Mum had exerted her independence and gone ahead with the wedding ignoring her mother's fears. My memories of my maternal grandmother are thin and faded. I can remember her dainty figure dressed in black with a black hat and I can remember her face and wispy white hair. All old people seemed to wear black in my early childhood. I remembered my father's sisters coming to visit one day and we children had to sit up very primly and appear happy and respectful and very well-behaved. We had never met them before and hardly knew who they were. The sisters seemed fond of their young brother and it was as if they were just checking how he was and how his family was growing up. Mum accepted them and she happily 'put on a show' for their visit. To the outside world, the Barkworths must have seemed a fairly ordinary family.

My father never went out except for work or the occasional walk to the shops. He had no friends and no interests that I can recall. He didn't go out for a drink with friends or to any meetings or even to the library although there was evidence that he had been a reader in the past as we had a large collection of Dickens' novels in our bookcase. He went nowhere and he saw no-one. Many years later, my mother told me that although Dad had had a grammar school education and a good upbringing he had, she thought, the mental age of a not very bright fifteen year old; he had never really grown up and had never reached adult maturity. His behaviour seemed to bear this out. My mother, however, was keen to portray an image of solid respectability and normality. She dressed her children well and we always had neat haircuts. When we were very young she bought matching coats and outfits for us. Hannah and I wore brown tweed coats with velvet collars bought in different sizes from C & A. We children were the outward sign of her inward strength, her determination to present a strong and successful image to the outside world.

~~~~~

On the whole my early childhood probably seemed to others to be quite unremarkable. I was happy playing on a little blue tricycle which I rode round and round in front of the garage at the end of the back garden. I adored my mother and the longest time I remembered being separated from her was when I was three years old. Hannah and Daniel and I were taken to nearby Ladybarn Park by a lady called Miss Robinson. It may have been when my mother was in labour with my youngest brother, Edward, because we had to be out of the house for some time or it may have been because my mother was attending the funeral of her own mother, who died just before Edward was born, I'm not sure. It was a sunny day in spring and we all sat on a bench overlooking the large grassed area of the park. Daniel was sitting up in the pram and Hannah was sitting on the bench at the other side of the old lady. I was looking at the back of Miss Robinson's hands. They were very wrinkly hands with prominent veins and freckles and large brown patches; I'd never seen such hands before. At that moment, the old lady seemed like a creature from a different species. I look at my own hands now and see the familiar signs of ageing and it takes me back to that moment.

When I started school at the age of four and a half I had scarcely been apart from my mother for more than a minute or
~~~~~

two. There was no preparation for this life-changing transition from home to school. I cried and cried when my mother left me. After a few moments the tears would stop but the hurt remained inside me all day long. I went for a few days without making too much fuss but, eventually, it hit me that this was going to be permanent. Then I really started to protest and screamed when my mother tried to hand me over to the teacher. Mum would pass me through an open window to get me into the classroom. I remembered feeling utterly desolate; I adored my mother so much, she was my whole life. I just wanted to be with her all the time and felt the physical and emotional pain of separation. This was the first hard lesson I had to learn like thousands of children have had to learn it before and since.

Soon I began to make friends. I remembered being outside my infant school, St Cuthbert's, with my little friend Katie Donovan and her very tall mother, Maureen. Katie had blonde corkscrew ringlets and was delicate and fair skinned. At five years old, she was my best friend. I usually walked home from school with Hannah but I had to wait for her and so it was agreed that I could walk with Katie and her mother. They lived across the park on Kingsway. We lived just near the edge of the park. Sometimes, as we walked along the street, a group of children would pass by on the opposite side of the road. They'd shout 'Catlicks! Catlicks! smelly old Catlicks!' Then the catholic children would call back 'Prodi dogs! Prodi dogs! Dirty old Prodi dogs!'

Our house was built in 1928, the year my mother and father were married. The estate was planned in a very orderly way and there were numerous options for walking home from school. The road names were very familiar: Brookleigh, Fairholme, Hartswood, Heyscroft, Ashdene, Hatherley. I loved the names.

In my child's mind they gave me security. They were reliable, they were always there. There was no feeling of confusion and, when I reached the age of seven or so, I wasn't afraid of being on my own. Around this time I became more acutely conscious of my own identity and separateness. There was in fact one single moment in which I felt as though my soul and body had parted and come back together again; I experienced a distinct sense of individual identity. In that moment of clarity, I was aware of who I was. I identified and accepted my own mind within my physical body; my conscious thinking mind was who I was. This was a pleasant and comforting feeling. I liked solitude and I found peace in withdrawing from the world into my own self where I could reflect. I had no idea where I was going in life but I had a desire to please and to do what was right. I knew, also, that I was not autonomous in the sense that all my thinking would be wise, for I was constantly seeking guidance and strength from outside myself. I already had an appreciation of body, mind and spirit. Maybe this came from religious teaching and, despite being very young, I felt this strong spiritual dimension in my life. Many years later, I felt free to choose; to unite myself with God, to somehow join with God in active work in the world. I discovered how, through deep reflection, we learn to discern the hand of God in our own personal experiences, in the challenges and frustrations of daily life and in the making of important decisions. We sift through our memories and we can see the way in which God has been alongside us over the years.

~~~~~
~~~~~

My home was typical of hundreds of thousands of semi-detached houses all over the country. The rooms were quite small. There was a dining room, a front room, three bedrooms and a bathroom with toilet. At that time the kitchen was a small square-shaped room with a heavy gas cooker and solid metal-framed cupboards. Some years later my mother had the house extended into the washhouse and this gave the family a separate breakfast room, where the kitchen had been, and a long galley kitchen. She was very proud of her new kitchen, especially when she was able to have a twin-tub washing machine and a fridge. Before this, I was going home to a mother who scrubbed the clothes in a sink on a washboard, soaked them in water with dolly blue and then put them in a boiler-type washer. She'd remove the piping hot clothes with a pair of wooden tongs into the sink or a bowl. Then she'd lift them out and put them through the hand-operated mangle. In the winter or on wet days, clothes were always drying in the dining room on large wooden clothes horses, blocking out the fire and creating heavy condensation on the windows.

There were numerous incidents that I recall about those early years. I remember learning the alphabet in infant school and practicing how to write my letters at aged five. I remember a school Christmas party when all the children were given presents. I got a table tennis set. Another child made me swap with them and I took home a cheap little jigsaw puzzle instead. I remember feeling pretty aggrieved by that, as though I'd been cheated, which of course I had. I was already developing a sense of fairness and justice. One of the girls in Hannah's class, Marian, was inviting all her friends to her birthday party. Marian invited me too. I enjoyed the party and saw for the first time what it meant to be part of a family with a loving and kind father who joined in the games and made jokes. During my second year in infant school I was taught by a young nun who belonged to the order of The Faithful Companions of Jesus. Mother Lucy was tall and slim and pretty and wore a tiny pair of round spectacles. The skirt of her black habit swept the wooden floors, her waist was draped with a rosary and her sweet face was framed in little white pleated frills under her black veil. Apart from the usual subjects, Mother Lucy taught music and the children played with a collection of percussion instruments. It was during these lessons that I became aware of the musical beat and the importance of timing; the practical side of playing music.

As well as one to one reading, the children learnt to read repetitively by following the text aloud together and, if any child was unsure, they could listen carefully and they usually picked up the words they were struggling with. We also took our reading books home and I read a little with my mother. The headmistress was another nun; Mother Immanuel was a rotund, slightly stooping figure who ruled the school with a cool degree of authority. Naughty children had to stand outside her door to be 'dealt with.' Mother Lucy and Mother Immanuel lived in the convent house next to the local grammar school and always travelled to school together.

Hannah and I and my brothers learned to ride two-wheeler bikes, helped a little by Dad, and when I was about eight I started to become more adventurous and rode up and down the pavements and round the quiet streets near our house. During school holidays we would play on the road in front of the house with two of the local children, Barbara and Ted. They lived across the road and weren't considered suitable companions for us. Mum thought their mother and father were 'common'; their father sometimes appeared in their front garden wearing only vest and trousers and their mother often wore a turban scarf with her hair curlers showing beneath. My mother would wear one of those wraparound aprons, which she called her 'pinny' if she was doing a dirty job, like cleaning the kitchen stove or dusting the picture moldings. Sometimes, she would wear a turban, but she would never be seen by the outside world in either of these. Perhaps this was one of the differences between working class and aspiring middle class. My mother certainly had her pride. She worked very hard doing everything herself as she could never afford help.

Most of the neigbourhood children didn't go to the same school or church which we attended but they were very friendly and I liked them. The girl next door, Janet Benson, lived with her grandmother and her father, Eric. I heard the story that Janet's mother had left her father. I didn't play with Janet very much. The boy who lived directly opposite our house was called Donald and he lived alone with his mother. He sometimes spoke to the children and told them about the animals he kept at home. We learned later that he had been cruel to one of his pets. Directly opposite were a lovely couple called Auntie Pat and Uncle Will. Auntie Pat invited all the children who lived nearby to play the piano with her and she taught us the basic scales and simple tunes. She would take us out to the country during the summer holidays. We would catch the bus on Parrswood Road and go up to Alderley Edge.[2] Walking through the woods, she'd tell folk stories of the wizard and the caves. She was kind and loving and my mother used to say it was sad that she couldn't have children of her own.

Defining moments are not always recognized as they occur in childhood but one experience was to be different. When I was seven years old, Katie invited me to go to her house for tea. It was arranged for Sunday afternoon and she was to call for me with her older sister, Margaret. Three o'clock came and I was dressed and ready in my best clothes, looking forward to the very rare treat of visiting someone else's home. The time passed but no-one came. I felt disappointed and puzzled. Perhaps they had forgotten. Perhaps I'd misunderstood and got the wrong date. The following day, Margaret called to see my mother. She explained that Maureen had suffered a severe stroke and cerebral hemorrhage and had died suddenly at home. She couldn't let us know immediately because she didn't have our telephone number. I was shocked to hear the news and thought how I might feel if I were Katie. I immediately felt a surge of love and sympathy for her. My heart felt dull and heavy and my mind focused on how devastated I would feel if I lost my own mother who meant everything to me. I sometimes wonder whether my sympathy for Katie came from the shock of realising that something similar could happen to me, and was therefore self-centred, or whether I actually felt genuine empathy for Katie and the feelings came from a true understanding of her loss and personal pain. Whichever it was, I don't remember seeing Katie after her mother's death; she was absent from school for weeks and then I heard that she was to leave our primary school that year to move to the preparatory school attached to the Convent Grammar School which Margaret, being four years older, already attended. My childhood friendship was over.

~~~~~
~~~~~

I don't know whether the saying, 'Give me the child until he is seven and I will give you the man', attributed to the Jesuits, is entirely true but there can be little doubt that the foundation stones which are laid in our childhood, are incredibly important. 'You are the product of your environment' is another well-used cliché. Yet, the future of a child is not preordained; I don't believe in fate. We all have to live our own lives, make our own choices and fulfill our own potential by following the opportunities which open up before us. This is, surely, what makes life so exciting.

As junior school passed by, I continued to be 'best friends' with Jillian and Rose and Anna. I sat next to Maria in her crushed velvet dress, which she seemed to wear day after day until it faded to an ashen pink and smelt musty. Lots of memories flood into my mind; impressions, anxieties, fears. In my final year, one of the boys in my class contracted polio and he was away in hospital for a long time. When he returned, he was wheeled into the classroom in a wheelchair, his legs encased in calipers. He managed to walk with two hefty crutches. One of his friends, Francis, would wheel him into school each day and I kept a picture in my mind of this caring, attentive boy who appeared to be so sensitive to the needs of his friend.

I seemed to cope well with the school work and was above average in mathematics and English. English was always my favourite subject and I loved writing compositions. My biggest hurdle was my almost total lack of confidence. Although I was not withdrawn with my friends, I was painfully shy with adults. As a very small child I had screamed and cried when I was handed over to the teachers by my mother; somehow that child lived inside me for a long time. I was described as shy or timid by my teachers and my heart would beat fiercely at the thought of having to read aloud or answer the simplest question. My mother described me as 'highly strung' or 'suffering from nerves.' Sometimes, it felt as though I was in the constant grip of anxiety.

My mother expressed her love by what she did for us in a practical way but kisses and hugs were rarely given. We were all very well cared for physically but we were not showered with affection. She was hard working, well organized and conscientious. I remember feeling very appreciative for what I had and feeling great sympathy for her and wanting to give her love and support. The adults in my life were going through great difficulties which I did not understand. They, in their turn, seemed to have little understanding of what we children were going through. But, perhaps that's how it always is. I had the companionship of Hannah and I was fond of my brothers and glad that I was not an only child. My overwhelming love and admiration for my mother continued; I tried my best to share the weight of her emotional burden and the disappointments within her marriage but there was only so much that a child could do. My understanding was limited due to the significant secret which she held which was associated not just with her own life but with all our lives.

~~~~~

Discipline at school was strict but usually fair. There was the odd time when everyone in the class was punished because the culprit would not own up. I was aware of the differences in children and that some lived in a children's home because their parents could not look after them. These children were under the
~~~~~

care of the Catholic Children's Rescue Society. From time to time, my mother would take a suitcase full of used clothes to their offices in Didsbury. From a very early age I knew there were children less fortunate than myself. Every year St Cuthbert's had St Joseph's Penny collections. Each child was given a card with twelve or thirty squares around the edge. You were asked to prick the square with a pin when you had collected a penny and when you had a shilling or half a crown you returned the completed card to the teacher. Later, when I went to the convent, each class would take carrier bags into school, full of items for sale to raise money for the same cause. The money went towards the Rescue Society and the children they cared for. Large packets of Kellogg's cornflakes were popular items because they half-filled the bag and were a staple item which most families would buy.

During my early childhood Dad was occasionally employed as a salesman. His contracts tended to be short-term and erratic. This caused arguments and frustration between my parents as Dad was often out of work for weeks at a time. My mother returned to work when Edward was five. Her smart appearance and fashionably styled hair left a good impression with customers. She was good with people and an excellent saleswoman, confident and positive in her approach. She worked for the owner of a ladies and children's clothes shop in Urmston and visited customers with samples of their stock and managed their orders. She would go onto housing estates with a suitcase of clothes, knocking door to door to find customers. She did this in all weathers and travelled everywhere by bus, although her boss would have provided a car if she'd been willing to learn to drive.

This she never did. When she was old, she stooped slightly to the right due to the weight she had carried around for so many years.

At another time she worked for a furrier. Fur coats were fashionable and she would visit customers and take their coats away for professional cleaning or remodeling. Her main source of income, however, was from her lodgers. She'd put an advert in 'The Manchester Evening News': Room available - Monday to Friday, bed, breakfast and evening meal. Tel: Didsbury 5331. Much later, when her children were working, they contributed and paid their share towards household costs. Mum was always struggling with money and, as she would put it, she managed by 'robbing Peter to pay Paul.' She was living from week to week and had to work very hard to maintain a decent standard of living. The house was mainly furnished with what she had bought when they were first married. There were bare floorboards in the hall and on the stairs long before they became fashionable. Mum longed to have it carpeted but it would be several years before she got her wish.

Dad wasn't able to contribute much money to the household and didn't appear to be motivated to do so. My mother told me that around this time he took out a mortgage on the house. This payment then became a heavy financial burden for her, as she paid all the bills; she bore the burden of responsibility because Dad was not earning. This must have been particularly upsetting for her as she had originally bought the house for cash from her inheritance. Therefore, to supplement their meager income my mother took in lodgers. The first one I remember was a man she had met during her earlier working days in the thirties. He stayed for several years; from when I was about six until I was thirteen or fourteen. He worked as an engineer at Hans Renolds on the nightshift and slept during the day. We called him Uncle Sam.

As my mother worked during the day she needed someone in the house during school holidays and Uncle Sam, although asleep most of the time, fulfilled that role. He was tall and slim; a kindly, sometimes volatile, northern Irish man with a strong Irish accent and always a cigarette in his mouth. He was single; his wife had died several years before, giving birth to their first child who had also died. He had a brother who lived and worked in Manchester, Uncle Stan. He would meet up with Stan and other friends at weekends and they would go drinking together. He was often drunk and in a bad mood and sometimes out of control. He would become very upset and get angry with my mother and argue and swear at her.

One day, when I was about eight, he came home from the pub and was unable to get into the house so he knocked on the door and shouted for my mother to open it. I begged her not to let him in. I was very frightened and felt threatened by the raging aggression on the other side of the front door. She hesitated but, after some considerable time and repeated banging and yelling, she opened the door and then told him that I hadn't wanted him to come inside. From that moment, he took his anger out on me, snapping at me contemptuously, obviously irritated and incensed because I had reacted as I had. My mother made a small attempt to defend me but she didn't ask me how I felt or why I was so frightened. After a few days, his anger with me seemed to dissipate and he became his usual self again. His aggression frightened me; I felt I had taken all the blame and punishment onto myself. I didn't retaliate or try to explain to my mother; if I had lost her love, I would have had no-one in the adult world to connect with and I couldn't risk that. Even though I was very unhappy following this incident, Uncle Sam was always generous and often bought sweets or little surprises. I remember delicious creamy whirls and blackcurrant and liquorice chews and sherbet dips. Like the black and white Scottie dogs in the Scotch whisky advertisement, Uncle Sam had two sides to his character and they were in stark contrast to each other. Part of me was fond of him but part of me feared him. I never asked Hannah or Daniel or Edward how they felt about him.

A year or two before, Uncle Sam had brought me two lovely dresses; a pink one with rosebuds and a green satin one with a circular skirt. He was given them by one of his drinking friends who had little girls of his own. I fancied myself as a ballerina, dancing and running up and down the narrow hallway twirling and skipping and turning circles. I loved those dresses and they transported me, like Mr Benn,[3] into my own fantasy world. I yearned for long thick hair which I could plait and curl. I attached ribbons with grips at each side of my hair and tied a bow at the end of them. I'd toss my head and watch myself in the mirror throwing back my hair like Miss Piggy.[4]

When we were older, Uncle Sam would buy comics on his way home from his night shift. Hannah and I would read 'The Girl', 'Girl's Chrystal' and 'School Friend' and Daniel and Edward read 'The Eagle', 'The Dandy' and 'The Beano.' As a child, Hannah was very quiet and serious. I loved her but we didn't always share the same interests. Hannah was a good reader and this kept her somewhat withdrawn and introverted. She did not play outside very much or join in physical games. I was more energetic and tended to play with my younger brothers, especially during the long school holidays. Aged eight or nine, we would go off on our bikes exploring the neighbourhood. When we were older, we cycled up to the airport to watch the planes taking off and landing. Sometimes I'd play ball against the side wall of the house with a tennis racquet or I'd throw and catch with one ball or two, waiting for the call to tea. Hannah was very bright and did well at school. At eleven, she passed her scholarship to the local convent grammar school 'The Hollies'. I was two years behind her at school and, although of good average intelligence, I didn't have Hannah's sharp memory. My mother thought there might be a slight doubt that I would pass my scholarship so she decided to send me to the convent's private preparatory school for one year to ensure that I would get a place in the grammar school with Hannah. I left my familiar state primary and moved to the large converted Victorian house which was 'The Hollies Prep.'

There's no doubt that the happiest of my schooldays were spent at St Cuthbert's. Although very structured, the children were allowed the freedom to play their own games in the playground; skipping, individually or in teams; Tag or Tig, a chasing game of two or more children, sometimes ending in a demand for a kiss; ice slides when the ground was frozen hard. We also played hopscotch, The Farmer's in his Den, Ring-a-Ring o' Roses, and old favourites like, Piggy-in-the-Middle; whips and tops and conkers. We'd use coloured chalks to design individual patterns on the tops. The educational standards were good and discipline was strict. The school rules provided the boundaries and were easily understood. They gave security and instilled just enough fear to be a deterrent. The ruler was used on the palm of the hand for misbehaviour. Fortunately, I was a well-behaved pupil – I didn't dare be anything else. I didn't want to bring further pain on myself or further worries to my mother by being badly behaved.

St Cuthbert's Primary School 1953
Martha, fifth from left second row

It was a well-run school and, on the whole, had good teachers whose methods followed the basic traditional principles of education at that time; imparting knowledge and building on that knowledge through rote learning. The main focus was on teaching adequate levels of numeracy and literacy along with sound religious and moral teaching. All this was evident at St Cuthbert's. Regular attendance was essential because if a child missed a link in the syllabus they could be greatly disadvantaged. There did, however, appear to be little interest taken in the individual child, their emotional state or their home circumstances. Nothing was asked and nothing was known. Physical disabilities were accepted and catered for wherever possible but we did not yet have the all-inclusive approach to mainstream education; children who had severe disabilities would have to attend a special school. The softer, child centered approach had not yet come into vogue and was something I would learn more about in later years.

Discipline at home was not harsh. My mother had certain well-worn sayings that would pop out from time to time; 'You'd try the patience of a saint!' 'If you don't stop crying, I'll give you something to cry about!' or she'd advise us how to cope with unkind comments from the children at school. Turn round and tell them, 'Sticks and stones will break my bones but words will never hurt me!' She also believed, 'Least said' meant 'soonest mended'. When I fell, my mother would smear Zam-Buk - the great herbal balm - on the graze and cover it with a piece of lint and plaster strips or a bandage if the knee was badly cut. She would give me a rare cuddle and tell me that all would be well. 'You'll get over it', she would say. I knew that she had the answers I needed. Time, however, would challenge my trust; motherly care would give way to the harsher realities of life and soon I would be left alone to heal my own cuts and grazes.

---

[2] Alderley Edge is a dramatic red sandstone escarpment, with impressive views from Castle Rock over the Cheshire Plain to the Peak District. The highest point on the Edge was originally a Bronze Age burial mound, later used as a fire beacon site which would have been lit as a signal to warn of imminent invasion.

[3] Mr Benn is a popular character created by David McKee who appears in several children's books and an animated television series of the same name originally transmitted by the BBC in 1971 and 1972.

[4] Miss Piggy was a well-known character on the American TV series 'The Muppet Show'. Known for her feminine charms, she featured in the series from 1976.

Chapter Two

'One looks back with appreciation to the brilliant teachers, but with gratitude to those who touched our human feelings. The curriculum is so much necessary raw material, but warmth is the vital element for the growing plant and for the soul of the child.'

Carl Jung

My first few weeks at prep school were traumatic. Classes were much smaller; around thirty as opposed to forty-five at St Cuthbert's. I'd been in the top ten of the class at St Cuthbert's for mathematics and English but joining the other children at the convent school, many of whom had been there since they were four or five, I soon realized the difference in standard. Our form teacher, Mrs Williams, was a no-nonsense type of woman; plump and grey and in her fifties, stern and unsympathetic. I was trying to adapt to all the changes, for which I was unprepared, and this, along with my anxious and nervous personality, made it very difficult for me.

One Friday afternoon I could stand it no longer and I went home at lunchtime. It was a fight or flight moment. The pressure I felt became overwhelming and the desire to flee kicked in. I had a key to the house so let myself in and waited for my mother's return. She was surprised by my behaviour and the weekend proved an anxious time as I knew I would have to face my teacher on Monday morning and explain my actions. My mother had received a telephone call from Mrs Williams as she was concerned that nothing awful had happened to me. She probably wasn't quite the witch I had believed her to be. Monday arrived and as I walked up the path to the front door of the school, one of the girls, Angela Bradbury, said to me 'Where were you on Friday afternoon? You're really in for it! You're in deep trouble.' In fact, Mrs Williams was quite kind and didn't make too much of the incident so I felt greatly relieved. I settled back and the crisis passed.

There was one positive thing about this change in my schooling, I rekindled my friendship with Katie and this proved to be a great help to me. Since her mother's death the family had been cared for by her Auntie Nelly. I remember her as a very small grey-haired lady, soft thin hair in a bun, wearing a beige belted raincoat and a headscarf. She would meet Katie every day from school and I joined them for the walk home. As soon as we were out of sight of school, she bought us an ice-cream or a toffee bar. Eating in the street was forbidden if you were wearing school uniform; the school was very strict about such matters. Auntie Nelly's generous nature didn't take these rules too seriously. My friendship with Katie became a constant in my life. She belonged to a strong close-knit family. Her two brothers were much older than us and even her sister seemed grown up although she was still only fourteen. I was to enjoy many happy hours with this loving accepting family. I didn't feel nervous or anxious when I was with them. My mother always did her best to offer us security but something was missing. Katie's family showed me how a family should be; humorous, supportive of one another, kind and caring. There were alternatives to the way I was living and I held on firmly to that belief.

Another enjoyable pastime was a weekly visit to the Palatine Picture House at West Didsbury to watch the Saturday children's matinee. Daniel and I would go together, sometimes with Edward too, to watch cowboy, adventure and comedy films in black and white; old films which were shown in serial form so the children had to attend the following week or they wouldn't find out what happened to their heroes. When I was in bed I would dream of riding a horse; of being a cowgirl. I'd sit astride the bolster, with a belt fastened around it, pretending it was the harness over the horse's head. Pulling back its reins, I'd gallop across the prairie to meet my handsome cowboy.

A child can escape reality by stepping into their imagination. The pretend world has been a refuge for many children but there comes a time when you have to wake up. It's sometimes hard to accept yourself as you are with all your weaknesses and shortcomings. In later life, I sought to love myself and to see myself clearly despite the negative elements of my character. I knew that the real challenge was to love others whether I liked them or not. I was to discover that when love exists, ignorance and prejudice can be set aside; anything can be forgiven.

Thoughts of school were never far away. I sat my scholarship, often referred to as the Eleven-Plus, in February 1953 after a gruelling first term of intensive work in maths, English and intelligence testing, trying as hard as I could to meet the expectations of my parents and teachers. By around March or April, I learned that I had passed. However, I was a 'borderline case' which meant that I'd passed to the technical high school but not outright to the grammar school. I then had to take an entrance examination for the grammar school. I passed this exam and the rest of the school year was very relaxed by comparison. I still felt a little out of my depth academically and, with my fragile self-esteem, this set the tone for the rest of my time in the prep. My grammar school experience, however, was just about to start.

~~~~~

During the summer term of that year the schoolchildren were given a day off. It was the feast day of St Peter and St Paul, a holy day of obligation in the Catholic Church. This meant that you were obliged to attend Mass. It was a beautiful summer's day, Monday, 29 June 1953. By early afternoon I was looking for something to do. Ed and I decided we'd go for a bike ride. He was only eight at the time so we weren't going to go far. Hans Renolds, the engineering firm where Uncle Sam worked, was about a mile from our house. Behind it was an abandoned area known as the Clay Pit where there was a large pond with an island in the middle. Men and boys used to go there to fish. We were quite interested in nature and had been learning about frogs so we went there to collect some tadpoles so that we could watch them develop. When we arrived we left our small bikes by the edge of the pond and started looking for tadpoles with our nets and jam jars ready. After a moment or two a young, fair-haired man came over to us and, noticing what we were doing, said he knew a place where there were lots of tadpoles. We followed him over a rafted bridge to the clump of vegetation that formed the island. Once on the island, he told Ed to go on ahead to the far edge of the path and we would catch him up in a moment. As soon as he was out of sight he led me into the low bushes until we found an area where I could stand up straight. He crouched down to my eye level. I was wearing a thin summer dress, a vest
~~~~~

and a pair of knickers. His eyes scanned my body, his hands reached forward and he began interfering with my clothing, placing one hand inappropriately on me and fondling me. He wasn't aggressive; he didn't say anything but it scared me so much that all thoughts were instantly eradicated from my mind. I now knew what it meant to be 'in the grip of fear'. I was literally paralysed.

It takes half a second to fall, a second to cut yourself, a second or two for a car to crash. Fear grips you in the same way. Shock locks you in and reality is somewhere on the periphery of your consciousness; but it is there and you are still in touch with it. Physically, I was frozen; unable to scream or even speak. I felt powerless. The water's edge was just a couple of feet from where I was standing. My heart was thumping in my chest, my throat constricted and, after a few seconds when my thoughts did return, headlines were flashing at me, 'Local girl found drowned in Clay Pit' in inch high letters in 'The Manchester Evening News.' At last I stuttered out, 'I w.w..want to go back to my brother....' I pulled up my knickers and he indicated to me to reverse back out onto the path. We walked the few yards towards Ed. The whole incident had probably taken no more than three minutes or so. Turning, we walked back to the shoreline. We netted some tadpoles and put them in our jam jars. I noticed the wild flowers growing in the gravel at the edge of the water. They were displaying their delicate little heads with leaves outstretched as if in a dance. The air was fresh and the sun was warm. We got on our bikes and rode home. Ed's passing remark to me was 'Wasn't he a nice man?' 'No', I groaned, but I didn't tell him why.

I couldn't sleep that night or the night after. It was a couple of days before I told my mother and I only told her because I wanted to stop the same thing happening to someone else. Mum didn't contact the police because she felt it would be too upsetting for me to have to retell the story. Fortunately, I never had a similar experience and I accept that the incident could be considered relatively minor when compared to the absolute horror of many assaults. If it had been reported, it probably would have been described as 'sexual interference.' Nevertheless, for an eleven year old child, it was frightening and traumatic. In my innocence I trusted this man and he abused that trust. It was a lesson painfully learned. I also rationalized that maybe everyone has to have some kind of experience like this and, if that is so, I supposed mine hadn't been too bad! It could have been so much worse; he could have been violent, he could have killed me! If Ed hadn't been with me, I really could have been left dead in the water.

I tell this story because it demonstrates how my mother sought, in her way, to protect me. She didn't choose to recognise that this man could re-offend and possibly do serious harm to another child; she didn't see the wider picture. She dealt with the immediate situation without consideration for the longer term. Her prime duty was to protect her child; she couldn't see any further than that. This was her judgement. It was an attitude that I would encounter again and again as I grew older. The incident was never referred to again.

~~~~~

The serious rows at home continued at a steady rate. I can't remember exactly what they were about. I just remember the
~~~~~

shouting and the levels of stress involved. Uncle Sam stayed on as a lodger to provide some financial support whilst my father was continually out of work. The house was cramped with Hannah and me and my mother in one small bedroom, Daniel and Edward and Dad in another and Uncle Sam in the smallest room of all; the little back bedroom.

One day, Mum invited a friend to stay. We called her Auntie Mary and she was a teacher who lived in Scotland. She had two small boys Andrew and Robert aged six and four. They had been in private residential care in Manchester whilst Mary completed her training as a teacher of the deaf. When Robert reached school age he had to leave the children's home and attend school. My mother agreed to look after the two boys while Mary found a permanent home for them all. The boys were accepted into St Cuthbert's and joined the other children there.

The two boys were accommodated in the little back bedroom so Uncle Sam had to move downstairs and sleep on a bed settee in the front room. It was soon clear that these two little boys were quite disturbed. Little Robert would wet the bed frequently and Andrew showed signs of deceit and other negative traits. My mother had little or no experience of dealing with these behaviours and the poor children were not treated very kindly. They were punished and marginalised rather than embraced and included within the family. I remember, with some shame, that while the attention was on Andrew and Robert, at least it was diverted from the rest of the family as Dad would take out some of his frustrations on them. This was the first time I had had an objective view of other children outside my immediate family. I realised later that the children were there, not out of compassion, but because they provided added income for the family.

With hindsight, I can understand why my mother took them on for the extra financial security which they provided but it also taught me how helpless children are and how self-preservation can overrule a child's reaction to injustice. The emotional maturity and empathy are not there until you reach a certain age and, even if they were, the observing child would be almost powerless to use them. Andrew and Robert stayed with the family for over a year before Mary eventually found a little house for them in Bolton. Many years later, I discovered that the boys were the result of an affair that Mary had had with a headmaster. One day, Mary was getting off a train in Glasgow with her sons, when they rushed down the platform shouting 'Daddy, Daddy!' The man on the platform was not meeting the train; he was boarding it with his wife and two daughters. The affair was discovered. When my mother told me this story she said, 'Oh, what a tangled web we weave when first we practice to deceive.'

~~~~~

Child centeredness did not seem to exist in my childhood. Everything was centred on the adults and the children were expected to fit in wherever they could. My first year at grammar school was to be far from easy and I'd lose even more confidence in myself. All the other girls seemed so 'established' and this didn't help my already fragile self-esteem. Of course, this was all in my own mind; they probably didn't feel in the least bit 'established' and many of them would be struggling like me.

The religious order of The Faithful Companions of Jesus (FCJ) was founded in 1820 by a French widow, Marie Madeleine d'Houet. Their philosophy was 'Education, Education,
~~~~~

Education' long before it became such a well-used phrase. This was the basic principle of the FCJs. They knew that the only way to change society was through a sound education. They had the intellectual courage and tenacity of the Jesuits and it was the Jesuit rule that they would follow.

'The Hollies'[5] convent, direct-grant grammar school and preparatory school were housed in four large Victorian houses, originally built as grand homes for Manchester industrialists and professional men during the mid to late nineteen century. 'The Hollies', 'Staneswood', 'Oak Bank' and 'The Acorns' stood on a tree-lined road, Oak Drive, among other similar grand houses in their own substantial grounds.

Image courtesy of http://rusholmearchive.org/

The imposing building which was 'The Hollies' housed the main school with a large hall extension to the left hand side. Image courtesy of http://rusholmearchive.org/

Katie and Martha

In the aerial photograph above, the houses which constituted the Hollies Convent & School can be clearly seen in the centre. Image courtesy of http://rusholmearchive.org

All of the buildings in this photograph were demolished in the early 1960s when Manchester University acquired the school and convent by compulsory purchase and several of their new halls of residence were built on the site. The school then moved to a new home in West Didsbury.

The entrance to the school was approached along its short formal drive, banked with holly bushes and rhododendrons. There was a science laboratory and further additions plus a corridor connecting the house with the white bricked convent 'The Acorns'. The convent school had a plain but elegant interior and a beautiful chapel. The preparatory schoolchildren were housed in 'Oak Bank', a pleasant Victorian villa at the other end of Oak Drive. 'Staneswood' had been added to the school later. This was another large house, neo-gothic in style and accommodated further classrooms and teaching facilities. During the 1850s many houses were built in Oak Drive by members of the prosperous middle class. Manchester University began to establish halls of residence from 1910, the earliest being Ashburne Hall. Increase in student numbers in the 1950s and 1960s required the acquisition of more houses or land for university halls.

Although the buildings of the old convent school had character they were not very conducive to learning. The rooms had high ceilings with carved coving, large shuttered windows and broad windowsills. The girls sat at formal desks in pairs. Life became relatively more settled during my first year and most of the teachers attended the classes in their designated form rooms. The graduate teachers wore their black gowns. One teacher was so small, about 4' 10", her gown touched the ground and fell off her shoulders. She was constantly readjusting it and wrapping it round her bosom. By the second and third years, the pupils, and there were about five hundred when I attended the school, had to move frequently from building to building in all weathers to attend classes, carrying their heavy school satchels with them.

The characters of the teachers were emerging. Many were graduates in their own field and taught with confident knowledge of their subject. Others, like the French teacher, seemed to be taken on by the nuns out of sympathy and were not known for their teaching skills. One or two teachers had problems with discipline but, even so, the disruption in class was kept to a minimum as a zero tolerance policy was enforced. The heating system was archaic, houses were draughty and the decorative state of the school was, in the main, drab and austere. Yellow musty distemper covered the walls with dark brown woodwork on doors and skirting boards. Some of the classrooms were a bit brighter with a paler coloured paint which at least lightened up the room when the sun shone in. Strict rules applied at all times. No running! Silence! Uniform had to be perfect. The school colours were dark brown with a ribbon of red, blue, green and gold. Shoes had to be brown, not tan or light brown but dark brown. The uniform consisted of a pleated gymslip with neat buttoned belt, a cream blouse, school tie and cardigan. A gabardine coat and beret or brown velour hat completed the winter outfit. There was also the popular addition of a school scarf. Brown socks or three quarter length beige stockings were worn up until fifth year.

Sixth formers could wear skirts rather than gymslips, and nylons instead of wool stockings. Trousers weren't considered a female garment, and no-one wore woollen tights, so knees would get red raw as the girls walked to school in freezing temperatures in the winter. Hats had to be worn at all times outdoors. In the summer the girls wore light green cotton dresses with cream collars and a tie belt, a brown cardigan or blazer and white ankle socks. A cream panama hat added a touch of fashion to the summer uniform. The school badge adorned the berets, the hats and the breast pocket of the blazers.

The nuns wore black habits flowing down to the floor – they appeared to float when walking. Their headdress consisted of a piece of very stiff white material, fitted flat to their forehead and reaching down to their eyebrows. Their faces were framed by a narrow white ruffle or pleated piece of cotton kept in place by a black veil which was pinned on top with neat little blob-headed pins. They were mainly older women in the convent and only a very few taught in the school. My fond recollections of Mother Lucy were like a distant memory. The nuns were very impersonal; they didn't relate to the pupils and so appeared to have little connection with us. There were many vulnerable girls at the school but I saw little in the way of compassion. I expected and hoped for some insight and understanding. Even the lay teachers appeared distant and, although not unkind, many lacked warmth. Later, Hannah found that the lay teachers were friendlier to the girls in the sixth form and I know she was left with more positive recollections.

The nuns were confined to the convent and rarely seen in the grounds as it was surrounded by a high brick wall. The headmistress, Mother Matilda, commanded authority, reverence and respect at all times. Her nickname was 'Tilly' and she appeared to be totally lacking in humour. She was a small, slightly crouching figure with a stern expression and held a little bell in her hand whenever she went around the school or into assembly. She would ring the bell to get our attention and speak in a solemn voice and always seemed to give instructions and orders rather than encouragement or affirmation. The majority of our teachers were women graduates and, unlike most convent schools, only two or three nuns were on the teaching staff. There were no male teachers. In fact, the only male I saw in my time at the school was the gardener/caretaker.

The religious order also included nuns known as sisters who were employed in the domestic work of the community and did not teach. Other nuns taught in local infant and primary schools and Mother Lucy, who had taught me at St Cuthbert's, had been one of these. My view of the school was, however, very subjective and narrow. I discovered later that Tilly was in fact an excellent head, and a very good administrator. She was admired by her colleagues and readily accepted the challenge of organising the grammar school with its varied and developing curriculum and relatively young and inexperienced teaching staff.

When I reflect on this time of my life, I can see quite clearly that much of what I recall was based on negative thinking which arose from my own unhappiness, lack of confidence and the depression which hovered around me at that time. We did have a lot of fun with our fellow pupils and, despite the gloom, I can look back and know that we enjoyed the friendships we made and the small successes we achieved. I feel sad that, despite the honourable calling of the FCJs, I didn't experience a softer and more understanding approach from the nuns and lay teachers – but, for me, it just wasn't there. For many teenagers, the world is a difficult and lonely place. Young people care so deeply and they are so vulnerable to criticism. Often, they feel that the world revolves around them, but they don't necessarily feel part of that world. As contemporary news reports indicate they are very open to bullying and victimization due to their extreme self-consciousness and sensitivity. I didn't detect any awareness or understanding of the teenage condition at The Hollies.

~~~~~

Our main focus in primary school had been on English, Mathematics and R.E. with the inclusion of intelligence tests to
~~~~~

get us through the Eleven-Plus. We'd also had lessons where we learnt about the lives of the saints or we listened to BBC school broadcasts. One, I remember, was about the order and form of Bach fugues.[6] I could relate Bach's Toccata and Fugue in D minor**♪2** to my own life. Two, three or four co-existing melodies are continuously moving, each one taking its own path. As a result of these transitions, the basic harmony is difficult to determine. It is obscured in a maze of transitory notes and suspensions. Sometimes, chords are incomplete and I have to use my imagination to fill in the missing sounds. My impressions of my life are similar to this, like the waves overlapping as the sea breaks onto the shore, leaving wavy lines in the sand. Countersubject and countersubject appearing in the narrative. Life is like that, we are called to play one theme against another. At one time one takes precedence, at another time it is another and so on. The dominant theme is usually the one which imparts the strongest emotion. As I reflected more deeply on my situation, I felt I was trying to fill in the missing tones; the tones which broke the harmonious flow. There was something missing; something seriously missing or something seriously out of place. But, what was it? It was the secret, yet I was totally unaware of its existence.

My music lessons at grammar school were spoiled by the fact that the teacher, Miss Mitchell, couldn't keep control of the class. We studied very little theory. It took all her time to keep the pupils' attention to enable us to sing a few songs. I could never understand why this didn't improve as I felt she had a new chance every year to gain control, but she never did. The grammar school introduced me to a much wider range of subjects; English Language, English Literature; French,

Geography, History, Art, Science, Music, P.E. Latin was introduced in our second year. I enjoyed English, art and Latin. Uncle Sam made me and Hannah smart folders for our artwork.

I recall the historical events[7] that were taking place as I lived through my school days. The Royal Tour, following the coronation, was the perfect project for geography lessons. The class followed the royal couple around the world and learnt about all the countries they visited. In 1956, the Hungarian revolution was brought close to home because some of the refugees were housed in homes nearby. The Suez crisis dominated the news. But the most memorable event was the Munich air disaster, which killed so many young Manchester United players. Many girls in my form were in tears as they or their brothers were keen supporters and felt they knew the players personally.

These early teenage years were a mixture of laughter and tears. I made new friends; Anne, Carol and Stella. We all had fun together during lunchtimes when, on wet winter days, we would learn ballroom dancing. We danced to the music of old gramophone records. Carol was tall and she took the position of the man to my girl as we learnt the quickstep, the waltz, the foxtrot and several old-time dances. Most of the girls came from south Manchester suburbs and from Stockport, Wilmslow and Alderley Edge but some were from the north of the city and beyond, as far as Middleton, Oldham and Warrington. They were from a wide range of backgrounds; daughters of doctors, lawyers and businessmen. Others were daughters of bus drivers, shopkeepers, nurses and teachers or from much poorer families who lived in inner-city areas or on large council estates. All were brought together by the Eleven-Plus system. We mixed together but rarely spoke about our parents or our home life. Only very close friends would have an inkling of your private family situation. Many of the children had been privately educated and were more prepared for the rigorous academic expectations of the grammar school. There was a clear 'pecking order' in terms of background. The nuns showed signs of snobbery and favouritism; they favoured the Irish children particularly, and they favoured the Irish children from professional families even more.

The school holidays came and went but Mum worked through them and we children were left to ourselves. Sometimes, we would have a delivery of coal and the black-faced coalmen would appear carrying their hessian sacks over their shoulders. Many of the older properties had small manholes or shutes leading down to their cellars but we had a coal shed and the men would empty the coal there, keeping it dry and separate from the house. The horse and wagon, later the coal and coke lorry, would pass through the streets at regular intervals with sacks of shiny black coal piled high waiting to be delivered. The coalmen would wear pointed blackened head-dresses made from a folded sack to prevent the coal and dust falling down their necks. They would drag one of the sacks to the edge of the lorry, turn round so that they backed on to it, and then pull the heavy sack onto their shoulders by tilting and gripping the top of the sack. Several pieces of coal would be lost from the overfilled sacks in this manoeuvre and these would be picked up later by the householder or passing children; one or two extras to be added to their fires. The coalman then threw the empty sack back on the lorry and they moved on slowly to the next house. One of our jobs was to count the number of bags they brought in so we could tell Mum that she'd had a fair and honest delivery.

Another trader was the rag and bone man. Some would use handcarts or drive round in a pony and cart. They'd give you 'donkey stones' or 'rubbing stones' in exchange for any clothes and other items they collected. The donkey stones were used for whitening your door step. They'd come round our streets shouting 'RAG-BONE! RAG-BONE!' A load might include rags, furs, shoes, scrap car parts, a settee or other furniture and an old cooker or washing machine.

I remember my first experience of watching television. It had all started when Mum met a lady, called Betty Jones, in the street and they stopped for a chat. Betty knew from our uniforms that Hannah and I attended the grammar school. Their young daughter, Glenys, had just started at the prep school. Betty was pregnant and unable to go up to the school twice every day so she asked if Hannah and I could meet Glenys from school and bring her safely home. My mother agreed that this would be fine and so we would meet Glenys and take her home where we would often stay and watch the children's programmes before dragging ourselves home for tea. I loved the serials and watched 'Anne of Green Gables', 'Black Beauty', 'Billy Bunter' and 'Robin Hood'. There was such a relaxing atmosphere at Mrs Jones's house. No raised voices, no arguments. Mr and Mrs Jones were a happy couple and being with them felt safe.

The Barkworth family's first television set arrived in time for the Coronation of Elizabeth II. My mother had been prepared to beg and borrow to provide the tiny ten inch screen for this historic event. She paid for the TV on hire purchase. Once she discovered this easy method of payment, she was able to replace the fireplaces, buy new carpets and pay for other improvements to the house. She was pleased to do this but it placed a heavy financial burden on her and she had to work extremely hard to meet all the payments. It wasn't called the 'Never, never' for nothing because it seemed like a never-ending age before it was paid.

Hannah had her books and seemed to fade away into some solitary activity or another. She would write long lists of married celebrities; Richard Attenborough and Sheila Sim, Michael Dennison and Dulcie Gray, Barbara Kelly and Bernard Braden, Bebe Daniels and Ben Lyon, Jean Simmons and Stewart Granger. Sometimes, there would be twenty couples on the list. Psychiatrists might say that this was her way of reinforcing her own beliefs in happy marriage. Another habit of Hannah's was to fill in the snow that topped the letters in advertisements at Christmastime. I took comfort in sucking my thumb and didn't give up this habit until I was nearly twenty.

Daniel and Edward were lively young boys who loved to wrestle and play. Many days during school holidays were wet or cold so we couldn't play outside. This meant that I was often the only one to keep any kind of order. The wrestling upset me a lot although it was really only the boys being themselves. I saw it as aggressive and I hated aggression. I also hated myself for my own anger-fuelled responses. I couldn't bear aggression but I would scream at them to stop, crying as I pleaded with them. They were having fun and didn't want to stop. Sometimes I would thump them on their backs as they coiled up into balls to defend themselves. Later, I realised that this was how I gave into and expressed my own desperate anger and frustration. Inappropriate expression of anger can be very destructive, and often humiliating to the one who is expressing it, but knowing how to channel it positively is incredibly difficult, especially for a child. I know now that this anger was justifiable but the way I expressed it was not. This memory highlights one of the ways I was affected by the high levels of tension and stress around me. How I missed my mother. I would stand at our gate and watch for her coming round the corner. I'd see the familiar walk and then, I would race to meet her. The great joy of seeing someone you love coming towards you. Your heart leaps and you're conscious of the smile covering your face in expectation. I knew her laugh, the tilt of her head and the warmth in her smile. My need was overwhelming. My love for her seemed perfectly balanced; I loved her because I needed her and I needed her because I loved her.

~~~~~

Despite feeling emotionally secure in my mother's love, my low feeling of self-worth moved into depression. I didn't understand what was happening but I knew I was deeply unhappy. It didn't occur to me that I could have asked for help at school, if indeed there had been any to receive. I was near the bottom of the class and destined to stay there. What a miserable and negative prospect for my future. During my second year, I became ill. The doctors diagnosed anemia and this explained my lack of energy, poor concentration and unremitting tiredness. I was off school for several weeks and felt very low, very negative and motiveless. I worried that I was missing a lot of work and that it would be even more difficult to catch up, particularly in French and maths. I was at the foot of a mountain and exhausted at the thought of taking the first step.
~~~~~

The rows at home continued – serious outbursts – shouting and intense anger; I sat on the stairs or cowered in the bedroom, hands over my ears, eyes tight shut to try and block out the noise. From what I can remember, no sustainable argument was taking place; no exchanges were being traded. There was simply an overwhelming noise, cries of anger and frustration coming from my father but, seemingly, going nowhere. These rows were not a daily or even a weekly occurrence. I remember them being every few weeks and they varied in length. They were about adult things; not something a child could relate to or understand. The intensity and anxiety of anticipation, however, were present every day. Sometimes, after things had calmed down, there would be a peaceful period and Dad would be quieter and would seek better communication with the children. I think his outbursts were cries of desperation and frustration. He hated having lodgers in the house, especially Uncle Sam, but he was powerless to prevent my mother from making extra money in this way. He must have felt very isolated and seemed to be completely inadequate in dealing with the conflict affecting his life. My mother's secret was at the very heart of this conflict but remained unspoken.

Arguing parents can give a child a sense of hopelessness – a sense of no way out. Often, parents have little understanding of the emotional impact they are having on their children. They seem to think that they can operate completely separately from the rest of the family. Perhaps it is some form of defence mechanism that they deploy. Consciously or unconsciously, they deny the turmoil they are creating; then, they naively convince themselves it isn't happening and they don't need to take responsibility for it. When we are depressed we can become obsessed with detail. This obsession feeds anxiety and flings everything into a sense of disproportion. I remember wishing that my father would die and put us all out of our misery.

~~~~~

I was constantly aware of the high expectation for all pupils which was made apparent by the huge board of university scholarships and academic achievements displayed in the entrance hall of the convent. The names of these high achievers were written in gold. I couldn't imagine myself being any part of this. When I returned to school, after my illness, no one asked me anything. There was no recognition of struggle. No help. No understanding. I was just asked to catch up by copying the lesson notes from a friend. These were the days before parent-teacher evenings and there was no contact between the home and the school for the majority of parents. On one occasion I remember breaking down in class and crying uncontrollably. My form teacher left me alone, didn't ask if there was anything troubling me and effectively ignored the incident. The crying was not an attempt to gain attention but it was a clear sign of the unhappiness that was just below the surface. I know now that they weren't to know how I was feeling because I didn't tell anyone. How could anyone know if I didn't tell them? Yet, I longed for someone to ask, 'What's the matter?' I needed someone who would allow me to express my feelings and make things better.

At around this time Uncle Sam ceased to be our lodger and found a flat of his own. We continued to meet him after we'd been to Mass on Sunday. He'd wait for us on the corner of Parsonage Road and Wilmslow Road, opposite the White Lion
~~~~~

pub. Sometimes he'd go on to have a drink there or, if it was a sunny day, we might all jump on the bus and go down to Platt Fields, a large park further down Wilmslow Road, where we'd have an ice cream and wander round the boating lake or feed the ducks. He always dressed smartly in suit and tie and his black ankle-high leather boots were well polished. He'd wear a trilby hat which he'd raise in greeting to people as we passed by. Casual clothes hadn't come into fashion and people really did have a 'Sunday best' outfit. He always walked on the outer-edge side of the pavement. He explained that this went back to the days of carriages when men walked on the outside to protect the ladies' dresses from splashes of mud from the wheels of the carriages as they sped along the wet roads.

During the working week, Uncle Sam wore collarless shirts with separate collars which had to be washed each day and, in winter, long one-piece combinations underneath his clothes to keep out the cold. He still worked nights at Hans Renolds and every evening Hannah or I would take him a bag of sandwiches, made hurriedly and surreptitiously by my mother. We'd meet him at the end of the road; a lone figure standing under a lamp-post. No matter what the weather, and we had plenty of rain in Manchester, this snack was passed on so he would have something to eat during the night shift. Occasionally, Katie would come with me, especially during summer evenings when she would visit to play. He often gave us a Fox's mint for taking the trouble to meet him. Once a week, he'd give us an envelope for my mother. This was his way of helping her with her expenses because he knew she was struggling financially. We always thought he was very generous. Although Uncle Sam had left, we had many other lodgers, usually businessmen staying four nights a week, Monday evening until Friday morning. At one time we had the two main bedrooms occupied by the family, as I've already mentioned, with a student in the small back bedroom, a business man in the dining room on a bed settee and another lodger in the front room, again on a bed settee. My mother was desperately trying to earn enough money to feed and clothe her growing family and to provide us with all that we needed.

During these early years I remained close to Katie and often visited her during the summer holidays and stayed all day, helping her to prepare the evening meal for her father when he returned from work in Manchester. At fourteen or fifteen, we'd read the women's magazines. I was fascinated by the illustrations of Eric Earnshaw, which accompanied the short love stories in many copies of 'Woman'. We'd listen to popular songs on the radio expressing our blossoming teenage notions of love and romance; Dickie Valentine, Elvis Presley and many others. Elvis was one of our favourites, Elvis singing 'Love me Tender'**♪3**. I had no experience of romantic love but I could dream about a love that was sweet and tender, lasting and complete. Being loved and loving back was something I held onto as my answer to prayers.

One day Katie made a perfect meat and two-veg dinner. She was carrying it into the dining room when she tripped and the plate flipped out of her hands like a pancake being tossed in the air. The dinner landed perfectly, entirely contained beneath the plate. At least it was easy to clean up and the damage to the carpet was minimal. Her father didn't seem to mind and happily accepted egg on toast instead. These times with Katie and her family were light relief from the unhappy atmosphere at home.

I was finding the schoolwork increasingly challenging and had difficulty in concentrating on homework and reading. The range of subjects and the work involved seemed overwhelming and some of the teaching was weak and unhelpful.

The pressure was kept up relentlessly. Do your homework on time! Prepare for testing, don't fall behind in class. 'Learn! Learn! Learn!' Be ready to answer questions. Be prepared for examinations. No-one at home knew how difficult I was finding it. There was no support within the school for any pupil who was struggling. If there was a clear reason for a child to be upset, such as death of a mother or father or brother or sister, then there would be sympathy for that girl and concessions would be made. I, however, gave no outward sign of my problems. As I've said, I'm not even sure that I could have expressed them clearly if I'd sought to do so. It was all held within me. Hannah was bright and doing well. She was in the top form and would go on to sixth form to study A-levels. Somehow, Hannah had the ability to put her energies into her schoolwork and she didn't realise how much I was struggling. Eventually, I seemed to freeze with a kind of inertia whilst desperately hoping for change.

During this time, Mum worked longer hours and arrived home after the children returned from school. I was usually home first. It was freezing in the house in winter as there was no central heating, so I would light the fire. We had a coal fire in the dining room. Sometimes the fire would be set and sometimes it wouldn't. I would lay the fire with coal and waxy firelighters. If we didn't have firelighters, we would use rolled up newspaper. I would light the paper and put up a large double page to draw the flames. One day, this piece of newspaper caught alight and flames were playing up the chimney breast. My heart raced as I pulled the burning paper down. It disintegrated into ash and fell on the tiled hearth. I got to be quite good at making fires but always watched it and whipped the paper away before it caught fire.

My mother tried to keep up to date with all the household payments but once or twice the electricity or gas would be cut off due to unpaid bills. The red letter had already come through the door – a final warning. If this happened during the winter, it would be particularly unpleasant and we'd go to bed very early because of the cold and dark. Then, she would have to find the reconnection fee on top of paying the bill. We had a store of candles in case of emergency. Sometimes the gas or electric would fail because of strikes. The trade unions, at that time, held considerable power and, if all else failed, they would use it. Getting dressed in the morning required imagination. After rushing back from the freezing bathroom, I'd get back into bed and dress with the bedclothes draped around me. Jack Frost would draw beautiful patterns on the windows, but they wouldn't be appreciated. We had a very old-fashioned electric bar fire which was useless. Speed was the best answer; the quicker you dressed, the warmer you would be. Mum had new gas fires installed downstairs so fire lighting was no longer needed and the coalmen stopped delivering coal.

As a commercial traveller, my father was out of work most of his life. It appeared to me that he was incapable of supporting the family either financially or emotionally. Around this time he got a dog, called Whiskey; a sweet little black and white mongrel. Mum banned the dog from the house and it lived in the old coal shed at the back of the newly extended kitchen. The dog stayed there for the whole of its wretched life. The poor creature was never taken for walks and was let out for a few minutes each day to run around the enclosed garden. Otherwise, he lay there, ate his food and slept on a smelly damp mattress or a pile of old coats. Summer and winter he remained in this squalid space, through stifling heat and extreme cold. My father was solely responsible for looking after him. He loved the dog in his own way but it seemed that he had no idea of its needs or how they should be met. The children weren't allowed near him in case he bit them. He was never bathed, so must have been riddled with infestation. He never received the veterinary care he needed. Whiskey would run round and round in circles chasing his tail trying to get at whatever it was that was irritating him. Today, my father would have been reported for cruelty and prosecuted. Mum used to say she should report him but she was afraid of his reaction. As he grew older, Whiskey's eyes became pale and watery, his ears were ragged and sore. He suffered from various diseases and developed a large growth on his stomach and I can't bear to think of what he endured in his final weeks. He wasn't seen by a vet and I remember hearing him wailing and crying as his body became weaker and weaker and he eventually died. I don't remember anyone referring to it again.

As a child I had some awareness of what was happening but I was powerless. It's not that I didn't possess the emotional intelligence to understand the suffering that was taking place but I didn't have the authority to do anything about it. Bravery is extremely rare in children. Altruism is almost unheard of. Children often lack the emotional maturity and the courage to act. They are trapped by their own self-survival mechanism and, like many adults too, find it impossible to compromise their own wellbeing. Dwelling on this later, I realised that it is the same for all children everywhere. Often, they are in far worse situations than this, when they or others are imprisoned or being persecuted. They are helpless against adults, against cruelty and the dominating power of the adult's will. My mother didn't do anything, the neighbours didn't do anything. That poor little dog lived for my father alone and died in misery.

This man was my father. I was being asked to honour him in the religious lessons at school. 'Honour thy father and thy mother', says the fourth commandment. The sad fact was that he was painfully inadequate as a husband and as a father. I felt the negative impact of this inadequacy. If only I'd been able to dismiss it, to ignore it and look at the positive things in my life but I couldn't. I couldn't honour him, I couldn't love him, I didn't even like him. I became more and more anxious and threatened by his presence as the years passed by.

---

[5] 'The Hollies'
Photographs reproduced by kind permission of Bruce Anderson http://rusholmearchive.org/fallowfield-brow-and-oak-drive

[6] Bach Fugues The Fugue is a musical form in which a theme is first stated, then repeated and varied with accompanying contrapuntal lines. Voices enter successively in imitation of each other; the first voice entering with a short melody or phrase known as the subject. ... A fugue usually consists of three or four parts (voices). Sometimes, there is overlapping of the subject, each voice as it gives out, not waiting for the previous voice to finish but breaking in, as it were, prematurely. In addition to the subject there is often a countersubject appearing in the exposition and probably later in the fugue. The voice which has just given out the first or second parts then goes on to the countersubject.
'The Concise Oxford Dictionary of Music' 3rd Ed. Michael Kennedy OUP 1980

---

[7] Historical Events - Royal Tour 1953 – 54 In November 1953, Queen Elizabeth II, accompanied by Prince Phillip, embarked on her first tour of the Commonwealth since becoming Queen. Travelling by steam, yacht, train, plane and car the royal couple toured for nearly six months, returning to the UK in April 1954.

The Hungarian Revolution or Uprising of 1956 was a spontaneous nationwide revolt against the government of the People's Republic of Hungary and its Soviet-imposed policies, lasting from 23 October until 10 November 1956. It was the first serious blow to Soviet control since the U.S.S.R. forces drove out the Nazis at the end of World War II. Despite the fact that the uprising was not successful, it had a large impact and would come to play a role in the downfall of the Soviet Union decades later.
http://en.wikipedia.org/wiki/Hungarian_Revolution_of_1956

The Hungarian crisis led to many refugees coming to Manchester. Around 800 refugees were housed at Styal Cottage Homes between 1956 and 1958.

The 1956 Suez Crisis - Egypt takes control of Suez Canal.

The Munich disaster 1958 - United players killed in air disaster.
Seven Manchester United footballers are among 21 dead after an air crash in Munich. The British European Airways (BEA) plane caught fire shortly after take-off this afternoon with 38 passengers and six crew on board. The footballing world is reeling from the loss of some of its most talented young players - known as the Busby Babes. Their average age was 24 and they included Roger Byrne - the captain - Mark Jones, Eddie Colman, Tommy Taylor, Liam Whelan, David Pegg, Geoff Bent and Duncan Edwards.
http://news.bbc.co.uk/onthisday/hi/dates/stories/february/6/newsid_2535000/2535961.stm

Chapter Three

'The unexamined life is not worth living.'

Socrates

I was increasingly influenced by religion. Through religion, I tried to make sense of my life and the lives of those close to me. From my earliest days at infant school I was aware of my inherited faith. The feast days and traditions of the Catholic Church were ever present in our daily lives. At primary school, we learnt the Catechism and were tested on it by regular visits from our parish priest. We were read stories about the lives of the saints, we celebrated Christmas with the nativity story and made paper lanterns and stars and pictures of the stable where Christ was born. We sang beautiful carols which shaped my view and love of Christmas. We coloured in sheets depicting biblical stories and miracles and learnt the meaning of the parables and the teaching of scripture. We were told we each had a guardian angel who was a spirit from God who would protect us. We were taught that we are precious in God's eyes, born unique and individual. The main simple rule of life, we learnt, is 'Love God and love your neighbour as yourself.' We were shown how to put this into action in our everyday lives. Central to this understanding would be the precept 'Do unto others as you would have them do unto you.' This fundamental rule applies in all relationships, whether among friends, in the family or in the community, and it links to all the universal values; respect, generosity, perseverance, integrity and responsibility.

We discovered we had a conscience; the ability to know the difference between right and wrong. We had a firm knowledge of the Ten Commandments, of God's forgiveness and the reason he came to earth; to love all mankind and to redeem us. We developed our relationship with a living faith; one that had deep meaning and relevance to our lives and to the lives of everyone with whom we came into contact.

From the age of five or six, I attended regular Sunday Mass with my mother, Hannah and my brothers. My father didn't attend because he wasn't a Catholic. He was a Christadelphian and based his beliefs wholly on the literal interpretation of the Bible, which was regarded as fully inspired by God and, therefore, error free. He didn't agree with the religious teaching of the Catholic Church. He rejected the doctrine of the Trinity and the immortality of the soul, believing these to be corruptions of original Christian teaching. Sometimes he would challenge one of us about this and would take his King James' Bible from the bookcase and quote from it, expecting us to defend Catholic teaching. As a child it's very difficult to be sufficiently articulate to competently argue for or against what is an individual's own interpretation. I was not prepared for a theological debate at the age of eight.

Passages from the Bible were beginning to have their impact and I especially liked the parables of 'The Sower', 'The Mustard Seed' and 'The Prodigal Son'.'

> 'Behold the sower went out to sow. As he sowed, some seed fell on the edge of the path and the birds came and ate it. Some seed fell on rocky soil but when the sun came up it was scorched and, not having any roots in the shallow soil, it withered away. Some seed fell into thorns, and the thorns grew up and choked it, and it produced no crop. And some seeds fell into rich soil, growing tall and strong,

and producing a good crop; the yield was thirty, sixty, even a hundredfold. And, he said, 'Anyone who has ears for listening should listen!'

Mark 4:3-9

And so we were taught how deep or shallow our own faith could be. Would it endure and yield growth or would it wither away?

I received my First Holy Communion and made my first Confession at the age of seven and was confirmed at eleven. Confirmation was a very meaningful rite of passage for me and I felt spiritually strengthened by the experience. God was with me that day and he entered into my heart. I took the confirmation name of Thérèse after learning the story of St Thérèse of Lisieux and her 'Little Way.' During my teenage years I became very devoted to her. She understood that we could all be disciples of Jesus by seeking holiness of life in ordinary and everyday things. This approach gave me a positive attitude to work and something to offer up to compensate for the boredom of the task in hand. It meant that anyone could become holy through daily tasks; I put this into practice through my schoolwork and homework; doing jobs around the house and trying to be good and sincere with friends. Of course I didn't always succeed and I was a long way from being a little saint, but I tried.

When I reached the grammar school, we had religious retreats once a year and we were meant to be in silence. As giddy young girls, we found this very difficult and we would often get the giggles and be told off for our lack of respect. Discipline was very strict but never physical. We were given detention or lines as a popular means of correction. Teachers would use the phrase 'Control yourselves, girls!' This became the comical expression which we would mimic constantly. As mentioned and as far as I can remember, there was no discernible warmth from the teachers or nuns. I think I had a subconscious need for someone to offer me reassurance and understanding. We knew our place and it was far below that of our elders and betters. Although there was zero tolerance in class, it didn't prevent a few girls stepping out of line and being disruptive in lessons. No matter how much they were corrected they didn't seem to listen.

The rules of the school cast a very controlling pall over our young lives. No running in the corridor, no speaking in class, single file on the stairs. Prefects, who were the older girls from the sixth form, and wore little metal badges, were placed strategically around the school and they could report girls for stepping out of line. We belonged to one of four houses, mine was St Agnes's. The houses competed against each other to gain top place for examination success, effort, good behaviour and sporting achievement. Perhaps it was a way of encouraging competitiveness. I usually got commended for 'courtesy', or 'trying hard.' The school encouraged girls to enter the Guild of St Agnes and later the Children of Mary; religious organisations for young girls which deepened their spirituality and helped them to understand the importance of their role in the Christian community. When I was fourteen or so, I joined an organisation called the 'Young Christian Students' which I loved. There were about seven girls in our little group. An older girl from fifth year, aged around sixteen, led the group and every week we would meet for a Bible reading which we would analyse for its spiritual message. This was called the Gospel Enquiry. Following that we would examine our lives at school or outside and discuss how we could be influenced by that spiritual reading and put it into practice. This was called the Social Enquiry. YCS was based on Faith and Action. Faith was the inspiration. Faith was the motivation. Action was faith in practice; living out our lives as Christians. This analysis of Christian virtues and moral values enabled us to discern how we should react to difficult circumstances. This model for Christian action was so simple yet it has remained with me during the most complex tangle of relationships and difficult times in my life. It is, quite simply, the blueprint for the Christian way of life.

The May procession

We also held the procession of the Blessed Sacrament on the feast of Corpus Christi in June. In my first year I was chosen, among others, to strew petals from a hand-held basket before the monstrance which was raised high by the priest beneath the ornately decorated canopy. All the girls wore long white dresses and were required to walk backwards, facing the Blessed Sacrament. 'Take, bow, kiss and strew' was the mantra we had learnt to ensure the movements were graceful and steady and in perfect timing. My dress had to be borrowed from another girl and, unlike my blue one which I'd worn for the May procession, it was too long for me. I kept catching my heel in the hem which put me out of sync with the smooth bowing, kissing and strewing. My movement went, 'Take, bow, jerk, kiss and strew', 'Jerk, take, bow, kiss and strew', 'Take, bow, kiss, jerk, and strew; not the most elegant of movements. What should have been a respectful and memorable experience was marred by the embarrassment of the ill-fitting dress and my awkward self-consciousness.

Many popular catholic hymns were sung at morning assemblies and they often reflected the liturgical seasons. In May and October we sang hymns to Our Lady and of course we sang Christmas hymns during Advent. In Lent we sang 'When I survey the wondrous Cross', 'Were you there when they crucified my Lord?' and at Easter 'Christ the Lord is risen today' and many others. One of my favourites was 'Amazing Grace' and another 'Lord for Tomorrow and its Needs'.

Lord, for tomorrow and its needs
I do not pray;
keep me, my God, from stain of sin
just for today.

Let me both diligently work
and duly pray;
Let me be kind in word and deed,
just for today.

Let me no wrong or idle word
unthinking say;
set thou a seal upon my lips
just for today.

Sister M Xavier

This hymn helped us all to live in the moment and reinforced the tenets of Catholic teaching. It was equal to a national anthem or a signature tune. I know it never failed to inspire me and helped me to focus on the important aspects of our school day. They say we should all try to live in the moment and Billy Jean King once said that that was why she won so many tennis matches, but I've always found this advice far easier to give than to put into practice.

I made regular visits to the beautiful chapel which gave my school life the added spiritual dimension which I was searching for. It was an inspirational place; a brief escape at lunchtimes or during retreats and I appreciated the peace and calm that it brought to me. One day, I took a wrong turn coming out of chapel and found myself inside the convent. I entered a large sitting room with low tables and several comfortable armchairs. The high windows were draped with thick curtains and looked out onto the contoured lawns of the garden. It was perfectly silent. My heart was beating loudly and I hardly dared to breathe. I turned quickly and retraced my steps. The convent was strictly out of bounds.

~~~~~

Of all human experiences, I believe that religious faith is the most individual; both a commonly shared experience yet an
~~~~~

infinitely personal one. Just as every mother gives birth, every birth is personal and unique to that woman. So I have found with my journey of faith. The paths are opened up before you and you choose to take them or tread another way. Another important aspect of religion is reflection; Catholics learn this from an early age by examining their consciences. Examining faults and confessing these to God, privately or in confession, enables forgiveness and the opportunity to move on; to wipe the slate clean. You don't have to let go of the past; you can wander its corridors and peep through its windows. The memories linger, good and bad. You can't change the past but you can reflect upon it and learn from it.

Like Socrates, Karl W. Palachuk[8] believes that people who examine their lives, who think about where they've been, how they got there, and where they're going, are much happier people. He says, no-one's life is free from trouble and strife but those who have some sense of where they belong in the universe also have a context for understanding how all the elements of their life fit together. There are two people, he says, one with a map and one without a map. Who has the better chance of reaching her destination? The one with the map, of course! When you examine your life, you get to choose your destination; you set the goals; you determine the path; you decide how long it will take; you are able to decide whether you're on the right path or the wrong path. In other words, you begin to know yourself and to take control of your life. You can decide who you want to be and begin to become the person you want to be. For me, my road map is my Christian faith. It gives me grounding and vision, a path to follow and a continuing challenge to meet.

A crucial part of our evolution as human beings is achieved through examining the world around us. Knowledge used positively for the good of others will give us the chance of making the world a better place. Many people avoid leading an examined inner life. It's not that they don't have time but they seem to actively avoid making time to reflect on their lives. Perhaps they think it will be too painful or just a waste of time and effort. 'Why bother, you can't change things that have already happened!' Yet, people who reflect carefully gain a degree of self-knowledge which may help them to resolve many issues in their lives and become happier people. Examining your life can bring tremendous challenges. You open up the possibility of doing something to address the negative elements that you discover. You may be forced to become pro-active; you may have to decide whether to act on the knowledge gained. In time, you begin to know yourself better and to take control of your life. Getting to know yourself is a lifetime's journey.

I was a child who reflected constantly on my life. I was not a child who thought 'Why me?' I thought 'Why not me?' I tried to understand what was happening and why it was happening. I was searching for answers but didn't know what questions to ask. My religious faith upheld and strengthened me. I clung on to it like a piece of driftwood in the sea. Would it save me? I didn't know. I did feel some sense of belonging and a sense that God was with me. At other times, I felt as though I was deceiving myself and I was completely alone. There was nothing there! There was no God! There was nothing and no-one except myself and all the millions of other lonely selves in the world. Even though I fought to hold on to my faith, it did not mean that I would start to experience success or that the problems within my family would be resolved. I tried to gain a balance by concentrating on the more positive aspects of my life. My deep feeling of gratitude for my mother, my friendships at school and my relationship with Hannah brought more constructive feelings. I became closer to Hannah and was thankful that we could share certain thoughts and experiences together.

The four children should have been equal in Celia's affections but it seemed that Daniel was the cuckoo in the nest. For some reason, Celia did not treat him in the same way that she treated Hannah, Edward and me. Daniel became closer to my father and seemed able to show sympathy for his situation. Celia made no secret of what she wanted in the house; she wanted new furniture, she wanted the house decorating, she wanted central heating. All these could only be gained by her own efforts and she worked very very hard to pay for them. She did home decorating herself, hanging wallpaper and painting woodwork. At the same time, she was providing for the needs of her children. She bought our uniforms from expensive suppliers. If we wanted ballet shoes or tennis racquets or cricket bats she would find the money to buy them. She paid for piano classes and ballet lessons. I dreamed of being a ballet dancer and when I was performing on stage I would call myself Margot Lycee.

If the boys wanted to go camping with the cubs and later the scouts, my mother would buy them sleeping bags, ground sheets and anything else they needed as well as uniforms and equipment. In later life, Daniel told me that he had loved John and had found him to be a deeply spiritual man much misunderstood. He told me that John had turned down several sales jobs because he didn't agree with the ethos of the companies. It wasn't his fault that he couldn't find work. Perhaps it was Mum's awareness of

Daniel's closeness to John that made her distance herself from him. One thing is certain, my mother was a powerful and dominant figure in our lives; she wrote the script and the players would act out their parts as she directed. My mother's secret was not included in her script and no-one else was allowed to recite it whilst she was in charge.

~~~~~

We were all now in secondary education. Daniel attended the boys' technical high school. He appeared to be coping in the best way he could on his own. Edward didn't pass his scholarship and remained at the secondary modern school. We all existed as individuals and we didn't ask one another how we were feeling. Perhaps we were too busy surviving, too afraid to ask or just trying to concentrate on the positive. I continued to get some satisfaction from doing jobs in the house, helping my mother in the small ways that I could. I remember doing housework and grabbing hold of the plug when I'd finished the vacuuming. Unfortunately, it was still in the socket! You learn from your mistakes and sometimes it's a painful way of learning. I went shopping regularly with my mother and helped to carry the heavy bags of groceries down Parsonage Road from Withington village. I became closer and closer to her. She confided in me. I became her companion, accompanying her when she visited her friends, supporting her in her trials and anxieties. One of these visits took us to Bolton to see Mary and her boys. She had found a job teaching and a little terraced house which was ideal for them. I loved Auntie Mary; she was smart and had a great sense of fun. A year or so later, Andrew and Robert told their mother about
~~~~~

the way they had been treated when they lived with us and we didn't visit anymore.

Life was certainly not all doom and gloom; there were sometimes periods of light relief. Christmases came and went. Mum worked hard to provide her family with good food and presents. She'd decorate the house for Christmas and Hannah and I would make silver and paper streamers and dress the Christmas tree. We helped her wrap the presents for her work colleagues and we'd laugh at the stories she told us about the people who worked in the shop. Mum began to visit friends she'd known before any of us were born and I enjoyed those outings with her. I met Auntie Eleanor and Uncle Charlie, Auntie Kathleen and Uncle Al, Auntie Hilda, Auntie Ethel and Uncle Bill. Meeting these friends from my mother's past life, I began to form a picture of her personality through interaction with her friends and I tried to learn more about her life.

My mother once told me that the biggest mistake she had ever made was marrying my father. Her own father had been in his forties and her mother in her mid-thirties when they had married. She was born shortly afterwards, the lone child of a late marriage. My grandfather had looked after his elderly mother and sisters before meeting and marrying my grandmother. My mother was much loved. Her father, who was an inspector in the police force, had considerable status in the Catholic community and was a highly respected man; people used to come to him for advice and counsel. My grandfather died of cancer when my mother was seventeen. She was devastated by his death and told me she thought she would never smile again. She was left a legacy of £2,000 which she would inherit at the age of twenty-one. In 1928, when she married, that was a substantial amount of money.

During my mother's childhood, my grandmother had been the stronger disciplinarian and grandfather would often defend my mother if she was being corrected. Following his death, she became increasingly unhappy at home as she had to stand up to her mother's strong guidance and control without her father's support. She felt trapped and repressed in the strict Catholic home and although she loved her mother she found it difficult to live with her. In those days life revolved around the church and, as a child, she would go to church three times every Sunday; to Mass, to an afternoon service and to evening Benediction. She had little companionship except her own school friends and perhaps people she met through work.

I don't know how she met my father but it was not through any connection with the church. She was, however, determined to establish her own independence when she married and inherited her legacy. She bought a house for cash and furnished it using her father's money and it was registered in the sole name of her husband. This meant that she was tied to him financially as she had no claim on her house and couldn't sell it without his consent. My mother told me that she should have been warned against the marriage. She was vacuuming one day and sucked up two rings by mistake which had been knocked off the mantelpiece onto the floor. She searched for them amongst the fluff and dust and found them. One was perfect and untouched, the other was mangled up. The mangled ring was her engagement ring. She always believed that this had been a sign to end the relationship but it was a sign she chose to ignore. She also told me that my father had threatened suicide if she left him.

My mother's desire to escape the dominance of my grandmother was stronger than her instinct to respond to the warning. All she really wanted was a husband she could love and admire, as she had admired her father, someone strong to love her and provide for her. She also wanted children. Just after her marriage a gypsy had come to her door selling clothes pegs. Mother bought some and the gypsy told her fortune. She told her she would have four children. She was married for eleven years before she became pregnant. It would seem that the marriage had never been very happy, although, photographs show that they did have friends who visited them and spent time with them as a couple. My father was always a keen motorist and he owned a car which I think would have played a part in her earlier attraction to him; in the late nineteen twenties a car was something of a status symbol.

In those early years of her marriage, before she had children, my mother was a fashionable young woman with hopes and ambitions and would have been proud of her new home and the lifestyle she had created. She set about working to maintain this standard of living and explored the newly opening opportunities for women in the years between the wars. With a relatively basic education and no formal training she found that she was good at selling and this was the type of job she would pursue. Newly founded foreign companies were beginning to establish themselves in England and my mother was employed by the Swedish company, Electrolux, demonstrating and selling vacuum cleaners, which were then being produced in the UK. During her time with the company she made several friendships which endured throughout her life. My father became a sales representative for several companies but the jobs were often short-term and the job market was very unstable.

The 1930s had begun and the economic depression was hitting hard. My mother began to struggle financially and was often the only wage earner. Many frustrations built up within the marriage. My father wanted to mortgage the house and my mother was helpless to stop him. She was proud and independent and unable to seek help from her own mother who had been against the marriage from the start. She kept in contact with her mother but I don't think she would have been able to confide in her. As my mother grew in maturity and confidence, my father's role was undermined even further and his relative lack of intelligence and ambition must have left her with feelings of despair and hopelessness. Everything they had, materially, she had provided. Now, she had a feeling of no control; she was trapped and everything was tied up in the house and in her marriage. She must have wondered how her life would evolve as she sought to fulfill her own inner yearnings and desires. I think she saw at this time that the only way she would be able to achieve her own ambitions would be to dominate the relationship completely and defiantly strike out alone. But, she couldn't walk away. She had no way of maintaining her existing lifestyle on her own single wage. As a couple, they had no shared interests. Their personalities were incompatible. They disagreed on religious matters. Mum appeared to have no love or respect for Dad but, I think, Dad loved her in a strange though inadequate way. From my mother's point of view, the marriage had certainly been a disastrous mistake.

~~~~~

My own relationship with my mother helped me through those teenage years and we had many happy times together and
~~~~~

were able to laugh and share experiences. My closeness to Hannah was also a positive aspect in my life. We developed shared interests. We loved settling down to the radio together, especially during the long summer holidays. We listened to 'Woman's Hour' with the daily serial. One that I remember was 'An Episode of Sparrows' by Rumer Godden; the same Rumer Godden who once said:

> 'There is an Indian proverb that says that everyone is a house with four rooms, a physical, a mental, an emotional and a spiritual. Most of us tend to live in one room most of the time but unless we go into every room every day, even if only to keep it aired, we are not a complete person.'

It's interesting to think of our existence in those terms. The ideal house has spacious and balanced accommodation. How difficult it is to provide such balance in our own lives.

Favourite programmes were 'Workers' Playtime', the 'Colgate Palmolive Show' on Radio Eireann – 'Keep that schoolgirl complexion with wonderful smooth Palmolive!' went the commercial jingle, or words to that effect. Our spotty faces weren't the best advert! The BBC gave us 'Hancock's Half Hour', 'The Archers', 'Dick Barton Special Agent', 'The Goons' and other popular shows. On Sundays, after Mass, we would do our art homework together on the dining room table and listen to 'Life with the Lyons' and 'Take it from Here'. Other programmes, not to be missed, were the Kenneth Horne shows; 'Beyond our Ken' and 'Round the Horne', and 'Twenty Questions' and 'Down your Way'.

I would listen to the songs of Kathleen Ferrier, her deep dark contralto voice expressing the dread that I feared if my mother were to die. 'What is life to me without thee, what is left if thou art gone?' What is life if thou art dead?♪4

Hannah and I went to the local cinema regularly, usually on a Friday evening, because we didn't have school the next day. We saw all the latest releases from England and America between the mid to late fifties down at 'The Scala' in Withington; crime, drama, comedy, musicals, adventure, mystery and our own particular favourite, romance. We didn't mind if it was dark and raining. We remember the bronzed wet pavements, the thick slippery leaves and the dirty slush following a fall of snow. Nothing deterred us from the escapism offered by a good film

When it was foggy, we had to be careful that it didn't get too thick as we had to walk back home after the show. These fogs were the 'pea-soupers' of the early 1950s before the Clean Air Act came into existence. Many times we walked to school and the fog would come down by lunchtime. The whole school would be let out early to allow us time to get home before dark. The street lighting was barely adequate in the swirly thick fog and the lamps would glow eerily. Sometimes, you couldn't see as far as the next lamppost. Cars would crawl along at a walking pace, headlights full on, clinging to the inner kerb and most drivers would abandon their cars and seek alternative ways home by bus or by train. Occasionally, even the buses would stop running and then the only way home was on foot.

You could easily lose your sense of direction and I remember an alarming feeling of what it must be like to be blind. Strangely, our hearing seemed to become more acute, perhaps to compensate for loss of vision. The thick taste of leaded sulphur hung in the damp air and coated the back of our throats. Our cream blouses and white underskirts would become grey and the toxic pollution affected anyone suffering with breathing problems. Death rates would increase and hospital admissions were higher than normal. Sometimes the fog would hang around for three or four days. Rain or wind would eventually disperse it and airports and transport systems would once again operate as usual. Then, there was what we called 'smog', a mixture of fog and drizzle, which was even more unpleasant. 1950s Manchester was a very unhealthy place. By 1956, the Clean Air Act was introduced. Scientists had influenced the policy makers and towns and cities were becoming cleaner. During the 1960s the effects of the industrial past were beginning to be blasted away from buildings in Manchester and its surrounding towns. All factory and household emissions were regulated resulting in purer cleaner air for everyone.

~~~~~

My relationships with my friends made life bearable at school. I prayed for my mother and my family. I prayed for myself. Katie left school at fifteen, for health reasons, without taking her GCEs. I was on my own again. I had other friends and they were beginning to think about what they wanted to do when they left school. Marie and Stella wanted to be nurses; Anne wanted to be a librarian. I thought I might like to be a children's nurse. I knew I wanted to work with children. I felt drawn to some kind of caring role. I struggled on as best I could, hopeful that the future would bring some positive answers.

Life at home did not change a great deal. Lodgers continued to boost the family income. My father still had his regular temper outbursts. He bought an old car, a Jowett, a former taxi. With
~~~~~

two extra seats behind the driver, it held five passengers in comfort. It had soft leather upholstery and a tortoiseshell-effect dashboard. Sometimes, he would take the family out on car trips into the country, to see the Blackpool lights or on holiday to St Anne's-on-Sea where we lodged with Mum's elderly aunt, Auntie May. He never stayed with us but would call to collect us when the holiday was over. He drove a little white van during one of his many fleeting jobs and Daniel had rides in it and kept him company during school holidays. Perhaps it was this attachment to Dad that distanced Daniel from the other children. I was constantly exposed to my mother's side of the story and I felt totally in sympathy with her situation. My father was regarded as 'the thorn in the flesh'; he was the reason for my mother's misery. How and when could that ever be resolved?

---

[8] Karl W. Palachuk 'The Unexamined Life is not worth Living' Relax Focus Succeed http://www.relaxfocussucceed.com/Articles/2003010002.htm

Chapter Four

'Laugh, and the world laughs with you; weep, and you weep alone.'

Ella Wheeler Wilcox

The years were passing by and I was now in my mid-teens. Hannah would start her second year of sixth form the following September and I was awaiting my GCE results with nervous anticipation. They arrived on a perfect summer's day but the results were far from perfect; I had passed in three subjects; Art, R.E. and English. I was bitterly disappointed; I had hoped for better, even though I knew it was unlikely that I would do well. Following the results, my mother and I attended a meeting with the headmistress. 'There's no point in Martha staying on.' she said. 'It would be a complete waste of time. She needs to think about what she wants to do.' There was no careers advice at the convent at that time. You were expected to be good enough to enter one of the 'preferred professions' which were firstly, the religious life; your highest calling was to be a nun, secondly, teaching and thirdly, nursing. The options for girls who didn't fall into those categories were seen as very limited and of far lower worth. Two of my friends became nurses and one became a librarian. Hannah wanted to train as a teacher. Katie worked as a receptionist at a leading Manchester hospital. She was settled and enjoying her social life. I decided that I would re-sit some of my exams and take a secretarial course at a local college. So, I left 'The Hollies' and embarked on a very different experience of education, one that would give me some practical skills which would ensure that I would never be out of work for the rest of my life.

I attended a local further education college, Fielden Park in West Didsbury and enrolled on a one year secretarial and business certificate and registered for re-sits in some of my GCE examinations. This was my first experience of mixed sex education since primary school. The college was led by a brilliant young principal called Mr Crouch, who set the tone for serious study. Most of the young people seemed to want to do well in their chosen courses. The characters of the students were diverse and far more interesting and unconventional than they had been at the convent school. I became close to a girl called Rachel who had been a pupil at one of the Manchester secondary modern schools, St Robert's. Rachel was a Catholic and lived in Longsight and was a member of the Young Christian Workers, the sister organisation of the Young Christian Students. The YCW was based on the same principles as the YCS but YCW included boys as well as girls.

At seventeen, I was introduced to the teenage social scene and I embraced it enthusiastically. One of the first friendships I made was with Eileen and her brother, Mark. They were the children of prominent Catholic parents who had founded an important support organisation for parents with handicapped children. I visited their home and met the family. There were five children, the youngest of whom had Downs Syndrome. The family accepted this little girl, so fragile and vulnerable, for who she was and encouraged her to be as independent as possible. They supported one another in caring for her and often had to put her interests before their own because priority care was needed for her. Eileen's father was a kindly man who was strict but gentle and very much the head of the household. He was a Justice of the Peace; a lay magistrate, appointed to hear minor cases and grant special licenses in Manchester. He was highly respected by his children and by those who worked with him. I wished that I had a father like him. He was a man of integrity and one who found great strength in his Catholic faith and its traditions.

We did not know it then, but many changes would take place over the following few years, not least in the church. At the instigation of Pope John XXIII,[9] foundations for the Second Vatican Council[10] were being laid. Society was changing. The Church was seeking to adapt to certain changes too. Maybe 'adapt' is the wrong word. The Second Vatican Council (1962-65) was the most significant event in the modern era of the Catholic Church. The Council was an instrument for renewal in the self-understanding of the Church, its inner life and its relationship to other Christian traditions, other religions and the world. Those participating in or who lived through the time of the Council felt a profound and exhilarating sense of renewal. Pope John set the tone when opening the Council:

> 'The Church should never depart from the sacred treasure of truth inherited from the Fathers. But at the same time she must ever look to the present, to the new conditions and the new forms of life introduced into the modern world'.
>
> http://vatican2voice.org/

Although not everyone in the Church was open to change, many Catholics would benefit from the new approach which was brought forward post Vatican II. The Council was presenting a softer more benevolent image. For me, it appeared to be more accepting and more compassionate in its moral judgements. Some of the priests were favouring a liberal rather than traditionalist view. There was a feeling that many issues were not simply black or white; there were many shades of grey in-between and I recognized a developing change in attitude which looked at every situation in its own individual setting rather than making a comprehensive judgement. There was a new sense of freedom, a sense of renewal and a feeling of anticipation. The swinging sixties had begun.

~~~~~

Apart from Katie, none of my friends had any idea of my life at home. My parents' relationship continued to be as dysfunctional as it had always been. Friends only saw me outside my home, enjoying the freedom and the friendships I was now developing with so many young people. After a year at Fielden Park, I improved my GCE passes marginally and attained all my secretarial qualifications. I was ready for the real world of work and got my first job as a shorthand typist at the head office of a large bank, based in King Street, the financial centre of Manchester. The Victorian building stood squarely on the corner of King Street and Pall Mall. The broad thoroughfare of King Street housed the impressive Bank of England and other important financial institutions. Pall Mall, unlike its namesake in London, was a narrow side street leading back towards Market Street and Piccadilly.

55 and 57 King Street housed the main bank on the ground floor with the trustee bank on the first floor. I worked in the trustee department dealing with wills and investments. The
~~~~~

typists' office looked out onto King Street. From a large bay window, I could watch the city workers passing by; men in their bowler hats carrying umbrellas and leather briefcases. Women, in ancillary roles, were yet to make a breakthrough into the higher echelons of commerce and most of them worked as secretaries, typists or clerks. I enjoyed my lunchtime breaks, shopping in King Street or meeting my mother for lunch at the Kardomah Café on Market Street, which at that time was an integral part of the British High Street with its strong smell of freshly ground coffee and hot buttered toast.

Hannah had achieved good A-level results and was on a residential teacher training course in north Manchester. Sedgeley Park College[11] was run by the FCJ order. The college was a Jacobean mansion called Sedegley House. One account describes it in 'its quaint austerity':

> '... the earnestness, industry and extraordinary lightheartedness of the students who, although spartan-like compared to our modern way of living, obviously enjoyed and benefited from the security of a close-knit, strictly disciplined community. The setting of the college, 'an agreeable region of seven to eight acres of well-timbered land was quite rural, with the front windows facing a green valley grazing milch cows.' 'May God fill those who here teach and learn, with knowledge, wisdom and reverence'.

Hannah returned home at the end of each term and appeared to be struggling with the sombreness of her life at college. It was extremely cold in winter and I think it was only her friendships and the thought that two years was not such a long time that carried her through.

At this time, we led our social lives largely through the organisations of the church. I, with my friends, joined two local

Catholic youth clubs, St Cuthbert's and St Kentigern's. I would play tennis at Fog Lane Park in the summer and table tennis in the winter. Three of my friends were keen walkers and I went on hikes with them in the Peak District, around Edale, Hayfield and Kinder Scout. St Kentigern's, or 'St Kent's' as it was affectionately known, had a lively disco every Sunday evening and provided a great opportunity to meet boys. It was the beginning of the rock and roll age with all the wonderful music and freedom which that era brought. I was entering upon one of the most enjoyable phases of my young life. I could forget about the stress at home and engage with the fun and emotion of popular music; the words giving expression to what I was feeling. These popular songs evoked the deepest of feelings. They helped you remember and they helped you to grieve. Rejected lovers could immerse themselves in the mournful words which spoke of their pain; while the songs reflected the pain back to them. It provided a legitimate excuse to wallow in your own misery. Emotions of every kind from happiness to despair were heightened by the music of Roy Orbison, Buddy Holly, Elvis, the Everly Brothers, Cliff, The Shadows, Bill Haley and many more who provided fantastic tunes to dance to or sad songs to mourn to and dancing was a great form of release. Whatever the emotion, we played those tracks over and over again. Buddy Holly summed up everything for us: 'It Doesn't Matter Anymore'**♪5** The sky may be blue but it's 'Raining in my Heart'**♪6**

I had a regular dance partner, Bob. He was tall and fair, a good ballroom dancer and great at jiving, so I danced mostly with him. It was still possible to dance with other boys because Bob and I were not romantically attached; we were not 'an item'. I went to dances at other venues and was open to meeting a wide range of boys from similar backgrounds to my own. The best occasions were the private Catholic dances held at 'The Plaza',[12] a dancehall on Oxford Road, close to St Peter's Square in the centre of Manchester.

These dances were often held on mid-week evenings and were organised by The Old Bedians who were the past pupils of St Bede's College, The Irish Association, The Catenians and several others. 'The Plaza' had a bar and a live band and the whole affair was far more sophisticated than a youth club dance. The ladies' cloakroom and powder rooms were up steep narrow stairs and were decorated with cream and gold furniture with individual lights set above each mirror. A variety of dances would be played during the evening; quicksteps, waltzes and barn dances and my lunchtime dance practice proved very useful. Finally, the lights in the ballroom would dim and the glitter ball would glisten as the band played the last waltz.

Many of the dances would continue until one o'clock in the morning. If I'd met a boy, he would ask to see me home. We would walk to Piccadilly and get a bus down to Withington and then walk for fifteen minutes towards our house off Parsonage Road. If I didn't meet anyone, I would walk to Piccadilly on my own or with Hannah or other friends and we'd have to face the drunkards who might be lolling around. I was a little anxious, but never frightened; there were always plenty of people about and it was all part of my night out. While Hannah was at Sedgeley, I attended these dances with Hannah's friend, Gemma, whose father had a car, and he would collect us when we were ready and drive us safely home. My mother was often still awake when I arrived home. She was now sleeping in the small back bedroom on her own, and I would slip in and update her on the events of the night. We relished those intimate chats and they brought us even closer together.

~~~~~

I enjoyed working at the bank and was beginning to feel more settled. I was soon promoted to work for one of the senior clerical officers. I was gaining in confidence. I made several close friendships with the other girls. My special friend was Millie. Millie was not a beautiful girl but she was startlingly attractive. She made the most of herself; she was funny and friendly and a free spirit. She was blessed with long thick dark hair which she wore in a French plait or a pony tail. She took great care with her make-up and her rather small eyes were accentuated with skillfully applied eye-shadow, eye-liner and mascara, giving the overall effect of a glamorous model. She always wore the brightest red lipstick. Her figure was perfect and she carried herself proudly and unselfconsciously. Millie appreciated the impact she had on others and was well aware of her strong sexual attraction. Men were charmed and fascinated by her. An only child from a wealthy family, her parents were much older and didn't appear to be 'clued in' to Millie's liberal minded lifestyle. She had attended Withington High School for Girls, which was then a state grammar school, and she had a string of good qualifications. She was very bright, good at languages, great company, vivacious and very very keen on boys.

Millie and I shared many personal and private conversations although Millie disclosed more to me than I did to her. Millie had many boyfriends and an active sex life. She was in a relationship with one boy, a doctor's son, which resulted in an
~~~~~

unplanned pregnancy. She tried to abort the baby by having hot baths and drinking gin. Those were the days before legal abortion and there were all sorts of methods which could be tried before resorting to outside help. Millie took what she considered to be practical action to solve a practical problem. I told Millie that if I had been in the same position, I couldn't have done the same thing, but I didn't judge her. Millie showed no outward signs of being seriously distressed by her situation although she was very concerned. She expressed her feeling of relief when she was finally restored to her single entity; one being again rather than two.

Sometimes, I would join Millie and other friends from the bank and go to the Saturday night dances at the Manchester University Union. Girls couldn't get in on their own because you needed to have a student card so we would wait on the steps of the Students' Union building and ask one of the male students if he would take us in on his card. Once inside, the girls would join up together and move around the three rooms set aside for music and dancing, waiting to be asked for a dance by one of the male students. Men outnumbered the girls by about three to one so the local girls were accepted as a welcome addition. Dances were still very formal; the boys standing together at one end of the room and the girls in their groups at the other. Girls were rarely seen to start a conversation and it was even rarer for a girl to ask a boy to dance. These University dances were often extremely crowded and it's not surprising that they got the reputation of resembling cattle markets. The annual Rag Week was a more exciting event when students dressed up and paraded in colourful floats through the centre of Manchester, selling the Rag Mag, the Rag Week magazine, and collecting small amounts of money for charity. The Rag Ball was the culmination of Rag Week and was considered the ultimate ticket of the social season.

~~~~~

Daniel and Edward were now young teenagers and had been Cub scouts and Daniel was a member of the Scout troupe at St Catherine's in Didsbury. They enjoyed collecting their various badges, Bob a Job Week and the camping breaks where they were able to put into practice what they had learnt. They both had paper rounds and had to be out of bed very early, summer and winter, to deliver the papers and magazines before setting off for school. Dad would make sure they were up and would cook them breakfast after their rounds.

Fashion was fun in the fifties and early sixties. Young girls wore full-skirted dresses with stiff net underskirts and pointed-toed kitten heel shoes or high heels. Daytime and office wear would usually consist of a simple dress or pencil slim skirt with blouse and cardigan. Girls would always wear nylon stockings with suspender belts. Going without stockings was very uncool. Shoes were either stiletto heels or neat little round-toed pumps. Accessories were particularly important and, if a woman wanted to be considered 'smart' she would wear gloves and a hat and of course carry a handbag to match her outfit. Trousers were rarely worn by women except for specific outdoor activities such as sport, gardening, camping or rambling. Silk scarves were popular, not for the way they looked; they didn't suit many people, but if worn as the Queen wears hers, they did protect hairdos from the rain and wind. New fabrics were being used such as polyester
~~~~~

and crimplene and a wide range of colours and designs were available.

The men would wear suits and ties for most occasions, work or leisure, or sometimes a plain or tweed jacket with trousers if they wanted to be less formal. Working men wore working clothes such as overalls and dungarees. Jeans had recently arrived from America and were just beginning to be seen as a fashion item. Previously, they had been known for their tough denim material and worn by cowboys or lumberjacks. Duffle coats were seen as trendy and were popular with students. Most students wore their distinctive college or university scarves and adopted a more casual look.

Whit Week was an important holiday and the famous Manchester Whit Walks[13] took place every year in the city centre. The Protestants would walk on Monday and the Catholics had their walk on Friday. I joined the lines of spectators to watch the children passing by in their pretty outfits. The clergy, with their top hats and walking canes, led their church communities from behind the brass band, which played popular church music. The band conductor walked at the front swinging a twirling baton in step with the band. Strong men carried colourful religious banners representing their parishes and patron saints. Religious statues would be carried and hymns sung as the spectacle made its way through the main streets of the city. Office workers watched from opened windows while crowds thronged the pavements. This was a display of religious faith and hundreds would come from all around the city to support their parishes as they took part.

~~~~~
~~~~~

The Plaza ballroom, Manchester

Manchester Whit Walks

Unlike many of my friends, I was not particularly interested in settling down and getting married. In the early sixties the average age for marriage was around twenty-three for boys and twenty for girls. Several of my friends were meeting boys and establishing serious relationships. This was in the era before the contraceptive pill and most young people got engaged before they were married and saved up for their new home together over a period of several months and often years. I was cautious about marriage; I held back in relationships. I was struggling to form my own ideal of marriage because my parents' marriage had been the exact opposite of what a marriage should be. There was no genuine commitment, no companionship, no loyalty, no shared values and no love. My male role models had not particularly distinguished themselves.

My own view of romantic relationships was similar to Isabel Archer in 'The Portrait of a Lady':

> 'Her thoughts were a tangle of vague outlines, which had never been corrected by the judgment of people who seemed to her to speak with authority. ...... Deep in her soul - it was the deepest thing there - lay a belief that if a certain light should dawn, she could give herself completely; but this image, on the whole, was too formidable to be attractive. Isabel's thoughts hovered about it, but they seldom rested on it long; after a little it ended by frightening her. It often seemed to her that she thought too much about herself; you could have made her blush, any day in the year, by telling her that she was selfish.' [14]

This light had not yet dawned for me and I felt unready for the commitment to one person and, although, it would have been the ideal escape for me, I wasn't tempted to opt for it. I had many casual or platonic friendships with boys based on mutual interests and my enjoyment of music and dancing. I loved going out with boys and the excitement of meeting someone new. I was a confusing mixture of cynicism and hope; quick to criticise boys for their shortcomings but ever hopeful that I would meet someone who would fulfil my romantic dreams. My social life was somewhat narrow. The men at the bank were old; thirty and over, which seemed old to me at the time and were either married or had girlfriends. I longed to feel the excitement of romantic love and the feeling that I had met that one special person.

I was nineteen when I met Ben at an Old Bedians dance. He invited me to dance and bought me a drink and chatted in a friendly and relaxed way. We danced together a few times including the last waltz and he asked if he could take me home. It sounds horrible now, but I remember the thought that passed through my head at the time. I thought he was very nice but I wasn't particularly attracted to him and I said to myself 'You're very nice but I'll probably have to finish with you someday'. Ben was six feet tall, slim, bespectacled with soft fair hair. He was twenty years old, a student, training to be a teacher, still living at home with his parents. Our first date was to a concert. He bought two tickets for the Hallé at the Free Trade Hall and we stood at the back of the stalls and listened to the music. A piece of music can wrap itself around you like a warm blanket. It is comforting and enfolding; it encapsulates your thoughts and emotions and soothes you like someone putting their arm around you or offering their shoulder for you to cry on. This was my first experience of live classical concert music and I loved it.

Afterwards we went to one of the popular coffee bars for a drink and shared our thoughts on the music we had just heard. I had my own small collection of classical records, mainly

Beethoven, Tchaikovsky and Mozart. Hannah and I enjoyed playing our LPs on the new radiogram which Mum had bought. We both loved Irish music; we would listen over and over to the music of Percy French.[15] One of our favourites was 'The Mountains of Mourne'.**♪7** For all the wonderful sights of London, the singer's heart was longing for the natural beauty and splendour of the mountains and his own Irish girl.

We loved the music recorded by Brendan O'Dowda. Nothing could equal his beautiful voice singing the emotive music of his homeland. French's haunting songs told of his love for his country, the sadness of mass emigration and the beauty of the Irish countryside. His comical songs drew upon the characters and culture of Ireland and painted a wonderful portrait of the richness and resilience of its people. To contrast with the nostalgia of French we would play folk music and songs of the troubles recorded by the Clancy Brothers and Tommy Makem.

I loved pop and this was the beginning of the pop culture that, for me, would reach its pinnacle during the 1960s and 1970s. The age of Twist came in and we were beginning to hear about a new pop group from Liverpool called The Beatles. Never again would the impact of popular music be so explosive. Artists were flooding onto the radio. Bill Haley and the Comets and Elvis had been famous in the US since the mid-fifties but now we were able to hear other great American singers such as Jim Reeves and the great Chubby Checker's 'Let's Twist again like we did last Summer'.**♪8** We had our own great singers too; The Beatles, 'Twist and Shout',**♪9** Tom Jones and Englebert Humperdinck, Adam Faith, Ricky Valance, Lonnie Donegan, Matt Munroe, Alma Cogan and Helen Shapiro. It seemed as though the world of music had been breached and was roaring forward like an unstoppable torrent. My love of music enabled me to exist in the moment, to articulate my feelings and to generate expressive energy. Music made me feel alive.

Certain aspects of my life were settling into a pattern. I worked from nine to five at the bank. I enjoyed my social life and was in and out of many relationships; boyfriends came and went; Michael, Kevin, Ray, Damian, Eamonn, never too serious, never too committed. I attended Mass every Sunday at St Cuthbert's and remained very close to my mother. We often stopped outside church for a friendly chat with one of Mum's friends from the Union of Catholic Mothers or the Catholic Women's League. My mother belonged to both these women's organisations and attended their meetings. She made every attempt to establish a normal happy life. She was a respectable married woman, with four teenage children. No-one imagined the struggle she had in coping with the fraught situation at home.

On one very rare occasion we had a home visit from Fr Chang, the curate. He was a Chinese priest, a lovely gentle man with soft dark eyes, who had escaped persecution in China and had been taken under the wing of our parish priest, Canon O'Leary. I can remember him sitting on a chair in our front room and talking to my mother. He was asking her whether everything was alright and of course she was telling him that it was. I wanted to speak out and say, 'No, it's not alright!' and I felt an uncomfortable twist inside me as I struggled to keep silent. The moment passed and he didn't visit us again. I knew there was something that was not right, something out of balance; relationships were not meant to be like this; marriage was not meant to be like this. If I'd known the secret, I would have understood.

Daniel left school and began working first for a firm of accountants and then as a trainee dispensing chemist. Edward trained as a dental mechanic and worked for a local dentist. Ben was a steady constant in my life. One of his best friends was Mark, Eileen's brother and he knew Rachel, my friend from Fielden Park and her friend Rita. He was in touch with several school friends and they would hold parties at one another's houses. Their parents would trust the teenagers to drink and play music, while they made themselves absent for the evening. It was all remarkably innocent and indicated the trust parents gave to young people in that generation. It was a different era but the trust was justified because we knew the boundaries that were expected and, for the most part, we respected them. I could never host a party. I was doing well to have the occasional visit from a friend. My father would not have allowed parties. Very few of my friends actually met my father face to face as he would disappear when visitors came. If he did meet anyone he would be polite and charming in equal measures.

Ben was the younger son of older parents. They lived in a modest council house in Chorlton very close to the River Mersey. You could gain access to their back garden along a path and through a small gate which led from the riverbank. Once inside the garden, a small green lawn surrounded by neat planting of alternate white and blue campanula came into view. Ben's brother, Louis, was ten years older than him and worked as a journalist in Manchester. He seemed a whole generation apart; he was married with a family. As an Old Bedian, Ben was very keen on rugby, which he had played at school. He wanted to be a writer and was interested in science fiction. He was fascinated by the Sputnik[16] satellite which had been blasted into space in 1957 and in the likely prospect of moon landings and further space exploration. In early 1958, the US had successfully launched its first satellite, 'Explorer'. He was intrigued by the American and Russian race to become the world's greatest space scientists. Russia's Sputnik II had been launched in November 1957 with a passenger aboard - a dog called Laika. The flight allowed Russian scientists to learn much more about the prospects for human space travel. The Americans' achievements were eclipsed in 1961 when the Soviet Union put the first human, Yuri Gagarin, into space.

Ben was a student at Hopwood Hall College up in the hills near Middleton, north Manchester. It was a men only teacher training college and this was one of the reasons why he made so much of his social life at home. Ben found it pretty bleak and lonely at Hopwood. I went up to the college one day and the cold wind was howling and the rain slanting in on us, and this was in the summer! He was teaching himself to play the guitar and was looking forward to qualifying as a teacher. One of his main interests was literature; he urged me to read 'The Catcher in the Rye'. I think he was hoping that this would help me to understand what it was like to be an adolescent boy. It did help and it gave me greater insight into teenage feelings and experiences. I kept in touch with Ben whilst going out with other boys. He invited me to my first Indian meal and to see 'How to Succeed in Business without Really Trying'. It was great to see a new American show so full of vitality and colour.

I resisted getting too close to any boy and resorted to safety in numbers. Relationships had their sexual dimensions of course and individuals did whatever individuals will do; I can't speak for others. I tried to show affection and respond naturally, depending on how I felt, but the boys I dated didn't put any pressure on me to have a full sexual relationship. It wasn't something I worried too much about. Ben and I became as close as we could be. On one occasion I put my face deep into his shoulder and cried. I didn't know why I was crying but I had the feeling that I wanted to bury myself in the softness of the moment and never raise my head again.

Despite the difficulties at home, I somehow managed to acquire the use of the front room and when Ben visited me we would lie down together on the settee and listen to the great Beethoven♪**10** and Brahms'♪**11** violin concertos and other intensely emotional music. The dreamy sounds would wash over us, taking us both to a higher realm which somehow expressed the way we were feeling about one another. We listened to many pieces of classical music; Beethoven's Pastoral symphony♪**12** was another favourite. Suddenly, out of chaos would come a sublime passage that would not have been nearly so sublime without the chaos before it. When common language is inadequate in expressing our feelings we reach for that expression in art.

I didn't know what I wanted and I didn't really know what he wanted. I'd walk with him to the 22 bus stop and we'd wait for his bus together which took him home to Chorlton. In the winter, I'd snuggle under his coat to keep warm and I'd breathe in the woolly smell of his tweed jacket with a trace of his aftershave, Old Spice. As I've said, we had very modest pleasures. Those were good times, probably the best we'd ever have. They were also confusing times; I began to feel under pressure because Ben was more stable and mature than I was. I was still not ready for a serious relationship. I was cynical, cautious, critical, fussy, guarded. In fact, I was inhibited and afraid of love. I could only think narrowly – 'What can you offer me? I didn't ask myself 'What can I offer you?' I found it very difficult to value myself but, at the same time, I felt justified in expecting the highest possible values in others. I was beginning to realise the difference between loving someone and being loved. Loving is giving and being loved is receiving but it's not as simple as that. To truly love you have to both give and receive over and over again. True love doesn't make demands. It's unconditional and it develops spontaneously and is on-going forever. The balance of that exchange determines the quality and depth of your relationship. I kept Ben at 'arm's length'. I thought, in my naivety that I could do better. I was soon to discover that this kind, generous and loving man, with his vocation for teaching and so many great friends was suffering from Crohn's disease. I tried to support him through those difficult times. He had to take time off college and had several stays in hospital when the illness flared up. I and all his friends would visit him regularly. He was treated with cortisone and steroids which caused his face to swell and left him feeling very self-conscious. He had to extend his teaching course by one year because of the time he'd missed. His teaching practices had to be fitted in when he was in a period of good health. Despite this, he was hopeful and always seemed positive about the future.

~~~~~

Now a qualified teacher, Hannah joined The Legion of Mary, a lay Catholic organisation, founded in Dublin in 1921. Its members were volunteers who worked with people in several
~~~~~

countries around the world. There were many dedicated young people in The Legion in Manchester at that time. Its members showed their commitment through engagement with prayer and active community work. The Legion saw as its priority the spiritual and social welfare of each individual. Members participated in the life of the parish by visiting families and the sick, both in their homes and in hospitals. Every legionary was required to carry out a weekly act of apostolic work in the spirit of faith and in union with Mary.

The Legion's work was usually parish-based but Hannah was based at St Gerard's Overseas Centre in Moss Side, one of the most deprived areas of the city. The centre was run by the priests of the Society of African Missions. Large numbers of immigrant African, Indian and African-American families were settling in Manchester and many of them were unemployed or in low-paid jobs and living in very poor housing. The children attended local schools and parents would find out about St Gerard's and the help they offered. Mothers and children could feel very isolated when they first arrived in Manchester but they soon became friendly with their neighbours and joined in community activities. Many of these activities were simple and practical and were provided by the Legion. There were knitting and sewing classes for the mums and outings and parties for the children. Members would visit local families in pairs and help them with housing issues, school enquiries and other needs. Sometimes, they would want to know about baptism or confirmation for their children and they could be helped with their approach to their local priest. When I heard about this work, I became very interested and joined Hannah at St Gerard's. I began to learn about the social and economic problems of families who struggled to provide for themselves and their children. I was becoming more aware of the political implications for such families. I felt empathy for the mothers and children and wished I could make a difference.

I was grateful to God for the relationship I had with my mother and realised how much worse life would be without her. In the meantime, I continued to work at the bank and enjoy my social life and tried to make the best I could of my life at home. Father Christmas did not exist, that I knew. I also knew that many adults were struggling to come to terms with the sense and purpose of their lives. You don't suddenly reach a magical age when everything is revealed. The people around you are just as lost as you are, sometimes even more so. This shock of reality hits us all at some point and how to resolve it is a challenge we must all meet.

Hannah joined The Gaelic League in Manchester. This was an Irish social club with a membership of working-class and professional men and women, many of them from politically active backgrounds who had been involved in Irish politics as far back as the earlier fight for Irish independence. The dances were held on Sunday evenings in premises in the centre of Manchester and I started going along too. Ceilidh bands would play and burly Irishmen would dance with the pretty girls, swinging them round in jigs and reels and the Irish waltz. These dance halls, which were active in most of the major cities in England, were an important social venue where Irish people could meet.

One New Year's Eve, I went along with Hannah to the celebration dance. I never dreamed I would ever meet a boy at The League but on this occasion I did. I met Francis. He was the boy at primary school who had looked after his sick friend. I fell in love with Francis at once. I thought he was very good looking with brown curly hair, a perfect smile and pale blue eyes. He reminded me of Dudley Moore, only Dudley had dark eyes. He was a student at Bangor University where he was studying Mathematics and Philosophy. His sister and her husband were keen members of The League and I had known his younger sister, Irena, at 'The Hollies'. We immediately had a great deal in common and I felt whisked off my feet, not only in the ceilidh, but in every aspect of my life. I was walking on air, thinking about him constantly, dreaming of being close and sharing everything with him. A few days later, he returned to university and I got up at some unearthly hour to see him off on the train back to Bangor. I felt very upset and missed him so much; living hour by hour, day by day until he returned.

My twenty-first birthday was approaching and Ben came round to see me and brought me a present. He took out a tiny red box from his pocket and my heart gave a sudden flip in case it was an engagement ring. But, it wasn't; it was a simple gold signet ring. He had had it inscribed with 'M' on the front and 'B' inside. It was the perfect gift, given with perfect understanding.

Francis and I wrote to one another until his return to Manchester at half-term. He told me then that he was seeing a spiritual adviser in Bangor and he thought he had a vocation for the priesthood. He also said that he had a girlfriend, Laure, an Austrian student, who was very keen on him and he didn't know whether to choose her or me or the priesthood. I was shocked and confused. I couldn't stand in his way if he wanted to be a priest; there was no question about that. My own emotions were of little importance if he had a religious vocation. I couldn't bring myself to express my true feelings for him. Jane Austen's Emma gives some understanding of how I was feeling; 'If I loved you less, I might be able to talk about it more' and I left it to him to make what he believed was the right choice. This was a heart-breaking time for me and a cruel irony. I now knew the difference between being 'in love' and being 'fond of someone', as I was with Ben. In my naivety I thought that my feelings for Francis epitomized real love, real passion and real commitment.

~~~~~

My love life was set against a backdrop of grave world events. The Cold War was a sinister presence in everyone's lives. The terrifying threat from the USA and USSR atomic conflict was palpable. The Campaign for Nuclear Disarmament was working non-violently to rid the world of nuclear weapons and other weapons of mass destruction. They tried to create genuine security for future generations and they had tremendous support, especially amongst the student population. The first Aldermaston March had raised awareness and the CND symbol appeared everywhere. CND members from all walks of life were marching. Young people were becoming more aware of the major political issues. This generation valued their franchise and recognised their responsibility in placing their vote.

There had always been political scandals but the media was now freer than ever before to comment upon and publicise the details. The Profumo Affair[17] undermined the Tory government of 1963 and seriously weakened the people's trust in ministers. The Macmillan quote: 'You've never had it so good' related to the financial strength of the pound, but the scandals were overriding the buoyant economy and this famous slogan was beginning to sound very hollow.
~~~~~

I was tired of my work at the bank. It was repetitive and there was little room for advancement. Some of my young colleagues had moved to other companies or got married but I didn't feel that this was the answer for me. Francis had telephoned me several times since his revelations about the priesthood and his other girlfriend. He seemed to want to continue with our relationship until he made a decision. We met often in the theatre coffee bar in the basement of Central Library; time snatched during my lunch hour. Each meeting left me sadder, more unsettled and more confused. I couldn't force myself to be assertive and my pathetic malleability did nothing to raise my self-esteem. I felt hopeless. Still enraptured by him but knowing there was no future with him, I knew I needed to do something with my life. I was growing older; I was feeling dissatisfied and became restless and depressed.

During the autumn of 1963, I was clinically depressed and on sick leave. This gave me time to reflect on my life and think about the future. Katie had made her choice and was very happy; she married Tom at twenty and was a mother when she was twenty-one. Hannah had a serious boyfriend and was at the start of her teaching career. I wanted to throw myself into something worthwhile that would give me the fulfillment I craved. I was at home when the news of President Kennedy's assassination[18] came through on November 22, 1963. The world had hit a new low. If there was ever a moment to cry: 'Stop the world, I want to get off', this was it. By Christmas, the depression had eased and I was back at work. The following year would bring major changes to my life; I was about to enter a whole new world, far away from my mother, far away from Hannah and far away from my father.

[9] John XXIII, was known as the 'Good Pope' because of his benevolent and jovial nature. Appointed Pope in 1958, he died in 1963.

[10] The Second Vatican Council Pope John wished the Council 'to increase the fervour and energy of Catholics, to serve the needs of Christian people.' To achieve this, the Church needed to be brought up to date, to meet the challenging conditions of modern times. Pope John, when asked to reveal his intentions, simply moved to a window and threw it open, to let in a draught of fresh air. He established a special Secretariat to promote further understanding of the beliefs and practices of other Christian bodies, and the need to work for the union of all in Christ.
http://www.christusrex.org/www1/CDHN/v1.html

[11] Sedgeley Park College
http://www.fcjsisters.org/ep/resources/about/hist_brit/Sedgley%20Park%20College%20history.pdf

[12] The Plaza Ballroom, Manchester Along with many other clubs the Plaza was the 'in place' to be in the early 60s.
http://www.manchesterbeat.com/venues/manchester_cbd/plaza/plaza.php

[13] Whit Walks At the height of their popularity, more than 30,000 people would attend the Whit Walks parade in Manchester.

[14] Henry James 'The Portrait of a Lady'

[15] Percy French Percy French is acknowledged as one of Ireland's greatest songwriters and entertainers
http://www.percyfrench.org/
Percy French, 1854 - 1920, with Brendan O'Dowda
http://www.youtube.com/watch?v=qKLWO2F3WgQ

[16] Sputnik and the Dawn of the Space Age History changed on October 4, 1957, when the Soviet Union successfully launched Sputnik I. The world's first artificial satellite was about the size of a beach ball

(58 cm or 22.8 inches in diameter), weighed only 83.6 kg. or 183.9 pounds, and took about 98 minutes to orbit the Earth on its elliptical path. That launch ushered in new political, military, technological, and scientific developments. While the Sputnik launch was a single event, it marked the start of the space age and the U.S. vs U.S.S.R space race. http://history.nasa.gov/sputnik/

[17] The Profumo Affair This took place in the early 1960s and has been described as the major political and intelligence scandal of the century. It helped topple the Conservative government and the Prime Minister Harold Macmillan. The story involved sex, a Russian spy, and the secretary of state for war. It captured world attention and discredited the government.

[18] The Assassination of President John F Kennedy The presidential party was driving from Dallas airport to the city centre when witnesses said shots were fired from the window of a building overlooking the road.

Celia, aged 16 with her parents

Celia, aged 7

Celia with her mother

John (left) with his family

Celia and John

Uncle Sam

Celia and family at St Anne's

Hannah, Martha and Daniel

Martha, Hannah,
Edward and Daniel

Martha and Hannah

Martha's 21st Birthday Party. Ben on left behind Martha

Daniel, aged 20

Edward, aged 19

Hannah, aged 23

Martha, aged 21

PART TWO
'The Secret'

Chapter Five

'A wounded deer leaps the highest.'
Emily Dickinson

In the early springtime of 1964, I was drawn to a particular advertisement in a Catholic newspaper. Plater College[19] was looking for students. It offered two diploma courses to young people who had missed out on formal higher education, one in Philosophy, Politics and Economics and the other in Social and Administrative Studies. The students would be selected by essay and interview and would have to show that they had a commitment to Catholic social teaching[20] and involvement in the community. I had been volunteering at St Gerard's for over a year and felt drawn to a career in social work. I wanted to work in the provision of children's services. I was motivated by the opportunity to expand my knowledge; to learn and develop so that I could pursue something more worthwhile. I sent for the application form and prospectus and arranged to meet Ben for a coffee to talk it through.

Ben looked at the literature on the table before him. He listened to what I told him about my ambitions and he offered encouragement. The first requirement, after completing the application form, was to write an essay, 'What are the main causes of juvenile delinquency?' I hadn't written an essay for over six years. I had never written an essay two thousand words long. Ben offered to help. We discussed the topic and I wrote down a few main points for further development. We arranged to go together to the Central Library in St Peter's Square which was the main academic public library in Manchester. Ben showed me how to find the right books and how to gather relevant information, how to structure the essay and how to balance the arguments. Then, I was on my own. I completed the essay and Ben read it through, giving his approval before final submission to the college. The essay was good enough to take me to the next stage. The interviews would be held in May and, if accepted, I would start the two year course in September.

I jumped off the bus one breezy spring evening; the pink and white blossom flying in the air. I had dressed sensibly in a new skirt and jacket but my fine hair was blowing and I felt self-conscious and extremely nervous. I crossed Wilmslow Road and entered one of Manchester University's halls of residence where a room had been set aside for the interviews. I had expected to be interviewed by three or four people including the principal but I was faced by a panel of twelve; the principal, various Manchester dignitaries and two or three former students. There were five candidates for interview. I struggled through the interview but within days received the news that my place was confirmed. A few weeks later my mother and I went by bus from Manchester to Oxford to see the college and to look around the city. We went to a wonderful musical show at the theatre in Oxford and enjoyed several restaurant meals together. We visited Henley and walked by the river. Mum was pleased for me but we were going to miss one another very much. I felt very lucky to be offered this second chance.

We were now more than halfway through the twentieth century but there were still very few opportunities for further education for men and women who had left school early. In 1964, if you didn't get straight to university or college via A-levels, you were more or less considered to have missed the chance. The main opportunities for learning were through polytechnics and night school classes but these only offered vocational or industrial training. The days of full life-long educational opportunities were yet to come.

During that summer, Ben was back in hospital. If what C S Lewis says is true, that: 'Affection is responsible for nine-tenths of whatever solid and durable happiness there is in our lives', then that was my true feeling for Ben; deep affection arising from friendship, warmth and genuine fondness and concern. He had been so encouraging and helpful to me; without his support and guidance I don't think I would have been successful in winning my place at Plater. Real friends help each other. They allow you freedom to be yourself - and accept you whatever mood you might present to them. They accept how you feel; positive or negative, it's fine with them. That's what real love is, allowing and accepting a person as they really are. When I left him for the last time, my eyes were stinging and hot with tears. Hopefully, he would be out of hospital soon and would be getting nearer to his first teaching appointment. Maybe, next time I saw him he would have a job and be over the worst of his illness.

Occasionally, I would call in to see Uncle Sam at his flat on Parsonage Road. He was now sharing it with his brother and his young nephew who had come over from Ireland seeking work. The three men lived the bachelor life, working, eating, and sleeping. Their main outlet was drinking at the weekends. As a heavy life-long smoker Sam suffered from bronchitis. Hannah kept in close touch with him, visiting him sometimes after a day's teaching and Edward, who worked at the local dental practice often called in for lunch or a cup of tea and a chat on his way home. Since he had left our house, I had developed a better relationship with him because I didn't have to face his drunken outbursts. These had been an additional trauma alongside the existing marital conflict. I could never put these unpredictable outbursts behind me and my relationship with Uncle Sam, although he was always kindly towards me, was often strained.

September was approaching and I was working up until the last moment. Even though I had a grant from the local authority, I needed the money. I would be resident within the college with all meals provided so I felt I would be able to manage my expenses. A year before, I'd saved hard all year for a trip to Spain; my first holiday abroad with friends from the bank. This would not be repeated this year as all my efforts were directed towards my move to Oxford. I'd been working through the reading list and buying a few books so I was beginning to get a feel for the subjects I would be studying. It felt like a fresh new start; it was a chance to prove that exam results are not the only indication of a person's worth. At the same time, I was apprehensive about how I would cope with the academic demands and, ironically, the exams at the end. I convinced myself, somehow, that this change of lifestyle would be a worthwhile adventure and an exciting challenge. I felt optimistic and I was ready to move forward.

University education was far beyond the aspirations of most working class people. The college sought to fulfill the vision of Fr Charles Plater, SJ providing the opportunity for a high standard of education to ordinary men and women, enabling them to train and return to their ordinary work in society, enhanced with the social teaching of the church. From its earliest beginnings, the college established close links with the Catholic Social Guild[21] and continued to offer education with an emphasis on Catholic social teaching. By 1960, the college was outgrowing its premises on Walton Well Road and the college moved to a large country house, south of the city, formerly the Bishop of Oxford's residence in Boars Hill. Joseph Kirwan (known by everyone as Joe) became its first lay principal in 1962 and, soon after, the college was renamed Plater College. Joe was a former student of the college with a distinguished war record in the Second World War. I became very fond of him, as a father figure, especially for his kindness towards me and he has remained one of the most significant influences on my life.

When I arrived in 1964, the accommodation at Boars Hill was somewhat haphazard and every inch of the house was used, as well as a croft in the garden and a lodge and caravan at the gate. Some years later, during the late 1970s, under Joe's leadership, the college moved to more spacious purpose-built premises on Pullens Lane in Headington.

Plater was recognised as the sister college to Ruskin[22] which was known as the Trade Union College. St Joseph the Worker was its patron and daily mass was offered every morning in the small chapel in the grounds just a few steps from the main entrance to the house. Students did not have to be Catholic to attend the college and students were welcomed from around the world. During my time at Plater, I enrolled on the course leading to the Diploma in Social and Administrative Studies. This diploma was approved and granted by the University of Oxford and was similar to a post-graduate course offered in the university to students with relevant degrees, so the academic standard was very high. Along with practical work placements, it would provide me with a basic qualification for social work. We were to study over two years and were invited to use many of the university's facilities.

We were offered membership of the Oxford Union and use of the Bodleian Library which included all the university libraries in the city and we were invited to sit our final examinations in The Schools. The college appointed its own tutors in Public Administration and Economics, History, Social and Political Theory, Social Ethics and Social Administration. A Dominican priest visited from Oxford to teach Moral Philosophy. Other subjects such as sociology, psychology, criminology and international relations were taught by post-graduates and students attended tutorials with them at their various colleges in Oxford.

The college, being founded by Jesuits, had a strong Jesuitical ethos. A statue of St Ignatius of Loyola stood proudly in the main library. The college was residential but a number of students lived in their own rooms either in Boars Hill or down the hill in Oxford. Most of the students came from the UK and Ireland but others were from Africa, Malta, Greece and Cyprus. There were two nuns in my year; one English and one German. They lived at a convent in Oxford but came up to college for classes and tutorials. Several priests were also studying there who planned to return to their appointed duties as administrators, social workers or parish priests.

The house ran efficiently with a resident housekeeper and a cook who lived nearby. Foreign au pairs would stay for a year or two and would carry out kitchen and household duties. They would attend language school in Oxford and would improve their English by mixing with the college community. Several love affairs developed among the students and the au pairs. The seasons in Oxford were a little ahead of Manchester; the leaves and the blossom appeared on the trees a week or two in advance of their counterparts in the north. The same seemed to be true about sexual activity. Maybe southerners were less inhibited; the so-called sexual revolution was now more evident and both sexes appeared more open to society's newly found freedoms and changing attitudes. It was also true that, although only twenty-two myself, I was now mixing with an older group of people and this was reflected in their more liberal attitudes and behaviour. What I was experiencing was a whole new world for me; a chance to meet interesting people, to study fascinating subjects and, hopefully, to leave at the end with the prospect of fulfilling my working ambitions.

The house was full of character with a huge wood-panelled entrance hall and broad staircase sweeping up to a galleried first floor. Two large rooms off the hall housed the libraries and quiet study areas. The light spacious rooms on the left of the hall were designated as the dining room and kitchens. There was a narrow servants' staircase opposite the kitchen door which led to the female accommodation on the first and second floors. The rooms on the first floor had been the original bedrooms and were quite large but those on the top floor were tiny and would have been used by the servants. There was a sweet smell of wax polish hanging in the air, especially in the library. The college stood in about seven acres of land with sunken lawns sloping to woodland at the rear of the property. Golden stoned gravel paths separated the house from the garden. A cupola topped the main house and offered views over the Oxford and Berkshire countryside. Fields stretched down to Oxford opposite the gates of the college and from a certain spot there was a beautiful panoramic view of the dreaming spires looking from the corner of Foxcombe Road.

I got the chance of a lift to Oxford with a former student, Michael. We arrived a couple of days before the start of term. The first day we went up to London to visit one of Michael's friends. The second evening, Michael and I were invited to dinner at Joe's home. He lived close to Oxford with his wife and his three young children. The children weren't present at the meal. Michael and Joe talked endlessly about politics and world affairs and justice and peace. I felt completely out of my depth. I had literally no adult conversation skills and no knowledge of politics. It's always better to keep quiet if you know nothing about a subject so at least I didn't embarrass myself by speaking out of turn.

I was glad when the first day of term arrived and I could meet the second year students and the new arrivals with whom I had the most in common. First of all I met my room-mates; Liz from Birmingham, Koula from Cyprus and Patricia from Nigeria. The four of us would share the large first floor bedroom for the next year. I was the youngest student at the college. I met Kathy, a second-year, an ex-nun with a spirited sense of fun and twinkling eyes. Mary, also a second-year, who was described as 'the keeper of the public morals,' was a Scottish girl in her late twenties. They were all eager to welcome the newcomers, to offer support and pass on their knowledge and guidance.

The two local pubs were 'The Fox' and 'The Flowing Well'. 'The Fox' was just a few hundred yards along the road from the college and was a stylish country pub with a comfortable lounge and large open fire. However, on that first night, I went with my newly made friends to 'The Flowing Well' which was about a mile away. We walked along the darkening lanes leading to the historic little village of Sunningwell. Coming into view was the pretty picture book image of a mock-Tudor style house. I could see the well, just beyond the wall and steps led up to a path through the rose filled garden. The building had previously been the village rectory and had only recently been converted into a pub. It had a great deal of charm and looked warm and welcoming. The convivial locals consisted of young farm workers or older village residents and the influx of students must have been a pleasant addition during term time. I hadn't had much experience of pubs. In Manchester, the majority of girls I knew didn't go in public houses unaccompanied. We piled into the public bar at the rear of the pub. A bar billiards table was on one side of the room with rough wooden tables packed closely near the bar. Several other students were joining us who had arrived later that day and I was introduced to all of them. One of these new faces was Harry and he was from the north-east. He had a pleasant lilting accent of which he was very proud. Almost immediately, I was aware of his forthright character. He was extremely friendly and confident and very enthusiastic. He was studying politics, philosophy and economics and seemed to me to be very knowledgeable and street-wise. He also appeared to be very popular with his fellow students.

Harry was quite short, perhaps two or three inches taller than my five feet four. He was both slim and strong; wiry might be the best description. His wavy hair, smiling eyes and almost continuous smile certainly made him attractive and interesting. The cook, Mrs Metcalf was particularly fond of him. 'I always like a boy who loves his mother' was her first comment to me.

I was to find myself in Harry's company from that moment on. He showed me around Oxford. He talked about his life in Sunderland and his interest in local and national politics. He had been brought up in a 'political' household and had several friends and labour party mentors who were on the local council in his home town. His ambition was to be a barrister. His background was solid working class and home had been a huge council estate. Before coming to Plater, he worked as a gas fitter. He seemed well educated in the 'university of life' definition of education. He would be twenty-five in December.

I felt like an empty glass waiting to be filled. My former life, for the moment, faded like a dream into the past. My new life became all absorbing and I had a very great deal to discover. Harry set himself as my guide and protector steering me through the labyrinths of this learning process. I wrote regularly to Hannah and my mother and looked forward to receiving their letters in return. Somewhat overwhelmed with the challenges I was now facing, I did my best to support Mum from a distance; the bond between us was indestructible.

My first subject was twentieth century social, political and economic history and I was struggling. I found it difficult to concentrate. It was as though I was on holiday and I hadn't yet found my feet. There were so many outside distractions. I was falling in love with Harry and very dependent on him. He was extremely attentive and, at times, possessive but I was not unhappy to be his little project. He loved being the guru; the expert, the authority, the leader, the specialist. He was also very kind and generous with his time and was always the first to roll up his sleeves to repair anything that was broken such as a cupboard door or the drains. Nothing was too much trouble and he was happy to work hard for the benefit of others.

~~~~~

That late September of 1964 brought with it an Indian summer; the sun shone on and on, lengthening the brightness of each day before the autumn nights drew in. The leaves were beginning to change colour. The semi-rural setting enhanced the transformation of the seasons. Manchester wasn't short of trees, particularly in Fallowfield and Withington, but the brightness of this autumn somehow set itself aside in a golden glow. Afternoons were given over for leisure or rest and Harry and I would stroll, hand in hand, along the lanes of Boars Hill. Harry took me to all the local beauty spots. He showed me Matthew Arnold's Field, a woodland and grassland site known for its superb views over Oxford and the surrounding countryside. The view is said to have inspired the poet's most famous line 'And that sweet city with her dreaming spires'. We climbed Jarn Mound and enjoyed the wide panorama encompassing three or four counties. Today, it has become so overgrown that the view has been obliterated. Taking the bus into Abingdon, we explored the quaint market town on the banks of the River Thames. We roamed the streets of Oxford soaking in the grandeur and history of the city, the colleges and its fine civic buildings. One day, we stopped at a small shop on The High and Harry bought me a pretty engraved silver ring.
~~~~~

It was customary for all first years to be invited to tea with the Misses Spooner, the elderly spinster sisters of the late Rev William Archibald Spooner.[23] We arrived at about four o'clock one Sunday afternoon at their well-presented house in the most genteel part of Oxford. They offered tea and tiny cucumber sandwiches with a selection of delicious home baked cakes and biscuits, all displayed on silver platters, engraved glass dishes or expensive porcelain. Our delicate china plates rested on lace napkins on our laps as we sipped daintily from the finest teacups with the smallest of handles. Both the ladies were diminutive. Their white and silver hair styled in a bun. They spoke with cultured cut-glass accents and were effortlessly confident in their roles as hostesses. We, mainly working class students, were trying our very best to enter with dignity and respect into this extraordinary but unfamiliar experience of a truly upper class tea party. Rev Spooner of Spoonerism fame was present in the form of a large sepia photograph perched on an elegant dresser. He seemed to smile down on us as we enjoyed the fascinating spectacle of courtesy, gentility and breeding served to us on plates by his gracious sisters.

Those rich and soft autumnal colours that would forever remind me of Oxford in late September were quickly fading. In their place were heavier shades of brown, rustic red and dull dark green. That palpable freshness of air; that sharp crispness on the breeze, that certain mellow perfume that lingers for a brief moment were all gone and Boars Hill lost some of its magical charm. The hydrangeas had long wilted, the camellia had lost its blooms and rain was a frequent caller. The days were growing shorter and I was engaged in an unrelenting struggle with my history essays. Baldwin and Gladstone's economic policies, among other things, were unfamiliar topics to me and it was with great effort that I grappled with the theories and consequences of political struggle.

All my experiences seemed to be heightened by my relationship with Harry. I had been open and expectant in this new venture and he had filled that space. He wanted to get engaged; he wanted to be sure that I had his full and undivided attention for the remainder of his second year. Part of me was challenging his possessiveness and part of me was embracing his strength and confidence and the assurances that he gave me. My friendships with the other students were deepening so I had the balance of female company as well and I would make friendships that would last through many years.

Meanwhile, I was adapting to the traditions of Oxford student life. A tutor would take the head of the table at supper time. Still painfully shy, I relied on Harry to sit with me to help me with conversation, especially with the tutors. After supper, coffee would be served in the hall and everyone would relax and stand around engaging with one another. I felt very self-conscious at such times; everyone else seemed so natural and spontaneous. I felt shallow, self-conscious and unresponsive. I longed to enter into this informal exchange but, somehow, my ideas, opinions and feelings seemed to evaporate, my insecurities dominated and I wasn't sure how to resolve the problem.

I missed my music and one Saturday afternoon went with fellow students to a performance of 'The Messiah'**♪13** at Oxford Town Hall. It was wonderful to listen to Handel's masterpiece.

> 'For unto us a Child is born, unto us a Son is given, and the government shall be upon His shoulder; and his name shall be

> called Wonderful, Counsellor, the Mighty God, the Everlasting Father, the Prince of Peace.
>
> Isaiah 9:6

Memories came flooding back to me. It was the beginning of December and the familiarity of Christmas was not far away. The weather was cold and wet and the winter nights were miserable. My term of History was almost at an end and I hadn't achieved a great deal, although I had, at least, produced a finished essay every week. The content and argument might not have been brilliant but the structure and format were definitely improving.

~~~~~

Around nine o'clock on the evening of Wednesday, 9 December, I was called to the telephone. My mother spoke and delivered some very sad news. Mum told me that Ben had died. He had been in hospital and his condition had worsened. The doctors had done all they could for him. The funeral would be held on the Tuesday of the following week. The blood seemed to drain out of my body; I was stunned with shock and couldn't stop trembling. I'd had no idea that this would happen and it was the last thing I had expected.

The news brought me crashing down to earth and I just wanted to return home and attend the funeral. I travelled to Manchester on the Friday of that week and would stay until the start of the new term in January. The funeral was well attended with a great many of Ben's young friends showing their love for him. His parents were celebrating his life as well as grieving deeply for his loss. I wore a blue wool dress because I thought Ben would like it. Saying farewell to him was one of the saddest
~~~~~

experiences of my life. Ben's mother invited me to visit and choose any of the books I wanted from Ben's bedroom. Among others, I chose his copy of 'The Catcher in the Rye'.

In my effort to be emotionally resilient, I became engaged to Harry over the Christmas holiday. He came to Manchester to visit for a couple of days and slept on the very uncomfortable bed settee in the front room. I was also on a work placement for two weeks with the Catholic Children's Rescue Society in Manchester. When I returned to Oxford in January I was relieved to find that my next subject, Public Administration, brought much better results. The civil service, local and national government, the monarchy, the police and the legal system were easier topics to study and seemed more relevant to me.

~~~~~

One thing I have discovered as I've gone through my life is that sad and negative events in people's lives can often have a very empowering effect. I call it my 'Arrow from a Bow' syndrome. It's like feeling a great need to propel yourself forward, to improve, to increase your knowledge and raise your aspirations, to experience intense motivation. I can only describe it as an arrow being pulled back in its bow and flying forward to reach its target. It sometimes happens when parents lose a child. They put all their energies into fundraising or setting up a support group. They are incredibly focused and determined to create good out of their sadness. I was unaware that this was happening at the time but, looking back now, I can recognise the change of pace, of momentum, of energy. This opportunity was a gift and I
~~~~~

was going to accept it and use it to the best of my ability. I embraced this second term with a new eagerness and enthusiasm.

Catholics have a strong belief that they are in God's hands. All we have to do is respond to that love and formation. He has his purpose for us if we will open up to it. He forms us and uses us for that purpose.

> Abba, Abba, Father. You are the potter,
> we are the clay, the work of your hands.

My mother's frequent letters didn't mention anything about the true situation at home. They were usually newsy and cheerful. I tried to put my memories of home to the back of my mind but I was always aware that she was missing me. Harry was talking about our future plans. He would graduate in May and was already exploring the possibilities of a career in the law. We visited London to meet with one or two of his political contacts in the labour party. This was my first ever visit to London. It was snowing lightly as we passed the Houses of Parliament and we had to ask permission from Joe to get the last train back to Oxford. Harry thought that he would be able to train as a barrister if he could just make appropriate moves in the right places. He knew all about entry into the legal profession and attendance at Inns of Court. His aspirations and his confidence were sky high.

Easter came and I was back in Oxford for the summer term. Around this time, I had another bout of depression. Harry accompanied me to the GP who prescribed anti-depressants over a period of several weeks. The illness interfered with some of my studies but I sat the end of term collections and was encouraged by better results. Harry was studying hard for his final papers which he would sit at the Examination Schools. To attend this formalised event, the men were required to wear black trousers, white shirts and white bow ties and the girls wore black skirts, white blouses and black ribbons tied in a bow. Oxford traditions were respected at all times and our special relationship with the university was highly valued. We had the honour of being presented with Oxford University diplomas although in later years this was changed to 'Special Diploma' status.

There were certain tensions in the air as all the second year students piled into the college van for their trip to Oxford on the first day of exams. Harry was calm and confident; his positive personality carrying him through. However, in that particular year, a number of Plater students failed their diplomas and, unfortunately, Harry was one of them. At first, he wanted to be based in London but he also knew that because I was so close to my mother I would want to return home. His career aspirations had to be modified. His inclination was directed now towards trade unionism and local politics and his ambition was to become a member of parliament, possibly even prime minister. A hiccup of failure had not dampened his ambition.

My feet, however, were firmly on the ground when I returned to Manchester that summer. I was to complete my first year with a six week summer placement with the National Society for the Prevention of Cruelty to Children in Macclesfield and Manchester. Each year, students had to vacate the college and take all their belongings with them. I had borrowed a trunk from Michael and sent this home ahead of my own arrival. My father refused to have me home and threw the trunk out onto the pavement outside the house. I think it was because he was jealous of my relationship with my mother but he gave me no reason.

Harry arrived in Manchester and we rented a small flat together in Fallowfield. I, as a student, was earning no money and Harry was yet to find work, so the relationship was under considerable strain. Around this time, I heard that Uncle Sam was not very well; he was suffering from chronic bronchitis and was in hospital at Baguley. I went to visit him there and spent an hour of so by his bedside. I felt a fondness for him. I knew he had been kind to us and, as a friend, he had tried to offer his support to my mother. He had kept in touch. He had shown concern if any of us were ill or troubled. I felt sad that he was suffering and wished him well.

During my work placement I was required to make the journey to Macclesfield for four of the six weeks. I accompanied the local inspector observing his work with clients and their families. The other two weeks I spent at the Manchester office where I met more senior inspectors and experienced the inner-city problems which their clients faced. My placement was very successful and I learnt a great deal about the real-life challenges of social work.

At the same time, Harry was having a claustrophobic effect on me. He was over-attentive and too intense. I applied for a provisional driving license and, unknown to me, Harry filled it in, leaving it for me to complete with my signature. Although it was a relatively unimportant example, I felt he was taking over too much and, although he was trying to be thoughtful and caring, I sensed his control and dominance. I was beginning to feel resentful. Harry's happy-go-lucky approach to life was not reflected in my own mood and I felt trapped by circumstances beyond my control.

The situation at home that summer was very fraught and Mum and Dad were never far from my mind. I felt guilty that I was not supporting my mother as much as I had in the past. I felt guilty that I couldn't love my father. Hannah was now spending most of her time with her boyfriend Simon and his family. She too needed to escape to another life outside the constrictions of the Barkworth household. Daniel and Edward were both working and remained at home and there were signs that Daniel was thinking of social work as a career move too. He was also planning to move out to share a flat with a friend. He applied to Plater and would have been accepted but decided instead to study at Manchester University. It took all of my defence strategies to present a normal face to the people I was working with. Due to my commitment and genuine interest, I somehow found the ability to flip between the two and could focus on the work of the inspectors and their clients but the strain was beginning to tell.

With the arrival of September, I was relieved to return to Boars Hill for my second year and escape from the repressive atmosphere of life in Manchester. This year I would share with an older student from Liverpool and we were in the small attic bedroom overlooking the drive. I managed to fulfill my academic work and continued to attend university seminars and tutorials. I particularly enjoyed sociology, psychology and criminology and had the opportunity of listening to the lectures of eminent academics including Professor A H Halsey and Dr Nigel Walker among others. A stream of new first year students presented themselves optimistically to college life. One mature student, Brian, a man of around forty, invited several students to his flat in north Oxford for music and drinks. I heard, for the first time, the superb tenor-baritone duet from Bizet's 'The Pearl Fishers' **♪14.** This plea for everlasting friendship seemed to me to express the extraordinary power of a love that will last until death.

~~~~~

A few weeks into term, I received news of the death of Uncle Sam. When I visited him in the summer at Baguley Hospital he was very ill with bronchitis and emphysema. His lifetime of smoking, heavy drinking and working in factory conditions had contributed to his poor health and he died shortly before his sixty-second birthday in October. I felt sad but didn't return home for the funeral. Harry visited me at college but I was beginning to have serious doubts about the future. I was confused about my feelings. I'd loved him when I needed him but I wasn't certain about his possessiveness, his overwhelming confidence and his unrealistic ambitions. I'd got to a stage when I didn't need him so much; I was now a little surer of myself, at least on a one-to-one level, and although not showing outwardly, I had begun to develop a quiet inner strength.

My mother had used my father's rejection of me as a catalyst. She moved out of the house into rented accommodation opposite the Red Lion pub in Withington. Hannah, Daniel and Edward moved in with her and helped finance the cost of the move and the furnishing of the spacious first floor flat. Hannah and Simon were now planning to get married and were looking for a house in Didsbury. My father remained in the family home with Daniel being the only one to visit and offer support. This move seemed to present an opportunity for change.
~~~~~

By Christmas 1965, I'd made the decision to end my engagement. Harry was very upset and begged me to reconsider but I couldn't stay in the relationship. We had been engaged for a year. I needed to be free to make my own way and to be responsible for myself. It was now clear that I would need another year at college to complete my diploma; the time I'd lost through depression in my first year had dragged me back. Studying sociology and psychology I became more aware of my own personality and the pressures that I was facing. I began to develop a more objective way of thinking. I was becoming a staunch pragmatist. Thoughts of the complexities of the relationship between my mother and father were sweeping through my mind. I was trying to make sense of something I didn't fully understand. There was definitely a missing piece; something undisclosed and waiting to be discovered.

During the summer term of my second year, I had a quiet period when I didn't have to worry about forthcoming exams. My fellow second-years were preparing for their final examinations but I was free to devote a little time to myself. We were in the middle of a heat wave and each day was predictably hot and sunny. Oxford is not only a city of dreaming spires; it is a city of real and achievable dreams. It has an indescribable aura of charm and romance which lingers in the air and never more so than on a beautiful summer's day.

The University's motto, 'Dominus illuminatio mea' means 'The Lord is my Light'. I'd heard about the long held dream that the city would be transformed into a place where Christ is its light. I was young and idealistic and very religious in my approach to life. My formation was rooted in my Catholic faith and my motives were governed by my beliefs. At the height of the heat wave I was introduced to a young man, Louis, who had been studying to become a Dominican brother. He lived at Blackfriars Hall and was at the point where he felt he should give up his vocation and return to a secular life. Originally from Liverpool, he was a gifted artist and we enjoyed a gentle relationship, walking by the river. We'd sit and watch the punters drift by, the pale green willows weeping and kissing the water. We'd stroll along the quaint and cobbled streets of the town. He gave me a couple of his pictures, a self-portrait and the interior of a Norman church. He visited me in Manchester during the summer but the relationship did not last. I mention it because it was like a dream, soft and misty; almost without substance. Two innocents drifting to who knows where? There was nowhere else for me to drift except back to earth.

I completed my final placement that summer, working within the family support team of a local voluntary organisation. We were dealing with families who were on the edge and were trying to avert a crisis situation. This preventive social work was demanding and often, if a crisis did arise, children had to be removed from their parents and taken into care. I found that I identified very closely with these families. If my mother had not been as capable as she was, I could easily have been one of those children. This was the point at which I decided to become a child care officer.

In my final year I was able to concentrate fully on my academic work. I went on dates, usually just to the pub, with several other students but didn't get emotionally involved with anyone in particular. My mother was no longer subjected to the rows and anxieties she had previously endured. Life was hard for her, none-the-less, and she relied heavily on Hannah and Edward for financial support. I knew I would go back to live with her and started to apply for jobs in child care in Manchester. I would be sad to leave Oxford but I had to return to the real world. The grime and reality of the north was part of me. The people I loved were there and it was where I was needed.

Harry settled in the north and worked tirelessly for the community. He achieved high political office in his adopted city.

---

[19] Plater College previously known as The Catholic Workers' College The college was founded in 1922, in memory of Father Charles Plater, SJ, who had been instrumental in founding the Catholic Social Guild in 1909 which gave the Catholic Social Movement its first organisational structure in England. Fr Leo O'Hea SJ was its first principal.

[20] Catholic Social Teaching - Encyclicals and Documents
Catholic Social Teaching is grounded in the values and principles of Judeo-Christian religious experience, which are reflected in the Christian scriptures and the Church's lived tradition. An active commitment to social justice is now recognized as essential to authentic Catholic faith.
https://educationforjustice.org/catholic-social-teaching/encyclicals-and-documents

[21] The Catholic Social Guild An organisation founded in England in 1909 to promote interest in social questions among Catholics, and to aid in the practical application of the Church's principles to existing social conditions.
http://saints.sqpn.com/ncd01771.htm

[22] Ruskin College Ruskin College is an independent educational institution in Oxford. It is named after the essayist and social critic

John Ruskin (1819–1900) and specialises in providing educational opportunities for adults with few or no qualifications. http://en.wikipedia.org/wiki/Ruskin_College

[23] Rev William Archibald Spooner (22 July 1844 – 29 August 1930) was a famous Oxford don whose name is given to the linguistic phenomenon of 'spoonerisms'. Few, if any, of his spoonerisms were deliberate, and many of those attributed to him, although legendary, are thought to be untrue. It is also said that Spooner disliked the reputation he gained for getting his words muddled. Examples are: 'You have hissed all my mystery lectures, and were caught fighting a liar in the quad. 'Having tasted two worms, you will leave by the next town drain.' (You have missed all my history lectures, and were caught lighting a fire in the quad. Having wasted two terms, you will leave by the next down train.) 'Let us glaze our rasses to the queer old Dean.' (...raise our glasses to the dear old queen.) 'Is the bean dizzy?' (Is the Dean busy?) 'A well-boiled icicle.' (A well-oiled bicycle.) 'He was killed by a blushing crow'. (He was killed by a crushing blow.)

Chapter Six

'The key to wisdom is this - constant and frequent questioning, for by doubting we are led to question and by questioning we arrive at the truth.'

Peter Abelard

I left Oxford with my Diploma in Social and Administrative Studies and joined the Children's Department of Manchester Social Services as a fledgling child care officer. Almost immediately, I realised the importance of being able to drive. The visits to clients were spread across the north-east area of the city. Sometimes, we needed to go further afield to Blackpool, Bolton, Rochdale or Oldham to visit children placed with foster parents or to attend meetings with other social service organisations. In the meantime, we were able to use a taxi service provided by the authority when we were moving children or, alternatively, we had to make our own way on the local buses to our various appointments. This was very time consuming. The authority would fund social workers for their first car, taking payment out of salary, but employees had to remain in post for at least two years. It would take me a while to get on my financial feet but I started to take driving lessons in the hope of simplifying my daily travel commitments.

The newspapers were full of the Moors murder trial.[24] Everyone was talking about it and shocked that it should have happened in a place like Manchester. Reporting of the trial revealed shameful and unbelievable acts of cruelty. The murderers seemed to show no remorse and blamed others for their crimes. The accounts made compulsive reading but it sickened the whole nation to think that such things were possible. Ian Brady and Myra Hindley became the two most reviled criminals in the country.

Hannah and Simon had married in July and moved into their own home in Didsbury. Daniel was now sharing with a friend. Mum, Edward and I left the temporary flat and, following their generous invitation, moved in with Hannah and Simon. Daniel, having completed his studies at Manchester, was also working as a child care officer. He was assigned to another area office but our colleagues met on a regular basis at lunchtimes or for social events.

Accommodation at the little house was very limited and I had to share a small double bed with my mother. It was not easy for me in my mid-twenties to share a bed with another woman, even though it was my mother, and I could feel the tensions rising in me. I couldn't relax. The stress was affecting my sleep and I felt drained of physical and emotional energy. The freedom I'd enjoyed at college was gone. I kept up my driving lessons whenever I could and my test was approaching. I took the test but failed.

My former social life was not waiting for me when I returned to Manchester; most of my friends had moved on. Katie now had two small children and was living in Yorkshire. I visited her from time to time and we kept in touch. Other friends were married or settled with partners and I no longer related to past interests. I had to make new relationships, new contacts and new opportunities to meet people. I was interested in my work and very committed but found it increasingly exhausting. I worked all day and returned each evening to this tense existence.

At work, I had my own caseload and was supervised by an experienced colleague. I took my turn at fulfilling the duty officer's role where virtually anything could arise. This was the cutting edge of our work and we were frequently dealing with crisis situations. It could involve life changing decisions about taking children into care or leaving them to remain with their families. Often, the risks were grave and decisions had to be referred to the manager of the team with the duty officer having to implement whatever decision was reached. This usually meant ringing round the support services in the city area and beyond to find foster care for children in crisis. These situations raised difficult challenges and I sought a lot of support from my senior colleagues, who, although extremely busy themselves, were very generous and helpful.

Most of my caseload focused on preventative care and involved responsibility and commitment as well as consistent communication with my clients and other social services. Keeping up with casework records was another major challenge and these notes were always outstanding. To complete my training, I was considering other one-year university courses in applied social studies which would give me the extra qualification I required as a social worker. This would mean a move to another city, further study, more disruption and greater financial strain.

My father was still living at the family home and Daniel visited him regularly. His working life, such as it had been, was over and he was not in the best of health. Daniel would see that he had enough food and was able to manage from day to day. Hannah and Edward chose to keep their distance. Time was passing. My mother made no contact with him. There were too many unhappy memories and any form of reconciliation seemed impossible. A few months passed and then the news came through that he had collapsed and died suddenly. I don't remember the exact circumstances of his death; I think I must have blotted them out of my mind. I can't remember attending his funeral but I think that all the children probably attended. A heavy load had been lifted from my mother's shoulders and laid to rest. I know I had felt the burden too but even when you lay it down the ache in your bones lingers on.

Hannah and Simon's kindness had been greatly appreciated but the house in Withington was now vacant and Mum wanted to return. I refused to go back; its associations were too painful. So she rented it out in the hope that the future might bring some sort of compromise. Several months passed but the troubling memories did not ease. My mother searched for a solution and decided to sell the house and move to another. She would need the help of Edward and me to secure a mortgage and to act as guarantors for her. We found a house in West Didsbury and Daniel joined us as we moved in. I took my second driving test and failed.

~~~~~

Not long after my father's death, I began to have deeper thoughts about my childhood. I felt there was something missing in the story I had been told and started to suspect that my mother was not telling me the whole truth. The more I thought about it, the more I believed that my suspicions were justified. These
~~~~~

concerns would not go away and they were taxing my brain. I felt unsettled and anxious, wanting to find out the truth but not daring to confront my mother. There was now an elephant living amongst us, sharing the space, getting in the way and blocking out the light and warmth from our relationship. Frustrations were creeping in all around me and I became increasingly irritable and cynical and immersed in negative thoughts. Was there a secret that was being held on to?

Gradually, I was slipping down a slope leading to despair. I wasn't coping; I was ceasing to function normally. One day, as I was sitting at my desk writing reports, I put my head in my hands and cried uncontrollably. My bewildered colleague tried to comfort me but I couldn't tell her my reasons for crying. I'm not sure I knew what they were myself. Now, my ambition to work as a social worker was being threatened and all inner strength was ebbing away. Many of the circumstances I was facing were not of my own making and were beyond my control. The mantra, 'It's not what happens to you that's important, it's the way you react to it' was coursing through my mind. I prayed fervently for help. I was questioning my faith. Christians are supposed to trust in God. He has the power to solve problems, to give answers; to heal and to restore. There was no sense of healing or restoration in my world.

I had embraced the opportunities life had offered. I was sure it had been the right path to follow; I had felt drawn to social work as a vocation and had no doubts about that. Now, I found myself out of my depth and lacking the means to overcome my anxieties and weaknesses. My response was to internalise my feelings. I didn't tell anyone about my worries; I felt unable to confide in Hannah or my friends so I tried to carry on and hoped that this difficult period would pass and that I would survive. In this state of anxiety, I took another driving test and failed.

I was called for university interviews at Swansea, Edinburgh and Liverpool. It was at the Liverpool interview that I was able finally to confront the true state of my health. One of the tutors who interviewed me questioned me perceptively about my wellbeing and I knew then that I was incapable of taking on the physical and intellectual challenges of another course of study. Within days of my Liverpool interview, I visited my GP in Didsbury. He listened to me for twenty minutes, not saying a word, and then he told me that I was suffering from severe depression and on the verge of a nervous breakdown. He prescribed anti-depressants, tranquillisers and sedatives, and signed me off work for three months. I was so grateful to this kind doctor for taking the time to listen to me. That simple act of remaining silent and enabling me to offload my feelings was in itself therapeutic. I have never forgotten the way that made me feel.

~~~~~

Not all depressions are severe but it is a common illness and one in four women and one in ten men will experience it in some form during their lives. Sometimes, it can be triggered by life events such as relationship problems, death, illness and loss. Depression leads to patterns of negative thinking and a gradual withdrawal from normal behaviour. A combination of events and life stress can spiral down into a form of reactive depression. No-one in my family had been prone to this illness, so genetics did not seem to play a part. My symptoms were clear. I felt
~~~~~

physically ill; this nauseous feeling was constantly with me. My mouth was dry and my throat constricted. My head felt fuzzy, my thinking blurred. I was aware of every act of swallowing. I could feel the stress and tension within my mind and body.

Persistent sadness hovered above me. I lost my concentration, couldn't read and there was a marked loss of interest and pleasure in activities that I normally enjoyed. My sleep was disturbed and I had little appetite. I lost weight and was tired all the time; even more so when taking the medication, for this seemed to numb my feelings and befuddle my brain. I was relieved to be away from work but my feelings of worthlessness heightened and dullness settled upon me like a black cold cloud. I would feel dizzy sometimes and my eyesight was affected by the drugs. Walking the streets of Didsbury was my best form of exercise. People say, don't they, 'Oh, she needs taking out of herself.' That is so true, and by walking I was able to face forward and look out to the physical world counteracting my feelings of self-centredness. I had nothing to offer anyone and there was little anyone else could do to change me. Recovery was slow, almost imperceptible. I didn't feel like socialising or visiting friends. Even listening to music involved too much effort.

Three months went by and there was no improvement. Another three months passed and my doctor referred me to a psychiatrist. I began to see Dr Thompson at the Psychiatric Unit in Swinton Grove close to Manchester Royal Infirmary. He started a talking therapy with me and eventually I was able to tell him about the suspicions I had regarding the situation within my family. I explained how I struggled with certain memories trying to make sense of them. Why did Uncle Sam give money on a regular basis? Why did he engage in discussions about family members on matters like education, illness or employment whilst my father did not? Why did we keep meeting up with him? I know he was lonely but was that the only reason? I knew he had been married before but didn't know any details. I knew he'd had a child but knew nothing more than that. Had my mother been in a relationship with him? Was he our father? Why hadn't she divorced and married him? I told Dr Thompson that I couldn't confront my mother and he asked me why. I said I couldn't bear to upset her and I might be wrong. I didn't want to lose her and feared it was all in my imagination.

My mother, for some reason, spoke to the psychiatrist, or he spoke with her. It's very unlikely that he would have discussed my fears with her, but, if he had and she had denied them, this might explain his reaction. She told me that he thought I was hyper-sensitive and he prescribed further medication. Another six weeks passed by and, still down in this deep dark pit, I had little hope of climbing out. Why didn't Dr Thompson realise the importance of this conflict within me and help me? With his support, I might have been able to communicate my feelings to my mother but I remained incapable of expressing myself. I was locked in a spiral of unremitting depression.

Much later, I learned that the key to successful relationships is good communication; this point was lost to me at that time. Even when you know that good communication is central to healing relationships, why is it so difficult to achieve? How often do we get 'crossed lines' and misunderstandings? We are all so wrapped up in ourselves that we don't listen attentively, we don't explain clearly and, consequently, we don't understand one another properly.

At my next visit, Dr Thompson offered me a course of Electro-Convulsive Therapy.[25] The treatment would involve placing electrodes on my temples, on one or both sides of my head, and delivering a small electrical current across my brain, while I was sedated or under anaesthetic. The aim was to produce a seizure lasting up to a minute, after which the brain activity should return to normal. It was suggested that I would have one or more treatments a week and perhaps more than a dozen treatments in total. I declined this treatment and desperately called on all my inner strength. I wanted to be transformed into someone else; one who could change. I hated being who I was, so dull and lifeless. I was missing out on life; I wasn't living, just existing in a colourless world, cold and lonely like being enclosed in chrysalis form, unable to feel any warmth and light.

Self-pity is a major element of depression. If you're consumed by pain, as with toothache, you can't take your mind off it. Depression is mental pain and is with you constantly. It doesn't enhance personality; it deadens the spirit. Any patience or humour, which existed before the illness is diminished by the effect of drugs. The humanity of the person is somehow sucked out, leaving a zombie-like personality in place of the former self. It's horrible.

My recovery from this depression was long and painfully slow. I realised that it wasn't just the secret that had led me here. The other important factor was loss; the loss of Ben, the loss of Francis, the loss of Harry, the loss of my career. The symptoms stayed with me for years rather than months.

I wasn't wallowing in self-pity, however, I was doing everything I could to fight it. I was trying to make a life for myself. My mother took in lodgers once more and this helped her to manage the finances without going out to work. Two of my single friends had babies which were not planned and I did all I could to support them. Daniel met his wife, Jane, and they married in her home city, London. He moved away, working in several social work posts, living in different places in the south of England.

~~~~~

One of the greatest struggles in life is finding meaning and purpose. Many of us just flit like butterflies from one pleasure-giving situation to another, indulging in whatever gives us the most gratification. Satisfying though these experiences may be, they are shallow and hedonistic when compared with how most people live their lives. Such ephemeral pleasures have no place in Victor Frankl's book 'Man's Search for Meaning'. He was writing as a survivor of the concentration camps and his life was as far removed from modern western society as it could possibly be. He gives great insight into man's endurance in the face of the overwhelming struggle between life and death. It may not seem relevant in the life of the average person but it surely can't fail to be inspiring to those who, for whatever reason, are suffering or have lost their purpose in life.

Depression, however deep, is not of course equivalent to the horrors of incarceration in a concentration camp but there are some parallels that can be drawn. Writing of the terrible deprivations and humiliation of the human spirit, Frankl said that no matter how desperate a person's situation may be there are always choices to be made. Every day, every hour, offers opportunities to make decisions which determine whether you
~~~~~

submit to those powers which threaten to rob you of your very self, your inner freedom. He believed that any man can, even under such circumstances, decide what shall become of him - mentally and spiritually. He may maintain his human dignity even in a concentration camp.

No prisoner knew how long his term of imprisonment would be; there was no date for release; his prison term was not only uncertain but unlimited. This is described by Frankl as 'provisional existence of unknown limit' which, along with imprisonment, is how life might be viewed when suffering severe physical or mental illness or other temporary states such as profound and overwhelming bereavement, depression or unemployment.

Frankl recognized that everyone needs to be able to look to the future and to set themselves goals. Sudden loss of hope and courage can have a deadly effect. Attempts were made in the camp to restore a man's inner strength by showing him future goals that he might attain. He quotes Nietzsche's words, 'He who has a 'why' to live for can bear with almost any 'how'.' Any man who saw no sense in his life, no aim, no purpose in carrying on was soon lost. Frankl concluded, 'We had to learn ourselves and, furthermore, we had to teach the despairing men, that it did not really matter what we expected from life, but rather what life expected from us.'

Frankl's balanced and unprejudiced reflections on his experiences have helped me to understand the importance of freedom, hope and courage and the vital central component, which is that our lives need purpose 'the why'. No matter what circumstances life throws at us 'the how', we must hold on to the overriding belief that we have a destiny to fulfill through self-determination. That destiny may not be heroic; it may be relatively simple but it is, nevertheless, one's own destiny and worthy of the struggle.

~~~~~

Forsythia heralded the start of spring and summer came and offered a touch of renewal. Another two or three months passed and I started to sense some very small improvements although these changes were almost undetectable. I began to hope and believe that I could get better. Very slowly, I began to think more positively. I realised I could not return to social work; it was too emotionally demanding for me at this stage in my life. I had absorbed other people's pain which had added to my own. I needed to detach myself emotionally, to stand outside and above my own pain and the pain of others; it was the only way I could survive.

Eventually, my thoughts were beginning to look to the future. When I was better, I would have to take some kind of office work. I continued to walk regularly and to benefit from this. My mind began to open up and I tried to connect more closely with the people around me. I was not yet ready for socialising and meeting new people but I began seeing old friends and showing an interest in them. I was still not inclined to pursue new interests, even practical ones, but with the reduction in my medication, my concentration was starting to improve and, slowly, I was able to read again. The improvement continued very gradually but some symptoms would remain with me for several years.
~~~~~

World events, of course, continued to play themselves out. In 1964, Dr Martin Luther King Jr, had won the Nobel Peace Prize for his work in the American Civil Rights movement. On April 3 1968, King arrived in Memphis a little later than planned because there had been a bomb threat before his flight had taken off. That evening, King delivered his 'I've Been to the Mountaintop' speech to a relatively small crowd that had braved the bad weather to hear him speak. King's thoughts were obviously on his own mortality. He concluded the speech with:

> 'Well, I don't know what will happen now; we've got some difficult days ahead. But it really doesn't matter with me now, because I've been to the mountaintop. And I don't mind. Like anybody, I would like to live a long life - longevity has its place. But I'm not concerned about that now. I just want to do God's will. And He's allowed me to go up to the mountain. And I've looked over, and I've seen the Promised Land. I may not get there with you. But I want you to know tonight, that we, as a people will get to the Promised Land. And so I'm happy tonight; I'm not worried about anything; I'm not fearing any man. Mine eyes have seen the glory of the coming of the Lord.'

On April 4, 1968, he was hit by a sniper's bullet. King had been standing on the balcony in front of his room at the Lorraine Motel in Memphis, Tennessee, when, without warning, he was shot. King was immediately taken to a nearby hospital but was pronounced dead. Violence and controversy followed. In outrage of the murder, many blacks took to the streets across the United States in a massive wave of riots. The FBI investigated the crime and an escaped convict, James Earl Ray, was arrested, but many people, including some of Martin Luther King's own family, believe he was innocent.

In the early-morning hours of June 5, 1968, an assassin named Sirhan Sirhan shot Senator Robert F. Kennedy,[26] who had just won the California primary. He died shortly afterwards having reiterated in his speech that evening his belief that the country needed and wanted unity between all people.

Months earlier, Senator Kennedy had addressed the death of Martin Luther King Jr. following his assassination.

> 'What we need in the United States is not division; what we need in the United States is not hatred; what we need in the United States is not violence or lawlessness, but love and wisdom, and compassion toward one another, and a feeling of justice towards those who still suffer within our country, whether they be white or whether they be black.'

~~~~~

It was difficult to feel optimistic as the western world brought forth new charismatic leaders, only for them to be shot down. These were depressing times and news headlines did little to promote optimism but, in my own life, there came a point when I had to move forward. One day, more than nine months after my initial diagnosis, I made the decision to go into Manchester and find a job. I went into an office recruitment agency and was offered a vacancy for a secretary to the cashier in a large industrial company in the city, The Manchester Ship Canal Company. The recruitment officer rang their personnel office and I went along for an interview.

Ship Canal House was a very imposing building, standing seven storeys high above a rusticated ground floor. The sixth storey had an inset row of classical Corinthian columns which spanned two floors. The whole building, reinforced concrete on a
~~~~~

steel frame, was clad in Portland stone. A statue of the god Neptune stood proudly on the top parapet and over the bronze doors of the front entrance was a sculpture of Atlas holding up the world.

I had a successful interview and started working for the cashier. I hadn't forgotten shorthand and typing so these skills returned immediately. I felt thankful to be back in work. I could now contribute something for my upkeep and I had taken the first step into the next phase of my life. I shared an office with another secretary. After three months I was promoted. I opted for the challenge of monthly accounts and year ends. Of course, it was not really what I wanted to do; the routine was repetitive and I worked in a tiny office which had just one high window overlooking a brick wall.

My main consolation was my relationship with my boss. He was sympathetic and generous and recognised my vulnerability. We shared a mutual love of classical music. He was something of the father that I had never had. Through our conversations, my love of music returned and I discovered many other great composers and numerous classical works. Mozart's 21st piano concerto♪**15** was just one of these pieces and it always takes me back to that period of my life. The concerto was used as a theme in the film 'Elvira Madigan'. Some people say it is the most beautiful film ever made. Almost every frame would do justice to a delicate watercolour painting. The scenes are flooded with muted shades of yellow, white and green. It is a film of pure romanticism relating the love story of two beautiful, selfish young people, obsessed by the legendary nature of their own passionate love. As well as music and film, my boss and I also shared an interest in literature and discussed the comparative nature, not of religions, but of Christian denominations; he was a Methodist. Our discussions put these issues into perspective and helped me to embrace an ecumenical view of Christianity.

I gave up smoking; a habit I'd had for nearly ten years and I passed my driving test on the fifth attempt. One day, I was on my way home, cutting though Spring Gardens, when I met Harry. We stopped and chatted for a few moments. He told me he was working for a legal firm a few streets away and that his political ambitions were being fulfilled. Sadly, the depth of feeling I'd had for him had long gone. I felt guilty. I saw him on many occasions through the years. He was always available and willing to help or offer advice. He gave his time generously and unconditionally. He was a good man who helped many people in difficult circumstances. We followed our separate paths but remained, tentatively, in touch. It took a long time for me to accept this second level of our relationship but, ultimately, I did and we remained friends until he died many years later.

During that year of 1969, the American, Neil Armstrong became the first man to walk on the Moon.[27] I was sad to think that Ben had missed seeing this momentous event. One day, I sat on the long seat of the bus going to work and the conductor looked at me intently, his face pushed forward into mine. 'Cheer up,' he said 'it may never happen.' A hot pain pricked somewhere inside me. He had no idea what he was saying. How I missed Ben. One night, travelling home on the bus, I saw the back of someone's head and I thought it was his. My throat knotted tightly and tears flooded my eyes. Sometimes, I would dream that he was still alive. If only I'd realised what I'd had with Ben. I loved all Roy Orbison's music and his song 'In Dreams'**♪16** explained my state of mind perfectly:

'In dreams I walk with you. In dreams, I talk with you …'

There was always a lump in my throat when I thought of Ben. He was so loving and accepting. I missed him and I had never needed him as much as I did then.

~~~~~

There was a community of Dominicans in our parish and I directed my thoughts towards a visit to them, hoping that they could give me some guidance. They lived in a large rather imposing house on Alan Road in Withington and I decided to call and make an appointment to speak with one of the priests. I wanted to explain to him how I was feeling and discuss how I might approach my mother in a sensitive and loving way in order to discover the truth. I climbed the broad stone steps and knocked at the huge wooden door. One of the young friars opened it and invited me in. I explained that I would like to see one of the brothers for help. At that moment an older brother came into the hall. He immediately took over and insisted that he was the one who should see me. I felt embarrassed and uncomfortable. It was almost as if I were at the centre of a competitive game. I felt like an object of prey rather than a person. It's difficult to explain the impact it had but, despite making an appointment, I never returned.

The late 1960s and early 1970s were passing me by. I tried to think positively despite my depressed mood; I struggled to hold on to the hope that eventually I would get better and reach a level plateau where my moods would be relatively stable. I wanted to marry and I wanted children. If nothing else, I kept up my
~~~~~

appearance even though it was a pale comparison to what it could have been.

~~~~~

Since the early sixties, young women had been growing more imaginative in choosing what they wanted to wear. Miniskirts had been popular for several years but now girls would wear a short mini skirt one day and a maxi dress, midi skirt or hot pants the next day. There was more freedom and variety. Trouser suits were becoming popular but were not yet worn at the office. For formal eveningwear, in the early seventies, women chose straight or flared Empire line dresses with, perhaps, a sequined fabric bodice and exotic sleeves or, less formally, full length maxi dresses, evening trousers or glamorous halter neck catsuits. The short flared skirt was very popular, and was a style I often chose. Casual separates, on a mix and match basis, were just beginning to come into fashion and the less formal look was becoming more popular. Women expressed their personalities through flares, platform heels and the peace symbol. The hippy look was in and nearly all the girls had long straight hair with a centre parting. Diana's 'flick' would come a decade later.

I was now in my late twenties and my social life was beginning to re-establish itself. I joined the Intervarsity Club with my friend, Joanne. It provided activities such as walks, badminton, tennis, record evenings, theatre and concert visits for young professional people. The events were arranged by the members themselves. A few months after we joined, Joanne and I decided to organise a record evening at my home and the activity was advertised in the club's monthly bulletin. I received calls from
~~~~~

several members booking their places. One was from David who said he would come and bring along some of his own records. We provided a buffet and a selection of wines and chose a good range of music. Edward was on hand to help and the evening was a great success. A few days later David rang again. He invited me to a Hallé concert.

Still very fragile, I embarked on this new relationship with both hope and trepidation. Just as mental illness destroys a person's approach to life, mental wellbeing can provide a positive change to the way you feel about life and how you approach challenges. Good mental wellbeing means feeling good about life and yourself and being able to get on with life in the way you want. Sometimes, we think about wellbeing in terms of what an individual may have; your income, home or car, or your job but evidence shows that what we do and the way we think have the biggest impact on our health. Part of this change is in becoming more aware of the present moment. This means noticing the sights, smells, sounds and tastes that you experience, as well as the thoughts and feelings that occur from one moment to the next.

When it comes to feeling good, other people matter. Most important are sound relationships with family, friends and the wider community. I began, very slowly, to build stronger, broader social connections in my life. For me, the strength of my relationships determines the quality of my wellbeing. They are, therefore, the most important single factor in my personal life. Investing in good relationships increases feelings of happiness and self-worth and can allow us to share our feelings and know that we are understood. Along with this comes emotional support, as well as the chance to support others. It seems reasonable to believe that being around people with strong mental wellbeing can improve our own mental health. Nurturing our relationships can help us feel happier and more secure and can give us a greater sense of purpose.

My life changed when I met David. He had very strong mental wellbeing and this was the beginning of one of the most important relationships in my life. He was solid and very independent. He had lived with friends in houses or flats since he'd come up to Manchester. Although he'd studied for a degree in chemistry, he'd worked in industry since graduating. He now worked as a computer systems analyst for a large textile company based in the city's Oxford Street. His home was on the Lancashire coast. Southport was an elegant small town community, nothing like the metropolitan city of Manchester. In its working class areas, families seemed closer knit; traditional values had survived rather better than in the big cities where many families had been rehoused following the Second World War and communities had been split apart. He was the sort of person who knew his roots and knew where he wanted to go in life. We shared many interests, music being the most important. Although, not a Catholic, David had been raised as an Anglican and had sung as a chorister at his local church. He was a keen sportsman and passionate about golf having played since the age of nine with his father. He always respected my Catholic faith and never argued against it.

When I visited David's family, there was always some discussion, hole by hole about their recently played game of golf. The family; his parents and sister and several aunts and uncles welcomed me warmly. One aunt had despaired that he would ever meet anyone he wanted to settle down with. A year passed by and the tentative bond was strengthening; we were still together. Once again, I was listening to beautiful music; Tchaikovsky's 6th Symphony♪**17**, Bruch's Violin Concerto♪**18**. I was sharing those special moments with David now and hoping that our relationship would fulfill my dream to settle down and have a family.

My attendance at church had been affected by my breakdown. I still had faith in God and my religious beliefs were unchanged but I questioned my commitment to the church as an establishment. I was aware that the church has always been made up of human beings, with all their personal faults but, somehow, I wasn't in the right frame of mind to concede these weaknesses. I hadn't been able to exhibit the kindness and compassion for others that I'd sought and needed myself. Meanwhile, I was hoping my mother would respond to my gentle questioning but I was constantly thwarted. She always found a way to deflect my questions and I couldn't find the courage to communicate more directly. I suppose a certain amount of resentment was creeping in. This resentment was slowly being replaced with anger and was being directed towards my mother.

David and I had been together for about a year when we talked of marriage. I expect most couples have a special romantic song; ours was 'And I love you so'♪**19**, sung by Nana Mouskouri. It expressed perfectly the way we felt about each other. David knew about my breakdown and he could see for himself how my health had slowly improved. We talked about family illnesses and I told him about my father's mental state. I explained about my family background and my uncertainties about my father and mother. I told him about my strong feeling that John was possibly not my real father. I showed him photographs of the family; John and Celia together, Celia and the children and Uncle Sam. He looked at the family photographs and had no doubt that Uncle Sam was our father based on a strong family likeness and the details I explained to him. Now that I had David's support, I felt that it was time to tell my mother about my discovery of the truth.

Auntie Kathleen, one of her oldest friends, was the person I decided to approach to ask for definite confirmation. I couldn't keep the secret to myself because I wanted to be honest with my mother and I wanted her to know that I knew the truth. One day, after work, I arranged to visit Auntie Kathleen. David said he would call for me at her house and take me home afterwards. I was rehearsing my conversation with her as I walked along. I was feeling sick with apprehension, my heart was palpitating and I was heaving and retching with nerves. Auntie Kathleen was a lively character, twice divorced, full of humour and very lovable. She listened carefully to my story and told me that what I was thinking was all true. She said Sam and Celia had always wanted what was best for us and felt they were protecting us by withholding the truth. 'What they don't know won't hurt them!' kind of philosophy, which was very typical of that time. She told me they had met while working for Electrolux in the thirties. Sam had become a widower a few years before he came to England. He needed somewhere to live and Celia suggested that he should board as a lodger with her mother. Her mother liked him and Celia and Sam's relationship developed from there.

When the war came everyone's lives were changed. Opportunities had to be taken as quickly as they arose. There was a 'Don't ask, don't tell' culture and as long as people were discreet, no-one need know. People, I imagine, went with their instincts far more than they would have done in peacetime. Everything became more urgent; seductions that might have taken months could be completed effectively in a fraction of the time. Feelings were heightened, intensified. There was a sense that the world might never be the same again.

Into this world, Hannah was born in 1940 followed, in quick succession by the rest of us. There was a brief moment when Celia and Sam were tempted to emigrate together to New Zealand but this didn't happen. Celia chose to remain with John on whatever terms were decided; if, indeed, any terms were decided. She must have stayed mainly for financial reasons because the house was bought with her money, a link she had with her own father. She wasn't prepared to let John take that from her. Both believed that marriage was for life; maybe this had been part of it too. Whatever had happened, the stage had been set, the lines were written and everyone had their parts to play. Soon, David arrived and he heard for himself the true story of my childhood.

The time came for our engagement and we planned to marry within a few months. I had to face my mother to explain what I had discovered. This prospect hung in the air like an approaching storm. How should I tell her? Should I confront her? Should I go through a third party? Should I write a letter? I knew there would be no single cathartic moment when all wrongs would be righted. I didn't know it then, but the rains would fall; they would envelop the valued treasure of our relationship. The water would seep into every available space, finding its own level and many unanswered questions would be left either floating on the surface or lost in the depths forever.

I found it very difficult to speak directly to her so I decided to write a letter in the hope of preparing my mother for the meeting. The original letter has been lost but the following is what has stayed in my memory.

Dear Mum

This is the most difficult letter I have ever had to write but I wanted to prepare you before speaking to you about it. I don't want there to be any secrets between us and I need to be as honest as I can with you. Please know that I write this out of love and without judgement for the people involved and it doesn't mean that I love you any the less.

For a long time I have suspected that Uncle Sam might be our real father and not John Barkworth as we have always believed. I now know for certain that this is so and I've had it confirmed for me by someone who definitely knows.

Now that I am getting married, I want to be certain that I know the full truth. I realise it might be upsetting for you but I hope you will understand my need to talk about this and to come to terms with the truth.

I will always love you.
Martha

I left the letter on the hall table and returned in the evening to face my mother alone. She had read the letter and despite the words in which it was framed she did not accept it with compassion or understanding. She was furious with me for having the audacity to uncover what I had discovered. What right did I have to know her business? She didn't seem to understand that I did have a right; in fact, I believed, all her children had the right to know the truth about themselves and their origins. There was no chance that she would be willing to tell my sister and brothers and she begged me to keep it to myself. I was very hurt by this response; so cold and unforgiving. It was as if I had committed some grave offence against her. She couldn't bear the fact that she had been discovered.

This disclosure changed our relationship irrevocably. I had torn down her meticulously constructed web of protection and exposed her to the dangers of confronting her demons. I felt the deep pain of rejection. I didn't realize it then but that feeling would stay with me for the rest of my life. Jacob Bronowski said, 'A lie can be good in the short term but wrong in the long term.' Celia didn't appear to know the difference. She had lived this lie for so long, I think, that she had begun to believe it herself. The option to lie is a serious consideration. You also have to have an excellent memory. It undoubtedly puts a strain on anyone to constantly have to remember the story they have previously told.

My mother clearly believed that it was her secret alone. She owned it; it was her property and she chose to deny that it had affected anyone else. If we're fortunate, most of us grow up in loving families. Frequently, however, there are many incongruities and it is a rare family that doesn't hold some sort of secret. Some secrets lose their power over the years, but others leave a damaging trail which never dries up. In families with more shameful secrets, communication becomes difficult. A child's natural curiosity may be met with hostility, even rejection. Often, questions are discouraged and lies are perpetuated. Sometimes, other family members are pulled under the cloak of deception and expected to collude with the perpetrator.

It isn't easy to keep secrets hidden. Sometimes the mystery lies in our enigmatic body language or in the expression on our faces. Other indicators relate to what we are prepared to talk about and when we choose to remain silent. In other words, information is suppressed. Although we feel that we communicate in many ways, verbally and non-verbally, some family members also develop instincts about certain issues. Much of my own suspicion was founded on intuition and only later, on more rational thinking. Whatever our feelings might be about keeping secrets in families, the secrets themselves have great potency. No amount of elaborate deception will guarantee that they remain undiscovered. Even if they are buried for what may seem like the right reasons, they can still be harmful.

Often, secrets are a defence mechanism. They exist because appearance is more important than reality. This was certainly the case with my family secret. They protect the one who holds the secret or can be rationalised as protecting other vulnerable family members and often they do. People say that it is a rare family that doesn't hold some sort of skeleton. While some of our buried secrets lose their power over the years, others leave a damaging legacy. Whatever the situation, there's something about the truth which makes us want to seek it.

The secret was Mum's great defence and she needed it to protect everything that she had worked for; her respectability, her appearance, her status as a Catholic mother and a widow. None of this must be compromised. She lived in a time when appearances were so important. She was recognised as an attractive woman; medium height with brown, now greying hair, styled in the latest fashion. Her nails were manicured, she wore carefully applied make up, smart clothes and well-heeled shoes. She was good company and loved theatre and music. She was generous to those she loved. She had a very strong character and an incredibly skillful way of presenting a solid exterior. I loved her; I will always love her. I admired her for her strength and determination. She had guts, stamina and resilience; was far stronger than I could ever be and utterly determined to survive. These outward signs meant the difference between pride and shame and she just couldn't bring herself to accept that her illusions of herself had been shattered.

> 'There can be no knowledge without emotion. We may be aware of a truth, yet until we have felt its force, it is not ours. To the cognition of the brain must be added the experience of the soul.'
>
> Arnold Bennett

And Pascal, the French mathematician and Christian philosopher said,

> 'We know the truth, not only by the reason, but also by the heart.'
> 'Once your soul has been enlarged by a truth, it can never return to its original size.'

I couldn't change the fact that I knew the secret and I had no choice but to take into account my mother's strong defensive reaction and her need for self-preservation. Perhaps it felt to her as though I had stripped her naked before the whole world. That must have been a horrible feeling for her. She was now desperate to cover herself up once more. I knew she had always done her very best for her children and I loved her for this, but did she genuinely believe that the truth would hurt us? It hurt her so much to know that I knew. Her whole existence depended upon the impression she presented and she was determined to continue the illusion – to herself if to no-one else. However, my mother must have known that she had had an adulterous relationship. I don't think she denied this to herself but I can't be sure. She must have been burdened by feelings of guilt and shame and maybe that's why she maintained her silence. There's a real danger that a long habit of not thinking a thing wrong, or rationalizing that it is excusable, gives it a superficial appearance of being right. Denying it doesn't mean that it didn't happen.

I can understand and accept that family secrets are best kept within the family. Outsiders may judge more harshly and Mum would not have wished her children to be classified as illegitimate. Perhaps this fear also influenced her decision to remain silent. At one point, she had told me that her marriage had not been consummated because John didn't want her to get pregnant as he feared she might die. They were married in a register office and my mother may have thought that this was not a 'proper' marriage as it hadn't taken place in church. I just don't know what she thought because she never told me.

Knowing that a thing is wrong is one thing, judgeing those involved is another. I don't seek to make judgements about the rights or wrongs. The placing in time of these events is important; wartime when normal boundaries were extended, her disastrous marriage and her love for my real father. Alongside this was her deep need to have children and perhaps Sam's need to be a father following the loss of his child. The general displacement of people during the war due to men working away from home provided the opportunity. Many strange things happened to so many people that would not have happened had it not been wartime. My mother and father acted out their responses to this unhappy situation relative to the strict morals in society at that time. In today's more liberal society, similar stories would not demand such an elaborate cover-up.

Sometimes in life we are offered the choice between truth and peace, you can take whichever you please; but you can seldom have both. I had to do what I felt to be right. Should I keep the secret? I'd be damned if I did, and damned if I didn't.

---

[24] The Moors Murderers The crimes of Ian Brady and Myra Hindley shocked the world and made them into two of the most notorious killers in British criminal history. Between July 1963 and October 1965, they murdered five children, all from the Manchester area. They kidnapped them and sexually tortured them, burying them on Saddleworth Moor in the Pennines above Manchester. The pair were jailed for life in 1966.

[25] Electro-Convulsive Therapy There appears to be no generally accepted theory to explain how ECT works. One of the most popular ideas is that it causes an alteration in how the brain responds to chemical signals or neurotransmitters. In the 1960s, ECT was used primarily in the treatment of severe depression, and psychiatrists saw it as the most effective treatment in many cases, particularly when depression hadn't responded to drug treatments.

[26] Senator Robert Kennedy appeared on the verge of greatness. President Lyndon B. Johnson had announced months earlier that he would not seek re-election over the growing unpopularity of the Vietnam War, which Senator Kennedy opposed. So, in the moments before Sirhan Sirhan fired the fatal shot, it looked as though Senator Kennedy would run against Republican Richard Nixon in the 1968 election.

[27] Moon Landing - 1969: Man takes first steps on the Moon. American Neil Armstrong became the first man to walk on the Moon. The astronaut stepped onto the Moon's surface, in the Sea of Tranquility, at 0256 GMT, nearly 20 minutes after first opening the hatch on the Eagle landing craft. Armstrong had earlier reported the lunar module's safe

landing with the words: 'Houston, Tranquility Base here. The Eagle has landed.' As he put his left foot down he declared: 'That's one small step for man, one giant leap for mankind.'
http://news.bbc.co.uk/onthisday/hi/dates/stories/july/21/newsid_2635000/2635845.stm

Chapter Seven

'Men stumble over the truth from time to time, but most pick themselves up and hurry off as if nothing happened.'
Winston Churchill

I had no-one else to be but myself and my conscience told me I shouldn't alienate anyone from the truth. My thoughts sometimes overrode my conscience and I questioned many times whether I should disclose the secret to Hannah and my brothers or whether I should protect and isolate them from it in case it hurt them or unsettled them. Seldom are we prepared for unpalatable truth, which is why it is often revealed to us gradually. If I told the secret now, there would be no period of preparation for them. They would have to hear it plainly spoken without the softness of time, without the means to process it slowly. Whatever I did, it would be difficult; a cruel intrusion disturbing their view of themselves and their own identity. My own manner of discovery had been gradual; bit by bit I had put my suspicions together to form the whole. Somehow, I knew intuitively that things just didn't add up; there was a sense of cover up; a sense of deception.

I remember going to Lyme Park[28] one day with my mother, Uncle Sam and the other children. I must have been about fifteen years old. We were having a very pleasant day, walking on the slopes not far from the Hall. Mum was at the top of a slope and she began to walk towards Sam. As she walked, the gradient took over and she ran forward out of control. He moved to save her and for the briefest second they were in each other's arms. I sensed something in that moment. I recognised the chemistry between them and kept that feeling close to myself. Any ideas or beliefs that I had, I realised, were mine alone. I didn't mention them to Hannah and I didn't mention them to my mother. No-one knows what another person is thinking or feeling unless they tell you and no-one was ready to speak.

The same thoughts had passed across my mind many times. Why had Uncle Sam helped the family financially? Why would he be so generous? I thought about the length of time Mum had known him and the desperate state of her marriage. I remember her consulting Uncle Sam from time to time about family matters, whilst never consulting her husband. I reflected on the behaviour of all of them, trying to make sense of it. None of them was happy. John was living a miserable life; no respect, no status, crazy frustration expressed with outbursts of rage. Frustration may not be as highly rated as anger, jealousy or shame but nevertheless it can be equally destructive. People can be 'driven mad with frustration'.

I've learnt the hard way that any emotion we feel has to be expressed in an appropriate way which gives the least harm to others. If we are angry and we express our anger violently either by word or action, we are having a destructive effect, especially if children are involved. The same applies to other emotions; jealousy is often projected onto others through sarcasm; resentment can make us cruel; rejection can be acted out in our own rejection of others. We instinctively seek some kind of compensation for our unhappy feelings and we seek it from those around us, especially from those to whom we are closest. This is often apparent when there's been criticism for some small matter; the other person invariably finds some way of criticising back; it helps to level out the transaction. Most of us don't even realize we are doing it.

The deceptive behaviour that was part of my childhood was clearly a sign of deeper personal issues. Some kind of defensive response needs to be learned to help the child cope with difficult situations and this is a natural means for helping us to cope with our insecurities. However, many of us become over-dependent on our defences and choose to hold on to them far beyond childhood.

~~~~~

Sam always drank heavily, perhaps to drown his sorrows. He was angry and volatile, especially during my earlier childhood. My mother was strong but she wasn't impenetrable. These thoughts and suspicions worked on my mind like sharp tools in their attempt to give character to my misshapen ideas. And so, eventually, I solved the puzzle. I discovered the secret. I discovered who I was and my genetic origin. Did my sister and brothers have the right to discover their true identities too? Did they know? Had they discovered it for themselves without telling anyone?

Of course, secrets and truths are no more the same than secrets and lies. It's far more complicated than that. Secrets can be lies. Secrets can be true. Then, there is interpretation. Sometimes, the truth becomes confused and what I think happened to me actually happened to someone else or maybe it happened to both of us. Every individual experiences truth in their own subjective way. Truth can be embellished. Truth and secrets can be discovered but concealed. For some people, facts are only true if they can be proven. Just knowing something is not enough. There have to be added elements of intelligence, comprehension, understanding and insight. The facts have to be processed before truth can be fully realised.

~~~~~

While I was wrestling with complex reasoning, my life was opening up new dimensions as I planned my wedding with David. The wedding day arrived and Daniel gave me away. We paused on the steps before entering the church. The registrar, for some strange reason, moved forward and asked me for confirmation of my father's name for the marriage certificate. My first thought was to say 'He's dead'. I looked at Daniel and made close eye contact with him. I thought 'If he knows I'll be able to tell from his reaction.' There was no reaction and I had to voice another lie. It stuck in my throat as I named John Barkworth.

We bought a house in Heaton Mersey, not far from Didsbury, which was perfect. It was a Dutch style dormer semi with a large open-plan lounge with staircase off, three bedrooms and a diner and kitchen combined. The front lawn stretched across both semis and was shared with the next door neighbour. The little back garden had a patio with steps up to a raised lawn. David's beloved piano took its special place in the lounge. During that first year we decorated and improved the house. Six months later, I was pregnant with our first child. Charlie was born in Stepping Hill Hospital in the early hours of a freezing cold morning in January, 1975. Outside, grey slanting rain was pouring onto the Derbyshire hills visible from my hospital room. The labour was traumatic and Charlie was born by emergency caesarean section. I didn't see him until he was about nine hours old. He was brought into my room in a little glass-sided cot. His eyes were wide open, his head facing towards me and he looked at me with an intensity that stole my heart. I felt that gaze reach into me and my love was absolute; how could I not give him everything I had; from that moment I would love him forever.

Charlie was fair skinned with blue eyes and soft blond hair, an enormous amount of energy and a very determined personality. He completed our little family and I felt a surge of happiness and fulfillment. I was now a mother and had a new life to focus on; a life I would need to put before my own. My world would revolve around a new vocabulary; devotion, self-sacrifice, acceptance, patience, tolerance, discipline and love; nappies, feeding, playing, wiping up, bathing, cuddling and love. I would have to grow consistently in these virtues and practices to fulfill my role well. Charlie was connected to me by an invisible thread, strong and unbreakable.

> 'One thing I know; the only ones among you who will be really happy are those who will have sought and found how to serve'. 'There are two ways to live your life. One is as though nothing is a miracle. The other as though everything is a miracle.'
>
> Albert Schweitzer

My miracle was Charlie.

~~~~~

Bringing up a child requires teamwork and David and I acted as a team from the start; each fulfilling our own designated roles, but often interchanging them too. Mum would visit me regularly and stay for the evening meal and I often pushed Charlie in his pram into Didsbury to see Hannah and Simon. Family members from both sides came to Charlie's baptism and Hannah and Simon were his godparents. The tensions still existed between me and my mother but I didn't want them to affect her relationship with her grandchildren. Nineteen months after Charlie's birth, I became a mother for the second time. My pregnancy coincided with the hottest summer of the decade, 1976. Lawns, fields and grassy banks turned brown, the earth cracked, the streams dried up and water supplies were at dangerously low levels. My
~~~~~

hair was constantly wet at the nape of my neck as my baby grew heavier and heavier.

This time it was an easier birth and Catherine appeared like a translucent angel, white blond hair, almost invisible on her perfectly shaped head. Her tiny fingers coiled around mine. She had blue eyes and the softest palest skin like the fine velvet of a petal. I was in heaven as I held her in my arms in our little sunlit garden on that early August day; my only desire to be her friend forever.

I'd sing to my babies whilst I was changing them:

> 'You are the sunshine of my life
> That's why I'll always be around.' **♪19**

It's a wonder it didn't put them off music for life.

Grandparents and other relatives visited and expressed their admiration. I enjoyed for the briefest moment the sweet delight of achievement. I now had a son and a daughter on which to shower care, protection and love. I would look after them with all that I could offer but never forget that they had free spirits. With two children under two my mind was often fuzzy and blurred but it was a bearable fuzziness, even though I was exhausted. There was a popular Bee Gees' song on the radio just then called 'Tis the Morning of My Life'. **♪21** It had a soft ethereal quality which reflected my mental state of slight disorientation due to the tiredness that comes with looking after very small children. I was off all medication by this time so I knew the feeling wasn't drug induced. I felt much more secure and there was a well-drawn path ahead of me. I made new friends through attendance at playgroups and meetings of the National Housewives' Register.[29]

David had his own interests; golf, badminton and singing. Charlie started school and Catherine was about to start when I was pregnant again with the third child that I had always wanted. Jack was born at the end of the summer of 1980. He had soft brown eyes, sturdy limbs and auburn hair, like his father. I had convinced myself that he would be a girl but it didn't matter. When he arrived, I was overjoyed to have another child. All my children had quite distinctive personalities. Jack was a contented and affectionate child and happy to play on the floor, arranging his cars into traffic jams and rescuing people with his emergency vehicles. He had a creative imagination and a loving nature.

I hadn't returned to the church at this point so the children were enrolled in the local non-Catholic school. The only time I attended church was at Easter; on Good Friday and Easter Sunday. The children went to Sunday school and learnt a little about the bible stories and the Christian way of loving and caring for one another. We had friends of all denominations and others who had no religious beliefs.

Charlie was outgoing and adventurous, always demanding attention and approval and thriving in the company of others. Catherine was artistic and self-sufficient; she would absorb herself in drawing and playing. She also had a very determined streak that asserted itself from the age of three onwards. Jack was very affectionate and couldn't tell a lie. He was capable of showing remarkable insight and understanding beyond his years. Dostoevsky said, 'The soul is healed by being with children.' It felt as if my soul was healing. My children were showing me the joy of life far better than I could show it to them. The funny things they said and did, the emerging language, the fascinating way children think and express themselves, so truthfully and literally. Their personal qualities shone through; fresh, honest and unblemished.

'Happiness is like a butterfly. The more you chase it, the more it will elude you. But if you turn your attention to other things, it comes and softly sits on your shoulder.'

Henry David Thoreau

The children were not perfect, of course; they were having to be corrected and boundaries had to be put in place constantly, but this seemed to give them greater security and trust. They knew what was required of them and, on the whole, they respected the rules. David was a strong figure in their lives. I was softer and more malleable but we were both consistent in our approach and supported one another in the task we had set ourselves. Bringing up a family is undoubtedly very costly in terms of time and effort but the rewards received in return are incalculable. I'm recalling those special moments, everyday moments, when your child runs into your arms as they emerge from a day at school; the feeling of peace and satisfaction when your children sleep soundly and safely in their beds at night as well as the relief that you can at last sit down and have a few moments rest. Nobody knows better than a mother how to tiptoe around a sleeping baby. There are places deep within the heart you don't know exist until you give birth to a child.

Eighteen months after Jack's birth, the family moved to a larger house in Heaton Moor,[30] just a quarter of a mile away. We moved in December 1981 and the piano was established in its rightful place in the dining room. Here, we would enjoy the space of a great family home with a larger garden and a laundry cellar. The snow lay so deep on the ground that it was early February before David could return to our old house to retrieve the balls from the back garden.

Family life went on with its ups and downs. The children were learning fast; they were developing their own interests; they loved watching 'Neighbours', 'The Wonder Years' and 'Home and Away'.

They had the usual childhood illnesses, the odd accident; the odd broken bone. As a teenager, Catherine would suffer for two years from ME and glandular fever. She would need courage and determination to recover herself and get back into the mainstream of life. When it was needed, she showed these signs of strength within her character and fought back to overcome her difficulties.

~~~~~

My mother's secret was never far from the surface. I was uncomfortable and the pretense often troubled me. I didn't want to judge my mother; I still loved her. Reason told me that I couldn't blame her or anyone else. However, the fallout was still affecting me and there were many examples where I took out my resentment. One day I was giving my mother a lift in the passenger seat of the car. Catherine was in the rear of the car. She reached forward and said to her grandma. 'Take your rain hat off, Nana. It's stopped raining now!' and she touched her hat to remove it. My mother flared up at her and said, 'No, don't, you'll spoil my hair! I've just had it done. Stop it!!' I was so annoyed with my mother. What did it matter if her hair was disturbed? She was so particular about her appearance. I was upset by her vanity and, in that split second I related it in my own mind, directly to the fact that she was holding on to her secret. Catherine meant no harm but Mum was angry with her for acting spontaneously, for doing nothing wrong. This was how silly little incidents could get out of proportion because of the underlying tension that existed between my mother and me.

All that had been done was in the past now. I couldn't change it. But, I thought about how we had been denied a father and it made me feel sad. I could have had a closer relationship with my real father if I'd
~~~~~

known the truth. We might have been able to meet his family, our grandparents and cousins, but this had not been possible. None of us had been able to acknowledge Sam as our father before he died. I thought about how John and Sam had both suffered. For all John's weaknesses, he didn't deserve the life he had. Equally, Sam was unable to acknowledge his children. Was his drinking a result of his fractured personal life? Perhaps he was drinking to dull his senses and to forget.

These thoughts were ticking away like a time-bomb inside me. If I told the secret would I be betraying my mother? My sister and brothers might wish they'd never been told. It may change my relationship with them for the worse; they may turn against me. They will be hurt. They will be unhappy. They will be angry. On the other hand, it will fulfil their right to know. It may strengthen our relationships; it may bring us closer together. They will understand what it's been like for me. It will be a tremendous relief to be free of the secret. We will remove the deception. We may develop a better understanding. They will have the chance to reassess their situation and face the truth, whatever that might mean.

'The Truth is heavy; therefore few care to carry it.' This quote by Winston Churchill describes the burden I was carrying. You would think it would be straightforward to tell my brothers and sister but my mother had begged that I shouldn't tell them because she thought they would think badly of her. You find out a secret. What do you do? You can dismiss it and think, 'Well, I know this but I don't need to concern anyone else with it.' Or, you can think, 'Who is affected by this? Do they have the right to know? How should they be told? Am I betraying anyone by telling them or by not telling them? Are there someone else's rights which overrule my own? Do I have the right to speak out? Will it benefit them or trouble them? What will be gained by speaking the truth? Will I be harming anyone by speaking the truth?

What will be the overall outcome if I speak the truth? There was also the troubling thought that they might already know; maybe one or all of them had already worked it out, just as I had, but had chosen to stay silent. Never judge anyone because you will never know what they're thinking unless they tell you and people only tell you what they want you to know!' Don't try to guess either. If you do, the chances are you'll be wrong!

Withholding the truth is, of course, a form of dishonesty. 'My mother's philosophy was 'Little white lies do no one any harm.' She had been raised as a Catholic; she knew the difference between little white lies and real lies; lies which affected people's lives, robbed them of their true identity. Such lies are difficult to justify under the guise of defence mechanisms, social appearances and pride. I believe she had a genuine fear of loss. She loved her children and wanted them to think well of her. She was aware of her own vulnerability; she was using her survival instincts. I respected her privacy and acknowledged her feelings but I was torn between protection of self, protection of parent and duty to my sister and brothers. There was a cruel incongruity in the whole situation. I had a great need for understanding; a need to let go of this built-up frustration that weakened my spirit and undermined my sense of integrity. I needed to tell someone!

~~~~~

Away from the church, I'd had no contact with priests. I searched for answers wherever I could. I continued to pray for guidance. I even consulted my daily horoscopes which, of course, were frequently contradictory.

One read: 'Some things can't, mustn't or shouldn't be said. Some sentiments are best left unexpressed. Some bones of contention ought not
~~~~~

to be gnawed on. Where there's a fire of conflict starting to burn in your world now, you can either feed it or starve it of oxygen. Look, this weekend, at the points you want to make and the debates you could get drawn into. Look also at the possibility of standing back and letting go. That's the braver and surely the wiser path.'

Another said: 'There will always be someone, somewhere, who thinks that you are doing the wrong thing or who fears that your judgement is questionable. They may well still be of this opinion, even if you walk down a golden road towards a citadel of success. Listen to your critics, by all means, this week. Some of their concerns may be valid and genuine. But don't be entirely deterred from a plan that inspires and excites you. Show some sensitivity, summon some understanding and then you may just inspire some support.'

And another: 'We all know that people have selective memories. Often too, they have selective perceptions of the present. They see what they want to see. If they find themselves seeing something they do not want to see, they soon find a way to see it the way they want to see it! June is due to be an exceptional month. A transit of Venus will soon occur, opening your eyes to truths that you have been reluctant to acknowledge, while opening your heart to a hope that, up until now, you have felt afraid to embrace. Trust this.'

So, I kept this heavy burden that had been placed on my shoulders. There seemed no way out of it; if I'd gone ahead and confided the secret, I would have risked ending my relationship with my mother completely. I couldn't do that. There was also a guilty fear that I would have been defying her. If I kept it to myself, there would be a sense of collusion. All that had happened was of its time. No further recriminations. No judgements. It was Celia's secret – mine secondary. I wanted to forget about it, but I couldn't.

~~~~~
~~~~~

All these events in my life were played out against a background of disturbing world events[31] - the Irish Troubles, the Munich Olympics Disaster, the trial of the 'Black Panther', the Israelis' rescue of the hostages at Entebbe, the IRA murder of Lord Mountbatten, Iraq's invasion of Iran, the Falklands War and the IRA bomb attack at the Conservative Party Conference in Brighton in October 1984. Frightening though these events were, people still had to get on with their lives. I remember having to leave the city centre shops and cinemas in Manchester because of IRA bomb scares. I remember the serious political and social tensions of the time. The Berlin Wall still divided Germany and religious and political hatred divided the great nation of Ireland.

I tried to introduce new interests into my life. Jack and I attended a mother and toddler group at Green Lane Evangelical Church in Heaton Moor. There, I met Jenny and her little boy, Robbie. As well as running the playgroup, the church also offered bible study classes and other short Christian courses. I started attending the bible study groups and became closer to Jenny. She had trained as a social worker, working as a probation officer, and we had a lot in common. She understood the reasons behind my separation from the church and helped me to return as a practicing Christian, firstly, at the Evangelical Church and later back to my own Catholic tradition. My ecumenical sympathies had led me back to God through the Bible.

All Christians, no matter what their differences, are choosing to seek and follow Jesus's teaching. I believe that God is present at all Christian worship wherever it is sincerely offered in his name. The prayers offered at the evangelical church expressed freedom and openness of thought; they came directly from the heart and mind. This abandonment in personal prayer brought me closer to the essence of God. One thing I am certain of is that all of us are trying to find meaning in our lives. We have so many things in common and we are all searching for love, forgiveness, peace and a home in which we are secure.

~~~~~

When Jack went to nursery, I applied for work at one of the hospitals in Stockport. The hospital social worker wanted a team of volunteers to visit his elderly patients. Some of them were in hospital and some were being rehabilitated at home. My role was to befriend these women and support them. I fitted the visits around school and nursery and began to feel that I was returning to the mainstream of life. I considered pursuing social work again but realised that I couldn't get on a course without being employed in the profession and I couldn't get into paid work without the necessary up-to-date qualifications.

Charlie and Catherine were developing their own interests. Charlie had joined The Manchester Boys' Choir[32] when he was eight and we were committed to regular rehearsals and concerts. We enjoyed meeting other parents and it was wonderful to belong to a very special organisation of which we were so proud. Charlie was invited to sing with the elite chorister section of the choir and he toured Finland, Hong Kong and Czechoslovakia as well as performing many concerts in the United Kingdom. Catherine enjoyed dancing and was learning ballet. Charlie and Jack were keen footballers, supporting Manchester City. Every spare opportunity would find them kicking a ball to one another down the hallway or playing in the back garden.

Jack was four and a half years old when he started school and I returned to work. I wanted to fit in with school times and found a job as one of the clerical team of the city's Education Development Service,[33] working sixteen hours a week during term-time. The pay was
~~~~~

very low but it was a way back into employment and after ten years at home I had a lot of catching up to do. Computers were replacing typewriters, Dictaphones had replaced shorthand. Noticeably, women were becoming more equal in the workplace; they were more assertive and commanded greater authority. The work was undemanding but interesting enough and I became aware of the new trends in teaching and the political undertones running through the education system in Manchester.

My life was full and incredibly busy with three young children, a husband, home and work commitments. Work fitted around the children's needs and I was happy with that. I didn't want a career; my priorities were focused on our children and their wellbeing. If any opportunities arose in the future, then I would consider them, but for now I was content to take this first step.

~~~~~

I'd been working at EDS for about two years when, one day, I received a personal telephone call. It was Francis. He'd heard from a friend that I was working there; the friend who, so many years before had been the boy in the wheelchair. He was now a head teacher in Manchester and Francis held a senior role in another educational service within the city. Francis had married Laure and had two children but the marriage had ended in divorce and he was now alone. He had custody of his children and seemed quite vulnerable. He wondered whether he could see me. I explained that I was married. Something pulled at my heartstrings and I agreed to meet him for 'old time's sake'. Other people in the office knew Francis and he had a bad reputation with women. One said to me, 'To be forewarned is to be forearmed.' I listened but thought I knew better. After all, I told myself, I'd known
~~~~~

him all my life. I didn't realise that it would be me who would be the most vulnerable; I was about to put my hands into the ashes of a still smoldering fire and it wouldn't just be my fingers that got burnt.

Although my work served its purpose for the moment, I sought other outlets to fulfill myself more purposefully. I trained as a voluntary adult literacy tutor and worked with men and women who had missed out on formal education in English and maths. These classes were held in the evenings at schools and colleges across Manchester. Francis and I arranged to meet in a local pub after one of these classes. Over twenty years had passed since our last meeting. His hair was greying but he still had the same smile and soft pale blue eyes. I listened as Francis brought me up to date with his life. He said he had done everything possible to save his marriage but his wife had met someone else and had left him and the children. He talked of the responsibility of raising his children alone and sought my approval of his parenting skills. I accepted all he was saying with sympathy.

In turn, I told him a few things about myself. I was struggling to find the words to help him, to encourage him, to offer some inspiration that might improve his life. He now knew that I was in a successful marriage with a relatively young family, he knew there was no place for him, nor did he seek it. He wanted to meet someone for a relationship; did I have any friends who might be available? When I reminded him of his kindness to his friend when he was a ten year old boy, he laughed and said, 'It was only because he lived a few doors away and I was asked to push him to school.' I knew he was joking, but I couldn't be a hundred per cent sure. Did he really care about anybody but himself? It was clear from the start that he only wanted to talk about his own concerns, his own difficulties and his own needs.

The contact between us could and should have stopped there, but my emotions were caught up and I would find it extremely difficult to disentangle them. I'd had no idea that this would happen; I was immediately transported back to being twenty years old again. I was in this desolate irrational place with no firm ground beneath my feet. Every move I made was with my heart, not my head. Logic and common sense would have said, 'Get away! Protect yourself. He's completely selfish. He's unfeeling, insensitive! He doesn't care!' But logic was absent and my own judgement was playing tricks on me. I simply couldn't judge him; why couldn't I judge him? Yes, I could judge him in my mind but not in her heart. Something was happening to me that I felt unable to control. Francis came into the education centre several times, but never spoke to me. My heart was ripped in two. We met on two or three more occasions and spoke very briefly but this game would have no winners.

I think it was Shakespeare who wrote: 'Love is the most beautiful of dreams and the worst of nightmares.' I was certainly experiencing a nightmare. My image of Francis as caring and spiritually-centred was nothing other than a naïve fantasy yet my feelings were overpowering. Again, I was like an animal trapped in a cage. Compassion and contempt were battling with each other. The person I had loved at twenty was a romantic image in my own mind as distinct from the real person. I could see him more clearly now. This unrequited love was totally overwhelming; I couldn't make any sense of it. How could I love Francis when I didn't really know him? I felt a very strong need to communicate with him and wanted to explain how I was feeling so that he would understand. At the same time, I knew how dangerous it was to get more involved with him. I was sick with confusion. I loved David; he was my rock and the father of my children. He had saved me and taken a chance with me, not knowing whether my depression would return to destroy us. I needed him like I'd needed no one else. He was strong and reliable, stable and consistent. I never had to worry whether he would go astray; I knew he wouldn't. That trust and stability strengthened me so much. It was like a strong thick rope that I could cling onto. No matter what chasm lay below me I could move my way along it to reach safety.

How could I love two people at once? I had no intention of leaving my family to rescue Francis from his loneliness and dejection but I had an irrational desire to help him because I loved him. I didn't choose to love him; it happened involuntarily. Or, perhaps I had always loved him subconsciously. If I had, it was a perfect example of unconditional love, because he had offered me nothing in return. Leonard Cohen's deep rich voice sang out: 'There Ain't no Cure for Love' **♪22**.

My love for Francis, which had been buried so deeply within me, had resurfaced. It was real enough. It didn't feel right but I was unable to cure it. It was one of those situations that you have to 'sit out' because nothing you can possibly do will change it. You have to become inactive and wait for healing to come and you have to accept that it might take a very long time.

My analytical gene was operating overtime; I was wretchedly miserable. It felt as though he had used me like a dirty rag to wipe his sweating hands and discarded me in a greasy corner. The pain of 'rejection' seared through me. You need perspective to deal with unrequited love but perspective was something I did not have. I tried to understand what was happening to me. I prayed to be rescued from this nightmare of tangled, twisted feelings. I engrossed myself in the analysis of 'love'. How could I love without any return? How does God love us? What is human love? What is divine love?'

Francis avoided me completely. Perhaps he realised that he had opened Pandora's box. Perhaps he had no idea at all. I'll never know because he wouldn't speak to me. For me, there was a distinct element of cruelty in his behaviour. It felt like an emotional rape, if there is such a thing. Perhaps this was me over-reacting but I can only tell you how the suffering felt to me. I couldn't know how I was appearing to others at that time; that would be for them to say. But inside, my heart was shrieking out in pain. Those who have had similar experiences will understand. Those who haven't may judge. I retell this experience not out of unresolved pity for myself but in an attempt to express the frightening emotions that were attacking me during that desperate time. A person can be cruel whether they are aware of it or not. I was brought to a point of frightening despair. I became the small helpless child reaching out for help and comfort.

When I listened to Charlie singing 'Mary Stewart's Prayer' ♪**23** with the Manchester Boys' Choir, my thoughts and prayers were immersed in the words and music.

Father in Heaven above,
All my hope rests with Thee
Jesus the heart of my love,
Turn Thou to me.
In chains unyielding I lie.
In deepest misery,
Calling for Thee, O Lord, calling for Thee.

Mary Stewart's Prayer - Donizetti opera

For some inexplicable reason I started reading 'The Confessions of Saint Augustine'.[34] I would go out in my car at lunchtime, eat my lunch and then read for the rest of the hour. No-one knew where I was or what I was doing. I was devouring the words. I had deprived myself of spiritual nourishment and now my appetite was overwhelming. God seemed to be speaking to me through the words of St Augustine.

> 'What agony I suffered, my God! I cried out in grief while my heart was in labour! But, unknown to me, you were there, listening. Even when I bore the pain of my search valiantly, in silence, the mute sufferings of my soul were loud voices calling to your mercy. You knew what I endured, but no man knew. How little of it could I find words to tell, even to my closest friends! Could they catch a sound of the turmoil in my soul? Time did not suffice to tell them and words failed me. But as I groaned aloud in the weariness of my heart, all my anguish reached your ears. You knew all my longings; the very light that shone in my eyes was mine no longer. For the light was within, while I looked on the world outside.'

Saint Augustine, Confessions. Book VII, 7 pg 143

> 'I have learnt to love you late, Beauty at once so ancient and new! I have learnt to love you late! You were within me, and I was in the world outside myself. I searched for you outside myself and, disfigured as I was, I fell upon the lovely things of your creation.
> You shone upon me; your radiance enveloped me; you put my blindness to flight. You shed your fragrance about me; I drew breath and now I gasp for your sweet odour. I tasted you, and now I hunger and thirst for you. You touched me, and I am inflamed with love of your peace.'

Saint Augustine, Confessions. Book X, 27 pg 231

It's incredible to think that Augustine's 'Confessions' were written as long ago as the end of the fourth century. I remember his writings as a skillful blend of autobiography, philosophy and theology. He offered eloquent explanations and critical interpretation of texts, especially the religious writings of the Bible. Augustine combined his remarkable intellect with profound humility. Many of the considerations he dwelt on gave forth both religious and philosophical revelations as he sought to return the work of creation to God. He spoke directly to God, and, it was in this context, that Augustine's 'confession' carried the dual meanings of an admission of guilt and an act of praise. In focusing on the events in his life that led specifically to his conversion, he revealed his personal struggle to become a Christian. This is a metaphor for the struggle of all Christians.

~~~~~

I wasn't seeking opinions and judgements; I was searching desperately for knowledge, understanding and truth. Like St Augustine, I was trying to bring reason into the world in which I found myself. Christians are often looked upon as brainwashed and unthinking but nothing could be further from the truth. They, like other intelligent human beings, are simply trying to make sense of the world and their lives and sense of their faith and beliefs. They don't always succeed but they are trying to lead good lives according to those beliefs.

I knew in my heart that, this time, my distress was partly of my own making. If you put your hand into the fire, you will get burnt. I hadn't wanted it, I hadn't planned it but it had happened and now I had to deal with it. My pragmatic approach to life came to the fore and I had learnt a great deal from the experience. As I reflected on my own little world, so small and narrow, I thought, 'We are like ants, scuttling about our daily affairs. We fulfill our natures and act according to our instincts, our genetic make-up and social programming. Ants are ants, human beings are human beings. We, as humans, can watch over the ants and make sense of their existence. Is God watching over us? Is the church and its teachings offering to make sense of human existence?'

Human beings can, at least, use their intellect to change their thinking and behaviour. Ants are ants! They adapt spontaneously through nature's laws. We can adapt consciously through our own enquiry, learning, reasoning and understanding.
~~~~~

'Ask, and it shall be given you:
Seek, and you shall find:
Knock, and it shall be opened to you.'

Matthew 7:7-8

How confined and limited was my own vision and understanding. How unprepared was I to offer anything but my own bumbling emotions to someone who needed more. I needed knowledge on how to communicate with people. I needed the skills to help others when they were in distress. My focus now turned once more to education and personal development both practically and spiritually. I read even more voraciously.

The great novelist Evelyn Waugh once said to Nancy Mitford, 'You have no idea how much nastier I would be if I was not a Catholic. Without supernatural aid I would hardly be a human being.' I felt that to be true of myself too. I knew what strength and direction I received from the faith given to me by my mother at birth and I could ignore it no longer. In 'Brideshead Revisited' Waugh describes an interesting phenomenon.

The second book of Brideshead, 'A Twitch upon the Thread', describes this image which is derived from one of Chesterton's Fr. Brown stories:

> 'I caught him (the thief) with an unseen hook and an invisible line which is long enough to let him wander to the ends of the world and still bring him back with a twitch upon the thread.'

Waugh's novel is about the process by which God calls his children back to the centre - even those who have drifted to the furthest edge. Waugh's character, Cordelia, offers us this metaphor of God with a fishing line tied to every Catholic. A baptised Catholic might wander away from God, but God can give a twitch on the thread and pull him back at any time. Lord Marchmain was never devout, but accepts the Last Sacrament on his death bed. When Lord Marchmain refuses the priest for the first time, Cordelia uses the thread metaphor: 'The worse I am, the more I need God,' she says. 'I can't shut myself out from His mercy.'

That's the thing about love, it never really goes away. I had played the cards I had been dealt. Before long I had returned to the true roots of my faith and started to attend Mass regularly at the local Catholic Church. I enrolled on a counselling course. The arrow had once more left its bow and it was flying who knows where.

---

[28] Lyme Park is a large estate located in Disley, Cheshire. The estate is managed by the National Trust and consists of a mansion house surrounded by formal gardens, in a deer park in the Peak District National Park. The house is the largest in Cheshire and has been designated by English Heritage as a Grade I listed building. http://en.wikipedia.org/wiki/Lyme_Park

[29] National Housewives' Register - now known as The National Women's Register. The NWR is a network of local groups and individual members who enjoy lively discussion and conversation, both serious and light-hearted. It is for women who like to be informed and share ideas. http://www.nwr.org.uk/

[30] Heaton Moor is one of the Four Heatons and borders onto Heaton Chapel, Heaton Norris and Heaton Mersey. It is characterised by the elegant Victorian housing built for Manchester's industrialists between 1852 and 1892. Its tree lined streets follow the field patterns of a former agricultural economy. The centre of Heaton Moor has an abundance of bars, pubs, restaurants and shops.

[31] World Events

1963 The Irish Troubles - The Troubles refers to a violent thirty-year conflict framed by a civil rights march in Londonderry on 5 October 1968 and by the Good Friday Agreement on 10 April 1998. At the heart of the conflict lay the constitutional status of Northern Ireland.
http://www.bbc.co.uk/history/troubles

1972 Munich Olympics Disaster - The Munich Massacre was a terrorist attack during the 1972 Olympic Games. Eight Palestinian terrorists killed two members of the Israeli Olympic team and then took nine others hostage. The situation was ended by a huge gunfight that left five of the terrorists and all of the nine hostages dead. Following the massacre, the Israeli government organized a retaliation against Black September called Operation Wrath of God.

1976 The Black Panther - Donald Neilson's trial started on 14th June 1976 and he was charged with abduction, making a demand for £50,000 with menaces and threat to kill, and the murder of Lesley Whittle. He received life imprisonment for these crimes.

1976 Israelis rescue Entebbe hostages - Israeli commandos rescued 100 hostages, mostly Israelis or Jews, held by pro-Palestinian hijackers at Entebbe airport in Uganda.

1979 IRA bomb kills Lord Mountbatten - The Queen's cousin, Lord Louis Mountbatten, was killed by a bomb blast on his boat in Ireland.

1980 Iraq's invasion of Iran

1982 The Falklands War

1984 IRA bomb attack at the Conservative party conference in Brighton in October 1984

[32] The Manchester Boys' Choir MBC was a highly successful non-audition choir, open to all boys who were interested in singing. The choir has since disbanded.

[33] Education Development Service - The EDS services were based in three centres across Manchester; central, north and south. Led by school inspectors, the teams of specialist teachers went into schools offering support and implementation of selected projects.

[34] The Confessions of St Augustine - Augustine's Confessions is a diverse blend of autobiography, philosophy, theology, and critical exegesis of the Christian Bible. The first nine Books (or chapters) of the work trace the story of Augustine's life, from his birth (354 A.D.) up to the events that took place just after his conversion to Catholicism (386 A.D.).
Quotations from: - 'Saint Augustine Confessions', Penguin Classics Translated by R S Pine-Coffin

David and Martha on their wedding day (23 April, 1973)

Catherine and Charlie

Catherine, Jack and Charlie

Celia with Catherine, Jack and Charlie

Celia on her 80th Birthday with Hannah and Martha

Charlie, Catherine and Jack (2012)

PART THREE
'Understanding'

Chapter Eight

'The aim of life is self-development. To realise one's nature perfectly - that is what each of us is here for.'

Oscar Wilde

I experienced a strange sense of disassociation but kept myself together and, despite the situation, was able to take myself outside it and somehow rise above it. Maybe this sense of objectivity was a defence mechanism. One of my main concerns was to understand what was happening to me and why. I enrolled at the Extra-Mural Department at Manchester University for the basic counselling skills course which ran over ten weeks. I was searching and had never been more open to learning. At the same time, I continued to read as much as I could to help me understand the nature of love.

Love is arguably the most complex emotion in the world and I read C.S. Lewis's 'The Four Loves'[35] to discover the meaning of what he believed to be the four different kinds of love. I found most of the answers I was seeking in that book. The natural loves of affection, friendship and Eros or being 'in love' are not sufficient without the saving grace of charity. If we love at all we will be vulnerable and our hearts will certainly be wrung and possibly broken. If you want to keep your heart intact, you must give it to no-one, not even an animal.

'Wrap it carefully', says Lewis, 'in the casket or coffin of your selfishness. But in that casket – safe, dark, motionless, airless – it will change. It will not be broken; it will become unbreakable, impenetrable and irredeemable.'

Lewis sees the Christian virtue of charity as the highest of the four loves. Charity is unconditional and is the only one of the four types of love that is self-sufficient. The love of God for his people is charity. Lewis believed that human beings, '…cannot love one another or love God without receiving God's love first and allowing His love to transform all their other loves. In God there is no hunger that needs to be filled; only plenteousness that desires to give. God, who needs nothing, loves into existence wholly superfluous creatures in order that He may love and protect them.' Victor Hugo in 'Les Misérables' explained how: 'To love another person, is to see the face of God'

Perhaps one has to love another person totally unconditionally to truly see the face of God.

~~~~~

While struggling with these concepts, I was still in touch with Katie and Tom and their family, visiting them first in Cleckheaton and then in Huddersfield. We always talked of the past, of our grammar school days and our time together as children. She was my oldest friend and the one with whom I had the closest bond. We had a connection through shared experiences. We knew we would be friends for life but I was not yet ready to confide in her. It would be some years before I would tell her Celia's secret. Each time I thought of telling, there was a sense of betrayal and that friends who had known my mother personally might feel the same.
~~~~~

Edward and his wife Helen now had two children and had moved from Chorlton to a house on Kingsway. Hannah and Simon had moved from Didsbury to Chorlton and Daniel and Jane were now living in Kent where they both worked for social services. Eventually Daniel would settle into teaching and an academic career. The family, as a whole, got together only occasionally and when this happened I was aware of the stress that I was feeling; that elephant in the room was ever present and I couldn't relax entirely and be myself.

~~~~~

One day I was at Mass when I saw a face from the past. Liz Williamson had been my supervisor when I was doing my social work placement at Didsbury. She asked me about myself and I updated her on all that had happened in my life; my marriage, the birth of my children; my return to secretarial work; my counselling training. Liz was working with young people who had been adopted and who were seeking their birth mothers. She asked me whether I would be interested in becoming an intermediary and counsellor for them. She invited me to her office for a more detailed discussion.

During this meeting the conversation turned in a more personal direction. I explained to Liz that I had been severely depressed and that I'd had to leave social work because of the emotional demands it placed on me. She questioned me further and I explained the situation within my family; the family secret and the impact it had had on me. She urged me to share this with at least one other member of my family as she felt it was too much for me to carry alone. She was aware of my mother's anger and her refusal to tell the secret but she still felt that it should be shared with another family member. I had no aunts or cousins with whom I could share it, so, I said I would confide in
~~~~~

Hannah and hope that she would understand my motives for telling her.

Once again, all the issues arising from the secret floated to the surface. I knew I could only tell the facts as I knew them. I didn't have a monopoly on the truth and was open to respect any other interpretation that might be offered. My memory might be impaired; I was willing to accept correction. From my own point of view, the story hadn't been twisted; the truth, as I knew it, had not been manipulated. Perhaps Hannah would be able to resolve the difficulties with my mother and enable her to tell our brothers so that we could all know and understand the true situation. I felt I should tell Hannah and then tell my mother that I had told her because I didn't want to be deceitful but to be open and truthful. The meeting with Hannah was tinged with anxiety and apprehension. She might already know. Perhaps she would say, 'Oh yes, I've known that for ages. I worked it out when I was fourteen.' I couldn't know what her reaction would be. Nevertheless, I told her what I had discovered and how I'd checked with Auntie Kathleen who had confirmed my suspicions. Hannah hadn't guessed the secret; she was shocked but didn't seem unduly surprised. Her mind was working overtime to take in the facts. She was digesting them until they made sense to her. She didn't, for an instant doubt that what I was saying was anything but the truth. Afterwards, we told our mother together. She was not pleased and said again that our brothers should not be told because it might upset them. Once again, she believed that the truth belonged to her alone. It was her life and her business, no-one else's.

This sharing of the secret provided some sense of relief. I felt I had gone as far as I could at that moment. Maybe I needed to put it behind me now. I had a feeling that I might be holding on to it in an unhealthy way but was uncertain whether this feeling could be justified or not. I remained confused and distracted. Such are the dilemmas thrown up by secrets. I prayed that the right time might come when I could be totally honest with Daniel and Edward. I wanted everyone concerned to know the truth and be reconciled to it and to one another. I had been an apologist, defender, ally and protector of my mother for most of my life. Why was the message so difficult to deliver?

~~~~~

'The greatest and most important problems of life are all fundamentally insoluble,' said Carl Jung, 'they can never be solved but only outgrown.' When would I outgrow it? Should I outgrow it? My return to my Catholic faith brought a degree of peace and helped me to look forward to the future. I now recognised a heightened sense of the importance of service in my life.

> 'God has created me to do some definite service. He has committed some work to me which he has not committed to another. I have my mission. I am a link in a chain, a bond of connection between persons. I shall do good and be a preacher of truth in my own place.'
>
> John Henry Newman (adapted)

All that I did every day, as a wife and a mother, were part of that service. I hoped that I would find other ways to serve in my professional life too. Since leaving social work, my working life had been confined to secretarial duties. I'd never lost sight of St Thérèse's 'little way' and so my wish to serve had been satisfied to some extent through this philosophical approach. I was drawn further into my desire to fulfill God's will in my life. I know it's a cliché but I felt as though I had been 'born again'. There was a clarity that had not previously existed which I couldn't explain. I felt, more than ever, that my life had purpose and meaning.
~~~~~

'Do not model your behaviour on the contemporary world, but let the renewing of your minds transform you, so that you may discern for yourselves what is the will of God - what is good and acceptable and mature.'

Romans 12:2

~~~~~

Manchester offered various opportunities for higher education and I was ready to take the next step. I'd read a great deal about the significance of body, mind and spirit. All three were important; all three had to be nourished. I hadn't let go of the moral philosophy and social ethics that I'd learnt at Plater; these teachings ran like blood through my veins they were so much a part of me. I decided to enroll on a part-time degree in Education, which could be fitted in with my family and working life. I studied two modules a year and sat the examinations in the summer term after submitting all the written work. It wasn't easy to fit the reading and coursework into my busy life but I took it on as an intellectual project and enjoyed my lectures and the friendships I made with other students. As a mature student, I was grateful for this opportunity to complete a degree and willingly immersed myself in the broad subject of education.

I studied the history of education, learning about the establishment of the state education system in the late nineteenth and early twentieth century up to modern times. I studied educational policy and provision throughout the U.K. and how further and higher education changed to meet the needs of all the population rather than the privileged few. I gained a greater understanding of how political, social and economic factors all influence the progress which can be made when attempting to deliver major services such as education.
~~~~~

Having studied social and political theory before, I now related this specifically to education. I considered the theories of Plato through to Rousseau, with his experiential learning with poor little Emile, and on to Piaget's twentieth century cognitive theory. I examined the psychology of education looking at the behaviourists, cognitive psychology, the humanistic approach with Freud, Maslow and Rogers and the child-centred model, where children's needs come first in contrast to the teacher-centred approach. I also studied comparative education in France, the USA, Russia and Germany. I looked at the place of computers in education and wrote a special paper on the nature of Jesuit education.

Half way through my degree course, I left the Education Development Service and went to work at Manchester University as secretary to a degree programme in a large long-established department. Here I gained an insight into the administration of the university and its internal policies in relation to staff and students. I was able to see the other side of academia; its characters, its stories and its disputations. I was thankful to work in a small office on my own where I could concentrate on my work without disturbance; I could talk quietly with the academics who were assigned to the various administrative tasks of the degree programme without getting too involved in office politics. The large window provided plenty of natural light and looked out onto the campus grounds. I could see the apple blossom in the spring and the little chapel building below. With this degree of independence, I was able to make the job my own and took a personal interest in each student.

It was a busy office with over one hundred and fifty students enrolled on the three year course. Much of my time was spent in keeping records up to date and chasing students who had missed lectures and seminars. I was particularly busy at registration time in

September and during the examination periods in January and May. I was involved in admissions, processing all the applications coming through and taking part in the University's open days. August was the busiest time; the busiest day of all when the A-level results were published.

I saw my most important role in student welfare. A programme tutor was appointed from the academic staff and he or she met with any students who were experiencing difficulties and I was often the go-between. Problems were personal and confidential and sometimes they affected the submission of coursework or the attendance at examinations and, if the student had good reason, these circumstances could be taken into account when results were being assessed. On one occasion, a student came into the office with his hand bandaged up. He said he wouldn't be able to sit his examination the following day because he couldn't write. When I asked him how he had hurt his hand, he replied that he had thumped the wall of his room in frustration while trying to revise. I arranged for an amanuensis to attend him at his examination.

Every effort was made to accommodate students and to deter anyone from leaving the programme. The majority of the academics were genuinely interested in the students; others were mainly focused on their own areas of research and had little time for 'whimpering' undergraduates. This degree programme was only one of the many which were administered through the main department. This was run by the senior departmental secretary who had great experience in dealing with the multiplicities of the academic year and was in charge of all the clerical staff and oversaw everything that took place in the departmental office.

Although much of my work was dull and repetitive, I tried to overcome my frustrations by focusing on the human aspects of my work; my relationships with staff and students and my interest in the academic content of the course. My own degree course was coming to an end and I graduated in 1993 with David, my mother and my three children attending my degree ceremony. The great Whitworth Hall at the university was filled with luminaries and was an elegant setting for the conferment of awards.

My mother was frail now and couldn't walk very far; she needed someone's arm to lean on. David provided his arm and I was grateful that she had been able to attend the ceremony. I hoped she was pleased with my success, although she didn't say anything. I knew she loved me deeply and wanted me to be happy. Over a period of years she had suffered a series of minor strokes and, sometime later, was extremely ill in Withington Hospital. The care she received there was kind and compassionate and she slowly recovered her strength. She now lived with Hannah and Simon in a specially converted apartment in their house in Chorlton. It was self-contained with a bed-sitting room, a kitchen and a bathroom. It overlooked the private garden at the back of the house. I would call to see her on my way home from work as it was quite close to the university. Mum continued to visit our family home and saw the children regularly. Charlie was applying for university and would soon be on his way to another life of his own making. I knew that Celia would miss him terribly; her first grandchild of whom she was so proud.

I had a sense that Mum knew that death was not far away. I became closer to her during this period but nothing was ever mentioned about the secret. The elephant was still there, blocking out the warm light which should have surrounded us. My heart was hurting by the rift in our relationship; there was a scar left deep inside which no-one else could see. I wanted to put my thoughts into words but the words never came; it was too delicate, too painful. It felt like an itch that needed to be scratched. But if you scratch, it becomes sore and if you scratch even more it can become infected. The anxiety prevented me from speaking.

A year had passed since my graduation and I was now embarking on another course of study. This time it was a certificate in counselling and I felt ready to pursue this next stage of my training at evening classes. The basic skills course had taught me so much. When I set out on my counselling training it was the start of a very long learning process; a path towards self-knowledge. After my experience with Francis, I wanted to find out if there was any way in which I could have helped him or indeed anyone else who needed help. I certainly didn't have the resources to do it then; I was too emotionally involved. But, I felt the need for change. I wanted to emerge as a stronger more capable person who could offer something to another person if needed.

~~~~~

At the beginning of my training I was learning how to listen, to accept, to be genuine and to address my prejudices. I was searching deeply for something – an answer, perhaps, to my own troubles. I realised that in counselling we need to become aware of our own actions and reactions, recognise them and put them aside so that we can face the person coming to us for help with a readiness to be present for them alone. The focus would be concentrated on the one receiving counselling even though I would undoubtedly be affected to some degree by the issues raised. We all have prejudices which are likely to interfere with our listening and it takes awareness of these prejudices to be able to keep them under control. I was challenged to see my own faults. Occasionally, someone may pass a remark and you realise how little you really know; how you've formed your own opinion and made
~~~~~

your judgements based on flimsy information and doubtful impressions. This made me recognise my own weaknesses.

The counselling course taught me why I needed to be focused, why I needed to listen intently; to become 'other-centred'. I learnt to be aware of my own reactions and feelings but not be distracted by them. I looked for other signs such as body language, sighs and facial expressions and interpreted these within the context of the listening. I trained myself to concentrate and offer the gift of real presence to the other person. 'At the heart of every counselling relationship,' Carl Rogers states, 'are the core conditions of counselling: Unconditional Positive Regard, Empathy and Congruence.[36]

After a while, these core conditions became a part of all my relationships whether therapeutic or not but they always needed to be acknowledged and improved. It takes a lifetime to perfect these interpersonal skills to the greatest degree and I know I don't always succeed. My first experience of being on the receiving end of counselling was, as I've mentioned earlier, when I was twenty-five and deep in depression I visited my GP to explain my symptoms. He listened to me intently for about twenty minutes barely saying a word. This was in the middle of his busy surgery and I hadn't expected to be with him for more than about five minutes. I remember how this made me feel and it made a lasting impression on me. He allowed me to explain and he listened without interruption or judgement. That meant so much to me. I wanted to be able to offer that feeling to others.

> 'In my early professional years I was asking the question: How can I treat, or cure, or change this person? Now I would phrase the question in this way: How can I provide a relationship which this person may use for his own personal growth?'
>
> Carl Rogers

Rogers' approach is the key to change and, ideally, should be fundamental to all those working in the caring professions. It opens the door to the process of counselling. Although Rogers' humanistic scientific approach is central to the teaching of counselling, many other theorists put forward different models, some of which offer a more directive approach. There are numerous models of counselling but no matter which model is used, the relationship that exists between the counsellor and the client is more important than the model the therapist uses. It is the essence of this relationship that provides the one in need with a peaceful quiet place where they are accepted for who they are. Over a period of time, I believe, the subconscious and conscious mind are capable of processing what has taken place between the two people and healing alteration can begin. All this is relative to the dedication of the client to the process, the expertise of the counsellor's skills and the dynamics of the special relationship.

~~~~~

In the wider world, revolutions and disturbing events were featured daily in the media.[37] I've always followed the news, nationally and internationally and tried to identify with the struggles of other people in other countries. Enough had happened in my home country; the Pan-Am 747 terrorist disaster in Lockerbie killed two hundred and seventy people, the Hungerford shootings were horrific and the murder of Stephen Lawrence shocked everyone. I was also aware of the broader issues of politics and social change around the world. When Mikhail Gorbachev became the leader of the Soviet Union, his political initiatives of perestroika and glasnost had brought feelings of guarded optimism to the west. Soon, Communist governments were losing power, first in Poland, where the communists agreed to free elections
~~~~~

that swept Solidarity into power. The Berlin Wall fell, East and West Germany were unified and demands for reform spread across the country from the east. The Romanian Communist Party was overthrown and President Ceausescu and his wife were executed. The parliament in Bulgaria revoked the Communist party's monopoly on power in 1990, and in 1991 popular opposition forced the resignation of the communist cabinet in Albania. Other eastern European countries then declared their independence from the Soviet Union. Further across the world, in China, many people died after troops cleared demonstrators in Tiananmen Square. Around that time, I had befriended a Chinese girl at university and, apart from seeing the reports in the media; I experienced through her the effect this had on its people, even though they were so far away. In another part of the world, Nelson Mandela was released in South Africa after twenty-seven years behind bars.

~~~~~

Mum had another stroke and was taken by ambulance to Manchester Royal Infirmary. I stayed with her while she was admitted. The Infirmary is within a few minutes' walk of the university so I was able to visit her every day, sometimes at lunchtime and sometimes in the early evening. Hannah and Edward and David and the grandchildren also visited regularly. Daniel and Jane came up to Manchester to see her. The consultant was not hopeful that she would make a recovery. Apart from the stroke, she had numerous other problems notably her breathing, a weak heart, digestive problems and arthritis. When she had been in Withington Hospital, they had done everything to build her up again, now the infirmary doctors focused on what they believed to be the inevitable outcome and provided palliative
~~~~~

rather than restorative care. Mum drifted deeper into a kind of semi-consciousness. She was vaguely aware but not alert. She seemed to know who was with her but found it difficult to speak. She slept a great deal and wasn't eating. She was assigned a nursing attendant who tried to ensure that she ate a little and drank when possible but she was not provided with tube feeding as she had been at Withington. This would have kept her alive, but artificially, and she could have laid in that state for months, perhaps years.

I was preparing myself for my mother's final days. I could no longer communicate with her. The spark of life was gone and her body was becoming a brittle shell, drying up from inside; the spirit edging further and further from its centre. She was visited by the hospital chaplain. I prayed that she would die peacefully and without pain. One month before her eighty-seventh birthday she gave up her tenuous hold on life. I had lost the mother I loved before our relationship changed when I told her I knew her secret. This single discovery estranged us and left me with the saddest loss I had ever known. All I could do now was pray for reconciliation beyond death.

Death is always a constant shadow in our lives. Although most of us don't dwell on it, it is ever present on the fringes of our thoughts. When we suffer the death of someone who has been very close to us we have to cope with feelings of devastation, loneliness and disbelief as well as overwhelming grief. Our sensitivities are raised and memories of our loved one haunt us in dreams. We live with shock and disbelief; grief enters into our bones. It seems to emanate from a damp misty shroud chilling and swirling around us and numbing our feelings of longing and regret, not unlike the dense, all-encompassing fog we experienced so long ago. We feel as though our life is hovering in an indeterminate state; it will never be normal again. Daily occurrences are a constant reminder of the one who is gone. There's an empty place at the table; one who shared with us is no longer there. There's a familiar telephone number which has been disconnected. We drift, as though in a dream, until reality finally takes over. Eventually, the process of grieving floats slowly away and we begin to live life more fully.

~~~~~

I believe that all men and women are stewards of the earth, as Sheila Cassidy describes so perfectly in her book 'Light from the Dark Valley'.[38]

> 'God, who is all-powerful and infinitely mysterious, made the world. He made it in his own way, intricate and beautiful, wild and dangerous. He filled it full of plants and living creatures, the most complex and self-aware of whom was man. God appointed men and women as stewards of the earth, to live on it, to cherish it but not to plunder and destroy it. It is in the nature of this world, of all God's creatures, that they are frail and vulnerable and that they die. Nothing and no-one lives forever. .... That is the way things are. On this earth we are all sojourners, because we are all destined ultimately to return to the Divine, to the heart of God from whence we come.
> ... If we were angels, of course, we would understand the truth that death is not a tragedy, that it is quite simply the beginning of the life for which we were originally created. But then we are not angels, we are creatures and we see, as St Paul puts it, 'through a glass darkly.' How then can we not be sad when we or those we love are afflicted or face death? This is what it means to be human; to be frail and vulnerable in our bodies, to be storm-tossed in our emotions, to be limited in our understanding. We forget, however, that this is the way the One Holy Transcendent God made people and that, when he had finished, he smiled upon his work and declared that it was very very good.'

Extract by kind permission of publishers Darton, Longman and Todd.
~~~~~

Our loved ones leave the earth and we remain. We live on it, we love it. All living beings and plants are destined to die and as such we are always vulnerable. Although there are many ways in which we try to manipulate it, we have to accept that nature defines what will be. As a Christian, I believe that when we die everything will be revealed to us. We will see things clearly and we will understand; our lives will be put into perspective.

Despite these beliefs, I still feel overwhelmingly sad when I lose someone I love. If I didn't feel these emotions I would not be able to empathise with anyone else's loss. I share my human nature and I accept others because of their humanity. I can appreciate what others are suffering because I can relate their situation to my own experience and so I am able to feel something of what they are feeling.

Our life on earth is sometimes described as a 'vale of tears'. This does not mean that we are in a place of despair but it is symbolic of our pilgrimage to heaven; the life after death which Christians believe awaits them. The vale of tears is a means of visualization; an acceptance of the human condition yet to be illuminated by the light of heaven. Christianity fits into my life like a giant piece of the jigsaw. Knowing that there are millions of fellow Christians in the world provides a great source of strength.

> 'As Christians, we need to begin again and again each day. The struggle to live a good Christian life does not diminish but with God's grace we are continually empowered. Christ on the Cross is the source of our strength and support. Whenever we feel sadness, experience misunderstanding or physical and mental suffering we can turn to Him who loves us and who, with His infinite love of God, helps us to overcome our trials. He fills our emptiness, forgives all our sins and eagerly draws us to a new path that is safe and joyful.'

Extract from John Paul II address 1 March 1980 (Scepter 1989)

Hannah and I organised our mother's funeral. Her favourite hymn was included at her reception into church; 'Sweet Heart of Jesus'♪24.

Sweet Heart of Jesus, fount of love and mercy
Today we come, Thy blessing to implore.
Oh touch our hearts, so cold and so ungrateful
And make them Lord, Thine own for evermore.

With the death of my mother, I was free to tell Daniel and Edward the truth about their real father. 'Freedom is the right to tell people what they do not want to hear.' said George Orwell. I agonised over this dilemma and longed for peaceful resolution. When would it come?

---

[35] C. S. Lewis 'The Four Loves' - The four loves C. S. Lewis describes are: Affection, Friendship, Eros and Charity.

[36] Carl Rogers - Personal-centred Therapy Selections from the lifetime work of America's pre-eminent psychologist, author of 'On Becoming a Person' and 'Client-centred Therapy' are contained in 'The Carl Rogers Reader' by Carl R. Rogers, Howard Kirschenbaum and Valerie L. Henderson (23 Apr 1990)
Theoretical approaches to Counselling
http://www.bacp.co.uk/seeking_therapist/theoretical_approaches.php
Models of Counselling - Person-centred, Carl Rogers;
The Helping Model, Gerard Egan; Cognitive Behavioural Therapy; Gestalt Therapy; Transactional Analysis and many more.

[37] World Events
Perestroika, which in English translates to 'restructuring,' was General Secretary Mikhail Gorbachev's program to restructure the Soviet economy in an attempt to revitalize it. Glasnost, which translates to 'openness' in English, was Gorbachev's policy for a new, open policy in the Soviet Union where people could freely express their opinions.
http://history1900s.about.com/od/1980s/qt/perestroika.htm

The Lockerbie Bombing - 1988: Jumbo jet crashes onto Lockerbie.
A Pan Am jumbo jet with 258 passengers on board has crashed on to the town of Lockerbie near the Scottish borders. In total 259 people aboard the flight and 11 on the ground died in the crash which took place 38 minutes after take-off. The subsequent police investigation became a murder inquiry when evidence of a bomb was found. Two men accused of being Libyan intelligence agents were eventually charged with planting the bomb. Abdelbaset ali Mohmed al-Megrahi was jailed for life in January 2001 following an 84-day trial under Scottish law, at Camp Zeist in Holland. In 2002 Al Megrahi's appeal against conviction was rejected.
http://news.bbc.co.uk/onthisday/hi/dates/stories/december/21/newsid_2539000/2539447.stm
Megrahi's release caused an international backlash and was met with fury and disbelief in America. Scotland's Nationalist administration ignored foreign opinion and freed him on Aug 20, 2009, on the basis that he had terminal prostate cancer and may only have three months to live.
http://www.telegraph.co.uk/news/worldnews/africaandindianocean/libya/9278166/How-release-of-Lockerbie-bomber-caused-international-backlash-which-refuses-to-go-away.html
Megrahi's death was announced on May 20, 2012.

The Berlin Wall - 1989: Berliners celebrate the fall of the Wall. The Berlin Wall had been breached after nearly three decades keeping East and West Berliners apart. At midnight East Germany's Communist rulers gave permission for gates along the Wall to be opened after hundreds of people converged on crossing points. They surged through cheering and shouting and were met by jubilant West Berliners on the other side. Ecstatic crowds immediately began to clamber on top of the Wall and hack large chunks out of the 28-mile (45-kilometre) barrier. It had been erected in 1961 on the orders of East Germany's former leader Walter Ulbricht to stop people leaving for West Germany.
http://news.bbc.co.uk/onthisday/hi/dates/stories/november/9/newsid_2515000/2515869.stm

Fall of Communism in Poland, Hungary, Czechoslovakia, East Germany, Bulgaria and Romania.
http://www.localhistories.org/communism.html

Tiananmen Square - 1989: Massacre in Tiananmen Square. Several hundred civilians were shot dead by the Chinese army during a bloody military operation to crush a democratic protest in Peking's (Beijing) Tiananmen Square. Tanks rumbled through the capital's streets late on 3 June as the army moved into the square from several directions, randomly firing on unarmed protesters.
http://news.bbc.co.uk/onthisday/hi/dates/stories/june/4/newsid_2496000/2496277.stm

[38] 'Light from the Dark Valley: Reflections on Suffering and the Care of the Dying' Sheila Cassidy Pub. Darton, Longman and Todd (1994)

Chapter Nine

'Christianity, if false, is of no importance, and if true, of infinite importance. The only thing it cannot be is moderately important.'

C. S. Lewis

Life often feels like a series of links in a chain. Some links may be weaker than others; there may be stresses in some places which affect the overall strength of the chain. How do we keep our strength in challenging situations? My Christian faith has laid down the guidelines of how to live in the world. In order for me to understand and develop my knowledge further, I have examined other belief systems to see whether leaving out God would be an easier way of dealing with life's challenges. I considered Humanism as an alternative to Christianity. Humanism denies any power or moral value superior to that of humanity and rejects religion in favour of a belief in the advancement of humanity by its own efforts. Therefore, it stresses the autonomy of human reason in contradistinction to the authority of the Church. The Humanist will see man as basically good; the Christian believes that man has a sinful nature and a tendency to do evil things. The Christian recognizes that people have great worth and value because every person is created unique and special by God who has a purpose for each one of us.

The differences in belief become clearer when considering the sanctity of life; Humanists believe that since man is merely a highly evolved animal, some human life is not so special and can be determined by man in whatever circumstances apply. Most Humanists will support abortion, euthanasia, and even infanticide in some cases. Christians believe that since man is created in the image of God and for the purposes of God, all life is infinitely precious.

Whatever you believe, there are no absolutes; only fools or people of incredible faith believe in absolutes. I know that there are Christians who are not truly Christian in their actions; the abusers, the bigots. There are Catholics who are not Christian. There are priests who are not Christian; there are nuns who are not Christian. Headlines such as 'Nuns cruelly exploited girls at laundry', 'Priest abused choirboy for nine years' are particularly shocking and challenging when you consider that the people perpetrating these crimes are thought to be steeped in their religious faith. These are not the majority, of course, and there are abusers and bigots among people of all faiths and none, but they are the ones who get the headlines because they personify hypocrisy.

If I'd relied on human elements alone I think I would have abandoned the church years ago. Most of the time, I could see beyond human weakness in general and my own weaknesses. I have met some truly good and holy people during my life. For me, Christianity gives hope and meaning, depth and structure to people's lives. Everyone is equal, created in the image and likeness of God. Despite its human organisation, the church offers divine inspiration through its liturgy, its sacraments and its teaching. Its ceremonies are a rite of passage. We all have good and evil within us. Our potential for either is, I believe, very great and it's always a matter of conscience which one we choose. If religion were to be eradicated it would create a vacuum. How would it be filled? It seems that there's something deep within the human psyche which longs to find meaning and a framework with which to live our lives. I see my Christian faith as a dynamic living element open to development and change. Every day I have the chance to begin again.

Two years after the death of my mother, I embarked on a diploma counselling course. This higher training would lead me to explore, even more, my search for meaning. I would learn more about the theories and models of counselling and in doing so I would learn more about myself. Philosophical considerations of human nature, human dignity, human value and human response are vitally important for us all but more so if you're seeking to counsel others.

~~~~~

The counselling process is, to some extent, the raking over of the client's thoughts and feelings and this can have a positive therapeutic outcome. Through exploring themselves and their situation, the client will understand that some issues will remain forever but many will be dealt with consciously and subconsciously. Changes can then be made in the light of what is discovered. If we are able to accept the challenges in our lives, we can gain from them and often they contribute to the richness and value of our experiences. They will certainly help to form our characters. This process continues until a point is reached where the client can accept what has happened and deal more effectively with what remains. Everything may not be resolved completely but the healing process has begun. Unfortunately, the process does not work perfectly for everyone but it works well enough for most people most of the time and real and lasting benefits can usually be gained.

~~~~~

By reflecting and looking at the complexities of my own life, I am becoming more aware of my own personality and my pattern of interaction with others. I am getting closer and closer to knowing myself. I am learning that love, patience and non-judgemental, non-directive acceptance on my part can do a great deal more to heal than intervention and guidance. The counsellor is, effectively, saying to the client: 'As a fellow human being, I accept and value you. I welcome you and want to understand you. My wish is that we will be open and honest with each other. I don't want to take anything away from you and hope that, through our relationship, we shall be able to work together for as long as you feel it to be helpful and worthwhile.'

Counselling is a helping activity in which the helper and client engage over an agreed period of time. Hopefully, this process leads to valued outcomes in the client's day to day life brought about by working through the issues together. It is the client who achieves the goal of helping himself, through the facilitation of the counsellor. In this way, counsellors enable clients to empower themselves and find their own solutions. Real progress is made when the client manages a problem situation and develops opportunities for change.

I believe that the psychological characteristics of counselling are on-going, even after the sessions have ended. Transformation takes place through the counsellor offering the client the self-healing process. By giving acceptance, time and attention, resolution can occur. Sometimes, the problem is unsolvable; it's a question of coming to terms with it rather than it being resolved. Counselling is a creative psychological process which occurs as the mind works away on the problem between sessions. It requires neither practical nor medical intervention. The giving of advice or opinion is not part of the counselling process and would reflect the thinking of the counsellor rather than that of the client.

An important aspect of counselling is to help the client engage as fully as they feel able with the reality of their situation including their pain, if that is a part of it. It is the ultimate acceptance of his situation that enables him to go forward to live as full and meaningful a life as he can in accord with his own wishes and needs. Whist providing a healing relationship, it is not a process without struggle. It can be like picking at a scab and opening it up in an attempt to cleanse what is below the surface; trying to heal an emotional wound that is still hurting.

Counselling seeks to empower the person to achieve personal growth and confront a specific problem or event in their lives. By listening and then reflecting back what the person reveals to them, the counsellor helps the client to explore and understand their own feelings. The individual is then able to decide what kind of changes they would like to make based on these reflections. This healing therapy can achieve significant personal growth and change lives.

The supportive relationship helps the individual explore important life issues in a non-judgemental way, helps them trust their own judgements about themselves and enables them to use their inner resources for healing and growth. It also helps build up self-belief and confidence. In this way, the counsellor creates a supportive, accepting environment in which the person is encouraged to be themselves and to come to terms with their own lives.

~~~~~

Far away from the world of counselling, changes were taking place at the university and office politics came to the fore; they became far too important to ignore. Certain people were acting in a Machiavellian way. Power games were being played. Certain individuals were jumping on the backs of others to gain a strategically better position. People were being undermined. I battled to maintain my own position but finally
~~~~~

came to accept that things would never be the same again. After about a year in this unpleasant situation, I'd had enough and was looking at other options. I had been offered a generous package of voluntary severance but wanted to continue working.

Judgement has become a dirty word and people are judged for having negative opinions about all sorts of things. Many are accused of prejudice if they don't accept certain behaviour. I prefer to judge the act rather than the person. The person may have all sorts of reasons for acting the way they do. It's always best to forgive, otherwise, you may carry a heavy weight of resentment that you can't set aside. Unfortunately, we can't like everyone we meet even though we can love and respect them as human beings; people often do things that we don't like or find difficult to accept. On this occasion, it was easier to step out of my working life and I started to consider other options.

One day, I was reading my emails when one came up seeking staff to act as support tutors for disabled students. I was now a qualified counsellor and with my degree in education felt suitably qualified to apply. Tutors were called upon to work one-to-one with students, helping them with study skills, organisation, time-planning and constructing and writing their essays. They would form a special enabling relationship with each student and work with them to support them in producing written work and attending to other demands within their degree programmes. I had a broad experience of university administration which helped me to understand the pressures on both the students and the academic staff. Training was offered and so I became a student support tutor. This role covered all the academic institutions in Manchester as well as the University of Salford.

Most of the students I worked with were dyslexic and many found it very difficult to organise themselves and to produce written work on time. Others had poor writing skills and needed someone to proofread their work. Some students suffered from mental illness or other disabilities and many had low self-esteem. All had their individual difficulties but were struggling to reach their potential. I was able to give them what I had not received myself but had needed so much. I felt I'd been fortunate to find this type of work; it involved personal service and it fulfilled all that I had been training for. My background in social work, my knowledge of education and different learning models, my counselling qualifications; all came together to make this job enjoyable and rewarding. There was something in my role which called upon all these strengths and I was, at last, fulfilling my career ambitions.

Meanwhile, my family life was changing and I was constantly adapting to these changes. What had once been a noisy and dynamic household was becoming quieter as the children grew up and went their separate ways. There were feelings of sadness and loss; there were occasions of satisfaction and achievement. Charlie had graduated from university and, after a year or so in Manchester, moved to London. He entered into business with a university friend and embarked on a successful business partnership which still continues today. Catherine had met her future husband and was planning her wedding. She had achieved good results despite the debilitating bout of ME and glandular fever which left her very weak and exhausted. She had had time off school but worked very hard to pass exams and study for a career in child care. I was very proud of her. Jack was completing A-levels and about to go to university. He was interested in a career in sports management. David and I would be alone once more. However, this mass exodus didn't work out as quickly as I'd feared and the children were back and forth many times before settling down with their partners and fulfilling their own independent lives.

The house was a family home and was still the cornerstone to which they could always return. It was like a base for a game of Hide and Seek; the players could return if they ever got tired of their hiding places. Most of life's problems seem to concern relationships and when relationships go wrong, we seek a safe place; somewhere we can go to lick our wounds, find comfort and recover. As parents we can accept this coming and going; it's part of the natural cycle of life.

Thomas Moore says:

> 'Love has to manifest itself in caring, nurturing, protecting; nurturing the human needs and the spiritual needs of one's children. Teaching them how to live and be alive for themselves and others. Loving and serving. Not loving and self-serving. Allowing the spirit of the child to breathe and be free.'[39]

Most mothers want their child to be free to be whatever they want to be, providing it is good. It is never easy being a parent; we can only try our best. Families may not always be ideal but they are the best natural support system in existence.

> 'Parents can only give good advice or put them on the right paths, but the final forming of a person's character lies in their own hands.'
>
> Anne Frank

Counsellors in training are expected to receive counselling themselves. I spoke to Hannah and we decided to go for counselling together to see if we could move forward with the problem of telling the secret to Daniel and Edward. There are many families with secrets; secrets as varied as the families themselves. The situations may be very different but often similar issues have to be faced. In these reflections, I have tried to analyse the dynamics of such a secret by telling my own story. It is my hope that this will be helpful to others. I am fully aware of the damage done by the concealment of identity. This search for my own identity was resolved when I discovered the truth but the ability and opportunity to pass on this information became an anguished process. It was difficult enough to ask the question. Why was it proving so difficult to communicate the answer?

~~~~~

Our chosen counsellor agreed that two people could come together to be counselled with the same issue. She listened and accepted our story and helped us to reach a decision. Daniel and Jane lived in the south-east of England, many miles from Manchester and it would not be easy to speak to them about the secret. We agreed that the next step would be to write to Jane to ask her whether it would be a good time to approach Daniel to talk about a family matter. We were feeling our way because we didn't want to rush in if the time wasn't right. He was working hard and might have been under stress. We were treading cautiously, realising that it might affect him deeply. At the same time, we didn't know whether he knew already; had worked it out for himself many years ago, and was perhaps struggling to tell us what he knew. Anyway, rightly or wrongly, we decided to write the letter. We simply said that we wanted to talk to him about something which related to our childhood which we felt he had a right to know. Was it a good time? Did she think Daniel would be open to hearing about it?

Today, I question why we didn't write directly to Daniel. I think we were trying almost too hard to be sensitive to his needs. There was also a feeling that because we had held on to the secret for so long we would need to apologise for that too. Perhaps he would think that we should have told him and Edward years ago, while Mum was still alive
~~~~~

but we could explain why we hadn't. Again, we would have to justify ourselves even though we had acted out of respect for her wishes.

The response to our letter was bitterly disappointing. Jane chose to stonewall us. She didn't seek any explanation or clarification. She spoke briefly to Hannah on the phone and said that it wouldn't be a good time to approach Daniel but didn't ask what it was that we wanted to discuss. The moment passed and the opportunity was gone. We settled back once more into an uncomfortable state of vacillation. The resolution we craved was out of reach.

~~~~~

We've now passed through the Clinton years and George W Bush is about to be inaugurated. Bombs are going off all over the world in various bloody conflicts and wars. It is 11 September 2001 and the US is under attack.[40] The World Trade Centre Towers collapse, thousands lose their lives. Shock reverberates worldwide and there is a sense that this is a life changing moment for everyone. I was meeting a friend in Bramhall on the day of the atrocity. It was a beautiful autumn day; the sun was shining, there was a light breeze and the trees were just beginning to change their colours. We went for a walk in Bramhall Park and had a sandwich lunch at a pub in Cheadle Hulme blissfully unaware of what was happening thousands of miles away. When I got home I switched on the TV and listened in shock and amazement as the story unfolded. Jack came home from college and I told him that this was a world shattering event which would go down in history as one of the worst terrorist attacks ever perpetrated.

Three years later, the world was shocked again by the Asian tsunami,[41] striking unexpectedly on Boxing Day in the Indian Ocean. We've spread across almost the entire planet and so, from time to time,
~~~~~

there will be disastrous calamities that hit local populations. I hope that one day we will be able to predict earthquakes and volcanic eruptions scientifically and we will eventually be able to anticipate other natural occurrences, such as tsunamis. All this will help us to reduce loss of life if we can evacuate the local population in time. We are constantly using our intelligence to overcome such natural events and will continue to do so.

Man-made disasters, however, are entirely different and they can be prevented. Many cause huge environmental damage and severe financial loss. Disasters such as the Bhopal Gas Tragedy in India, the Deepwater Horizon Oil Spill in the Gulf of Mexico and the Chernobyl Meltdown in Ukraine or climatic changes as a result of man's exploitation of a region are caused by negligence, greed or human error.

> 'I do not accept any absolute formulas for living. No preconceived code can see ahead to everything that can happen in a man's life. As we live, we grow and our beliefs change. They must change. So I think we should live with this constant discovery. We should be open to this adventure in heightened awareness of living. We should stake our whole existence on our willingness to explore and experience.'
>
> Martin Buber
> 'Encounter with Martin Buber' by Aubrey Hodes (1972)

I have wrestled with the complex interpersonal theories of Martin Buber[42] and cannot hope to explain them adequately here, but, for those who are willing to pursue them, they give an extraordinary view of how every individual, man or woman, can perceive the living world and their fellow men. We all have many paradoxical experiences in our lives, it's no wonder we get confused. I find it easier to follow certain well-founded rules as this enables me to focus on my chosen path and it strengthens and reinforces my way of seeing the world.

I've learnt that in life we need, primarily, to be givers not takers. We need to work towards reconciliation rather than conflict and look for forgiveness rather than retribution. Our past, once reconciled, can be a source of great strength and resolution. Life is a wonderful and fragile gift which we need to embrace and hold near to us. That's why truth is so important because when we lose it we let ourselves down and diminish our own authenticity. It is increasingly difficult in our modern society to live according to Christian teaching even though the rules laid down are there for our own benefit; there to prevent us getting hurt. We are tempted to moderate the teachings to enable our lives to fit in with society's norms. Christians have to be very strong to avoid these compromises. The young always want to fit in and it takes special courage to move against the general thinking within their peer groups. What we know to be right, we must transmit to others and act out in our daily lives. Human passions and emotions do not change; society's rules change to condone different behaviours for different generations. These behaviours then become the accepted standard and those who don't go along with them are considered prejudiced, old-fashioned and out of touch.

Everyone knows that change is not always progress. We need to evolve but we also need to improve, otherwise there is no advancement, only regression and a weakening of the values that were once held paramount. I try to hold on to these core values and to present them to my own children and grandchildren. I see them as part of my legacy to them; I believe I would be failing them if I withheld what I truly believe to be right; tried and tested as they are by a lifetime of careful consideration and experience. My children will, of course, make their own choices based on their own thinking and reasoning. I love and accept them but, at the same time, I always urge them to make informed decisions based on careful examination of all the facts at their disposal.

~~~~~

The new millennium opened up many new opportunities in my life. Working part-time as a support tutor, I was able to take up other interests. I visited Charlie in London as often as I could. I went over to Yorkshire where Jack was studying and spent time with him. Catherine was working and settling down to married life with Steve. Our first grandchild would be born within a couple of years. I joined a national pregnancy care charity as a voluntary counsellor. This was the work I wanted to be involved with; offering positive and practical support.

Friends and I established a book club and I happily returned to reading fiction, reviewing each book and sharing what others had learnt from it. Over the years we have read and analysed many writers and their stories. Semi-retirement also meant that I was able to see more of Hannah and make new friends. I visited older friends too; Katie, Jenny, Tania and Sue and reconnected with them. It was good to build stronger relationships; for true friendship, time is not important; the genuine essence of the relationship remains irrespective of the frequency of contact. I was also preparing for the time when I would retire fully but that was a while off yet. I wanted to be sure that I would have enough interests to enjoy and feel engaged with. It was all part of my way of adapting to my changing life.

'You are never too old to set another goal or to dream a new dream.'

C. S. Lewis
~~~~~

[39] Moore, T. 'Care of the Soul' Piatkus (1992)

[40] World Trade Centre On 11 September 2001, terrorists hijacked four aeroplanes and deliberately flew them into targets in the United States of America. These acts of terrorism killed almost 3,000 people and triggered the subsequent conflict in Afghanistan. http://www.bbc.co.uk/history/events/the_september_11th_terrorist_attacks

[41] Asian Tsunami On 26 December 2004 more than 200,000 people were killed when an earthquake beneath the Indian Ocean triggered a devastating tsunami. Places as far apart as Sri Lanka, Thailand and Somalia were affected by the disaster.

[42] Rabbi Martin Buber: 'I and Thou' This book was first published in 1937and became one of the most influential books of the twentieth century. Buber believes that we become fully human only when we enter into the I-Thou connection with other people - relating to them as person to person. Love exists between people as an I-Thou meeting. 'The man who does not know this, does not know love', says Buber, and he goes on to give a moving and profound account of what love really is. The I-Thou inter-relationship is also possible with other living things: a tree and a pet animal, for example. God is the Eternal Thou and we can meet him only in the I-Thou concept. God can never be 'It'; He is always 'Thou'. He meets us as Thou and is present in every Thou. The I-Thou relation cannot be planned or contrived. It simply happens, but only if we are open to it. To be fully human we have to be open to this possibility. The evils of the world are, in Buber's view, the result of our failure to be open to the possibility of I-Thou and being content with I-It.

Chapter Ten

'Each person should judge his own actions and not compare himself with others. Then he can be proud for what he himself has done.'

Galatians 6:4

When we face difficult times in our lives; the death of a loved one, a child leaving home, the breakdown of a marriage, the loss of a close relationship, how do we seek healing?

> 'Healing requires a number of steps,' says Fr Brian D'Arcy. 'Step one is a time for reflection, openness and perspective. We should acknowledge the positives. Step two on the healing journey is facing the causes of the hurt as honestly and as objectively as possible. Step three requires us to sift through what can be changed and accept what cannot. Step four is realistically looking to the future with courage and hope. Healing demands that we give up hope of a perfect past so that we can have a better future.'
>
> Extract courtesy of Father Brian D'Arcy C.P.
> 'A Little Bit of Healing'

Seeking help through prayer, I believe I have been led along various paths and through countless relationships to the place I am today. If we can see life as a journey, we can see each step on the road to our formation. We can look back with a sense of accomplishment and we can look forward with hope because, in knowing ourselves more fully, we are strengthened and better equipped to deal with future challenges or diversions along the way. We can learn from every single person we meet and, in turn, we are capable of having a positive effect on all those around us. I need to acknowledge the rationality and thinking of others and respect the value of their freedom as well as my own. I need to live in the present, taking on my own social responsibilities and develop a mind which is constantly curious about the human condition and human destiny. In order to progress, I need to know my faults as well as my virtues.

'The greatest of faults, I should say, is to be conscious of none', wrote Thomas Carlyle.

> 'To discern what weaknesses and faults separate you from God, you must enter into your own inward ground and then confront yourself'.
>
> Johannes Tauler[43]

If I don't confront my faults and change, I will never evolve into the person I want to be and I believe it is a conscious and personal choice we can all make. Christ is at the centre of my life and it is as natural for me to ask him for guidance as it would be to ask a loving human father. Women are said to have the best network of friendships and I have found that female friends have always been a great source of support to me. Women, in general, seem more able to share and to be intimate and honest with one another. On the other hand, I have also found that many men are capable of great insight and understanding. When I told my children, when they were teenagers, about my family secret, they all accepted my story with love and understanding.

~~~~~

It still remains for me to tell my brothers the same story. And so I embark on yet another soul-searching exercise in the form of this book. But to be truthful, this is the way my life has been since I first discovered the secret. That desire, or maybe it's an unfathomable need,
~~~~~

to tell my brothers, has never left me. I decided I would write everything down as a therapeutic exercise in the hope that I would discover some way of bringing about closure. I can see the frustration of procrastination in others but I must be the greatest procrastinator of all. I arrived at a certain point in the story and I knew that I had to make a decision. I couldn't just hand my brothers a book and say 'Right, this is the family secret; it's all written down there. Read it and let me know what you think!' I explained to Hannah that I was writing my story and she supported me. Then, I came to the part where the secret had to be passed on and this is what happened.

~~~~~

Daniel and Jane were coming up from Kent one weekend for a family party. Hannah and I decided to tell Daniel and Edward together. Dan was travelling up on Thursday so we planned to meet with them at Hannah's house sometime on the Friday. All the old conflicting torments rose to the surface. Fears and anxieties: Do they know already? I am betraying my mother! They may wish they'd never been told. It will change our relationship for the worse. They will resent the fact that we didn't tell them earlier. They will be hurt. They will be unhappy. They will be angry. It may strengthen our relationships. They will understand what it's been like for us. They will have the chance to reassess their situation and face the truth. It will be a tremendous relief to be free of the secret. How will it affect them? Will they be shocked? Will it upset them? These arguments and many more wracked my brain whenever I thought of the secret.

~~~~~

As I write this account I'm getting nearer to some sort of resolution. Hannah is a great support and has shown sympathy and understanding each step of the way. I'm so glad she has been able to share this with me. We now come to a crossroads but this time we can't stand still or turn and go back. We have to face forwards and take our next step together. A special birthday is on the horizon. The years have gone by so quickly and I can hardly believe that I've reached this age, but I have, and I want to celebrate by having a joint 'Martha and David' party for all close relatives and friends. I feel so fortunate to have my precious family and want to share some of this joy with others. Our idea is to see Daniel and Edward on the day before the party and tell them the story of Celia's secret. All the preparations are in place; Daniel and Jane have been invited, Edward will be there with Helen.

A couple of days before the party, we receive a telephone call. It's been snowing heavily and Daniel and Jane don't think they'll be able to make it up to Manchester for the weekend. They're very sorry to have to miss it but can't risk being stuck for several days and unable to return. So, our plans to tell Daniel and Edward together are thwarted once more. The party goes ahead and is a great success. My children and grandchildren are my greatest joy and I am grateful for the opportunity to bring everyone together and celebrate what we have as a family. Daniel and Jane say they will come up to Manchester as soon as they can.

Several weeks later we are attending a concert. A very old folk group will be playing and singing; you know the kind, founded in the 1960s and now geriatric, but still very good. Hannah and Simon, Edward and Helen have all agreed to attend. Hannah thought it would be a good idea to ring Daniel and ask him if they'd like to visit and join us for the concert. He said they would. I rang Edward and, with Hannah's agreement, arranged for him to call in at Hannah's on Friday morning for coffee. I said we had a bit of family business to discuss. 'Helen won't be able to come, is that alright?' he asked. 'Yes, that's fine. We just need you to come on your own'. On the Wednesday of the concert week Hannah had a call from Jane. 'Daniel has been very sick for several days and isn't fit to travel' she said. 'He will have to see the doctor and have some more tests as he had a similar bout of illness a year or more ago'. The trip is off. Another chance to disclose the secret has gone by.

I have shouldered the secret for most of my adult life and prior to that I was suffering its ramifications as I've been able to express in the story of my childhood. I want to be free of it, even though I know I will never be completely free. It's part of me now, part of who I am and will always be with me. But, even after all these considerations I still asked myself whether it was the right thing to do? I recently consulted a priest and he said 'It wouldn't be wrong to tell them and it wouldn't be wrong not to tell them.' I can't say that was the most helpful response I could have expected.

I spoke again to Hannah, 'I think we should tell Edward on his own'. Hannah agreed that, although Daniel couldn't be with us, we should go ahead with our plan to tell Edward. Friday morning arrives and I reach Hannah's house. Edward arrives. We have coffee and we chat for half an hour or so about the various members of the family. Edward's son has just bought a house and he has been helping him to modernise it. Edward has been suffering from a pulled stomach muscle and has been in pain. He eventually asks 'Well, what is this piece of family business you want to discuss?'

I start by saying, 'Ideally, we'd have liked Daniel to be with us too because it concerns us all.' I said, 'It's something which Hannah and I have known for a long time and we'd have liked to have told you many years ago, but circumstances didn't allow it, as I'll explain. We know that Uncle Sam was the father of us all. I found out in my mid-twenties and confronted Mum about it just before I got married.' Edward's eyes filled with tears. 'I thought I might have been his son,' he said slowly, 'but I didn't think he was the father of all of us'. 'There is no doubt that he was father of us all', I said and Hannah confirmed that this was so. I then went on to tell him about how I had suspected it and how I'd confirmed it with Auntie Kathleen and written a letter to Mum and how she had reacted with anger and insisted that no-one else in the family should be told. I went on to explain how David had seen the photographs and had said he had no doubt that Sam was our father as he could see the strong family likeness. I told him about reaching the point where I shared the secret with Hannah and how we told Mum about sharing it. She had again insisted that Daniel and Edward should not be told. We shared out thoughts and talked of family situations which came to mind. We told him about having counselling together, our approach to Jane and what had happened. We talked of Mum's difficulties and the very hard life she had faced and we all agreed that we couldn't judge her or Uncle Sam. We looked at photographs of us all as children and a few rare pictures of my father on his own and with my mother. We have just one photograph of the six of us as a complete family.

Edward said he got on well with Uncle Sam. He liked him and felt he had a good relationship with him. We thought about the secret in the context of its time and how people covered up the truth and how similar things must happen in many families and in many more where it never comes to light. I explained, 'Mum didn't want to tell because she thought you might think differently about her or think less of her.' We recognised that she was fearful of the truth coming out and of other people's opinions and judgement of her. Edward began to cry. I moved over and sat beside him, putting my arm around his shoulders.

'I'm so sorry if we've upset you. I didn't want this to happen. I don't want our relationship to be harmed by us telling you'. He raised his hand and said, 'No, no it's not that. It's just so upsetting to think that Mum couldn't bring us together and tell us when she was alive. We would have understood. It's happened and we can't change it.'

Edward said he was glad we had told him and, although it had been upsetting, he was pleased to know the truth. Then, he laughed and said 'You know when you said you had something to tell me which affected the whole family, I thought you might be telling me about winning a million pounds on the lottery or something.'

I've always felt close to Hannah, especially so since we shared the secret. Now I feel closer to Edward too. Since telling the secret, I feel there has been a noticeable improvement in our relationship. I'm sure I'm not imagining it; there's deeper feeling, a greater understanding that didn't exist before. For that I am grateful.

About six weeks later, Daniel and Jane visited Manchester to attend another fundraising event. They would stay at Hannah's as usual. This time there would be three of us to tell the story. Daniel and Jane were ready for coffee when Edward and I arrived. The circumstances were exactly the same as they had been for Edward except Jane was with us. I didn't know what to expect. There was no easy way to introduce the topic and I was fairly direct as we told them in the same way that we had told Edward. Daniel was in shock – he had no idea. Jane was attentive, showing her concern as she bent towards him like a mother with her child. He had been researching his Barkworth ancestry back to four generations. He loved John as a father and described him as a complex character. He told us how he had refused sales contracts on moral grounds due to disapproval of certain products. He found him a deeply spiritual man. Daniel recalled going out in the van, sharing time with him and building a relationship. John woke him for his paper round, cooked his breakfast on his return. He encouraged him. Daniel had felt marginalised and excluded from the family. He thought Mum had treated him very badly. He had a very low opinion of her; considered her selfish and he didn't have anything positive to say about Uncle Sam; he neither liked him nor tolerated him. Sam had been a member of the Orange Order[44] and didn't relinquish his ties with them during his lifetime. Daniel appeared to have a somewhat polarised view of life; he seemed unable to acknowledge the cultural implications of people's actions. He was against the Orange Order and thought that Sam should have left it by the 1960s. But, Sam was a Presbyterian and most Presbyterian Northern Irishman at that time were members of the Orange Order; it was part of his Northern Irish culture. The serious impact of The Troubles came a little bit later in 1966 and Sam had died in 1965. Many of Daniel's memories didn't match up with ours. He was defensive of John yet judgemental of Uncle Sam and Celia. He seemed to have no understanding of Mum's desire to change things in the house. He remembered it being John who struggled to pay the mortgage. Yet, we all believed that the house was bought for cash by my mother in 1928 and that John took out a mortgage later, which he was never able to pay back; at least that was Mum's version of events. He had memories of the sandwiches taken to Sam each night but he was aware of not being a part of it. He thought Sam and Celia were having an affair but had no idea of the true situation.

This is why secrets are so pernicious. They harm people and they harm relationships. This disclosure was proving to be very difficult and upsetting. Once said, it can't be taken back. Daniel was clearly troubled by the news; he had lived his life with positive memories of his 'father' John Barkworth. He said, 'I'll always think of John as my real father.'

Everyone is a victim in this story because deprivation is a negative word and we were all deprived of a true father. Again, I asked myself: 'Have we done the right thing in telling him?' Edward and Hannah reassured me that we had. We couldn't justify three of us knowing the truth and not Daniel. Now we had gained an understanding of Daniel's personal memories, thoughts and feelings and his individual perspective, which could be acknowledged and respected. It felt as though we had been raking over our memories like coals in a dying fire. We all have selective memory and we can only make sense of life through what we know and remember. A few days later, I wrote:

Dear Daniel

..... Please don't take this in a patronising way. There are really no words to express what I've been thinking and feeling since our disclosure to you this weekend. It proves how individual we are in our experiences and you're fortunate to have the positive memories you have of John which are very special to you, and you were very special to him during his lifetime. I hope that we will be united in what we have shared rather than divided because of our differences.

We've all had to get on with living our lives as best we could and I have gone way past the point of making judgements about any of it. I pray for Mum, for John and for Sam and I pray for us all that we come to terms with the truth (as we see it) and find peace and forgiveness at this stage of our lives. .....

With love to you both,
Martha

~~~~~
~~~~~

Anthony Trollope said, 'No man had a right to regard his own moral life as isolated from the lives of others around him.'[45] Our actions reach out like circles in a pool. I hope that anyone I have hurt in the past will forgive me for all my faults and hurtful actions. I contacted Daniel and Jane again later in the summer and invited them to Jack's engagement party. They were not able to attend but I said I hoped we'd see them soon. I wrote to him again in January to update him on family news and wished them well for the coming year. Soon, there will be a wedding in the family. I hope they will be able to attend. No further recriminations. No judgements.

If I could have written to my mother as she was dying I would have said:

Dear Mum

If our souls are infinite, as I believe they are, then the essence that is me will meet again the essence that is you. We will be reconciled and we will both understand.

With love always,
Martha

This letter might have helped to remove some of the barriers which were set up after I told my mother what I knew about my birth father. Maybe she would have understood what it was like to be me and would have smiled on me and forgiven me. I know my mother loved me. I felt it as a child and I felt the loss of it as an adult. The first step to resolution is truth. The second step is forgiveness; it won't change history but it may make it easier to live with. The third step is reconciliation and communicating the love which stems from the first two steps. Finally, the hope is that healing will occur. This seeks to remove the barriers of misunderstanding which separate one human being from another. We can only seek to make the best decisions we can with the information we have. There is always a limit to human understanding.

> 'Thus in this oneness Jesus Christ is the Mediator, the Reconciler, between God and man. Thus He comes forward to man on behalf of God, calling for and awakening faith, love and hope and to God on behalf of man, representing man, making satisfaction and interceding. Thus He attests and guarantees to God's free grace and, at the same time, attests and guarantees to God man's free gratitude.'
>
> Karl Barth, 'The Humanity of God' [46]

It is by such experiences that we come to know the redemptive power of God's love and mediation. I was a slave to the secret; now I am free, or as free as I can be given the human condition. The human person encompasses body, mind and spirit. The body, our physical entity, is the functional container for the mind and spirit; it has to be fed to be kept alive. The mind enables disassociation; we are able to operate as individuals, amidst the chaos yet outside it. No matter what the situation, we can each take ourselves outside it or rise above it. People can tell you how to live your life but each individual is free to look at various options, decide for themselves and act upon those choices. The power of the mind determines the logical choices we make but the intellect has to be informed if we are to behave morally.

The spirit, or the soul, I believe, is the moral conscience and the sentient awareness of beauty, truth and feeling. It enables us to be profoundly aware of love and the deep, unfathomable mystery of being. Anything that brings joy touches the soul. The soul reflects our sensibilities and our empathy with others; this is sometimes experienced when we feel the impact of judging others or being unjustly judged ourselves. Body, mind and spirit come together in the individual's unique intelligence; in the realisation that God upholds those who are willing to help themselves. We are free and self-determining.

Sometimes, it's helpful to remind ourselves of the choices we have made, to evaluate them and adjust them. As a Christian, I accept the Ten Commandments as the guidelines of honouring God and living in society among our fellow men. This is the basic starting point. St Paul says:

> 'We must, bear with each other, and forgive each other. If someone does wrong to you, forgive that person because the Lord forgave you.'
>
> Colossians 3:13

'Your actions, and your action alone, determine your worth', said Evelyn Waugh. We cannot claim ignorance of this fact and it is only by realising our own potential and having faith in our own abilities that we can build a better world.

~~~~~

I have found that nothing comes easily. How many of us can live our lives far away from the world's troubles with only ourselves to focus on? However we view our lives, world events are key players and are dependent upon the time in which every story is set and the events running parallel to it. Everything takes place on our own individual stage, in the role we are playing and in the spot on which we stand. Few of us can ignore the scenery and the various characters playing alongside us. Wars, atrocities, murders, all manner of crimes are taking place around us. Love, service, sacrifices are being offered every day too. We have to be aware of all this to keep a balance and to make
~~~~~

choices about the parts we want to play. Nothing is fixed; we can set the scene and we can write our own script.

~~~~~

In my search for forgiveness, reconciliation and healing, I now know that healing requires a number of steps. It demands time for reflection, openness and perspective. We need to face the causes of the hurt as honestly and as objectively as possible. We are required to sift through what can be changed and accept what cannot. Finally, we are urged to look honestly and realistically to the future with courage, hope and the determination to act if that is what is required.

Before we can claim healing, however, we must discover the meaning of forgiveness and reconciliation. For me, forgiveness is excusing someone for a fault, an action or an omission; it is offering an open hand and setting aside anger and resentment. I will be reconciled if I resolve any differences or misunderstandings. I will need to accept my own faults and the faults of others if the lost relationship is to be re-established. I believe I must also practice compassion; have sympathy and understanding for the suffering of others. If I can achieve all this I will be healed.

---

[43] Johannes Tauler German Dominican, one of the greatest mystics and preachers of the Middle Ages, born at Strasburg about 1300; died at the same place, 16 June, 1361. http://www.newadvent.org/cathen/14465c.htm

[44] The Orange Order The Orange Order is a Protestant fraternity with members throughout the world. Autonomous Grand Lodges are found in Scotland, England, the United States of America, West Africa, Canada, Australia and New Zealand. The name comes from William III, Prince of Orange, and is kept because his victory over despotic power laid the
~~~~~

foundation for the evolution of Constitutional Democracy in the British Isles. Support for William of Orange in the British Isles led to the formation of Orange Societies to commemorate his victory at the Battle of the Boyne in July 1690, but the largest and longest lasting groups were the Boyne Societies in Ireland.
http://www.grandorangelodge.co.uk/what-is-the-orange-order

[45] Anthony Trollope: 'Dr Wortle's School'

[46] Karl Barth, 'The Humanity of God' Pub. Fontana (1967)
Born in Basel in 1886, Karl Barth was a Swiss Reformed theologian. Barth is often regarded as the greatest Protestant theologian of the twentieth century.

Chapter Eleven

'Where there is injury let me sow pardon.' 'While you are proclaiming peace with your lips, be careful to have it even more fully in your heart.'

Francis of Assisi

When I think of the concept of forgiveness, I'm not looking to forgive my mother for the fact that she had children outside marriage. I can understand and accept why she did this. I'm not looking to forgive my father or the man I believed to be my father whose angry outbursts frightened me as a child. I'm looking for a kind of mutual forgiveness between my mother and myself, between myself and John and Sam. Yes, my childhood was traumatic at times and the emotional pain and the fear and anxiety definitely contributed to my nervous and insecure personality but that is my nature and I don't feel I have to forgive anyone for that. Anyhow that has resolved itself slowly as I've got older. What has been much more difficult to change has been the feeling of resentment towards my mother because she refused to confide in her children when they were old enough to know the truth. Not only that, I felt her anger and loss of approval which resulted in damage to the relationship we had and which I treasured so highly. I had to live with the elephant; I was left in its company, constantly having to relate to it; I felt its size and its weight. It was too big to ignore, impossible to remove and it stood between me and my family relationships because it prevented me from being truly genuine. It takes lots of energy and effort to carry resentment and you feel its pressure resting heavily upon your shoulders. She left me on my own;

she gagged me and tied my hands behind my back. I couldn't tell the secret, I couldn't even write it down. We both made serious mistakes in dealing with the situation and I want to forgive her for her mistakes and I want to ask forgiveness for mine.

There's an appropriate balance to be made when sharing problems. When we are children, we should not be made to bear the weight of our parents' problems. As adults, however, we can appreciate the effect certain problems are having and we can support our parents. Part of the parental role is to share the problems of their child but not the other way round. I am searching for forgiveness and reconciliation and healing. These are difficult philosophical concepts and I am very much a lay person in such matters but I do know that forgiveness is a freeing experience. It puts anger back in its box, it eradicates the need for revenge and it opens the way to new thinking and feeling. Changed behaviour emanates from that new thinking and leads towards a path to reconciliation and healing.

I'm returning to Victor Frankl for further insights and he believed that the health of our bodies is often dependent on the health of our minds. I've always known this to be true. Therefore, the physical and the psychological are intimately linked. We all need the 'will to live' to thrive. Frankl believed that 'humans must have meaning in their lives in order to have the will to live'; he concluded from his horrific experiences during the Second World War that man 'can only live by looking into the future ….. and that many men and women in the concentration camps survived ….. because they clung to hope for future happiness and fulfillment.' Frankl recognized this human need for purpose, and he worked hard to give that purpose not just to the patients he treated in his own practice but to the world as a whole through his writings.

Refusing to forgive sets up a barrier and, where the cause is serious, it acts as a block and holds on to an injury like a heavy load. This heavy load can have a depressing and destructive effect and can be described, as attributed to Freud, as 'frozen anger'. Often beyond articulation, the sufferer may not even know it and, therefore, be unable to express it. The anger becomes impenetrable, solid and gripping. How do we lay down that load and forgive? I have found that before I can forgive, I need to understanding that I am at fault too. When I fail to live up to my own standards of reasonable reaction and behaviour, I feel low in myself and regretful. If I can forgive myself and understand why I reacted in a certain way, then I can begin to empathise with others and begin to forgive.

> 'Forgiveness is the conscious decision to let go of the anger and resentment I feel toward someone who has hurt me. Forgiveness is, first of all, an act of the will, a decision. We all know something about making decisions. Every day we make hundreds of decisions, some big, some small... The more serious the offence, the more time it takes to come to the decision to lay anger aside. We all know that it takes a certain amount of time to feel right about any important decision.
>
> When the hurt is so serious and so deep that we are left traumatized or permanently scarred, we may need professional help to be able to come to forgiveness. But in all cases, forgiveness is the goal, because not forgiving is self-destructive.'

Courtesy of Fr Thomas Richstatter, O.F.M.
Original Source: 'Exploring Forgiveness' By Robert D. Enright
Wisconsin Press, 1994. ISBN 0-299-15774-1

Before we can progress, we need to acknowledge our pain and accept that forgiveness is a process which will take time. We need to recognise the negative feelings that we feel. When we are hurt, when something of importance or someone we love has been taken away from us, we feel anger and resentment and this is natural and we have a right to these feelings. However, because these feelings of anger and resentment weigh on the one who carries them, they are a significant burden. They are injurious to our physical, mental and spiritual health. That is why finding a way through them, and ultimately setting them aside, is so vital.

The decision to forgive the person and let go of the hurt and pain does not imply that I condone or excuse what the person did. It doesn't necessarily demand that the one who offended me is sorry. Although forgiveness is more difficult in these cases, it is still my decision; it does not depend on anyone or anything else. It is my decision to lay aside the burden of hurt and pain and if I resist, it allows the person to continue to harm me. It means that I persist in carrying the burden of anger and resentment, a burden which restricts me from getting on with my life.

Fr Richstatter talks about 'reframing' the picture. Reframing refers to the process of seeing the situation, the one committing the offence, and/or ourselves in a new or different way so that we have a better context in which to make the decision to forgive.

> '….. Seeing someone in a larger context can give us an insight into behaviour. Reframing is not intended to excuse the perpetrator, but it can allow us to have some insight into what might have caused him to do such a thing. What were the circumstances which led her to act in this way? When I consider my own context … and when I am aware of my own sinfulness - I am in a better position to make the decision to forgive. This is the heart of compassion - the ability to 'walk in another's shoes.'
>
> Courtesy of Fr Thomas Richstatter, OFM
> 'Forgiveness in Our Church Today: Key to Healing'[47]

'Do we really know how much we hurt each other? When one considers the depth of the human personality and its endless complexities and impenetrability, good sense shouts out that we should learn how to forgive.'

Fr. James Lloyd, CSP[48]

The tiny seed of forgiveness is in us all. Only we as individuals, making our own choices, can decide whether it shrivels or whether it flowers. Forgiveness is brought forth through love. It is the ultimate expression of kindness and compassion.

I thought about the beautiful song, 'The Rose'♪**25**, sung by Bette Midler. There is a seed of forgiveness deep within us which love can raise to the surface.

'God is the Father who is full of mercy and all comfort. He comforts us every time we have trouble, so when others have trouble, we can comfort them with the same comfort God gives us.'

St Paul's 2nd Letter to the Corinthians 1:3-4

~~~~~

Nations, like individuals, can also be reconciled. The nation of Ireland has shown us this. They stopped fighting, started dialogue and established peace and the process of reconciliation. They have demonstrated how the vision of a 'Shared Future' can emerge from even the most bitterly divided and bloody past. They will never forget the misery and suffering that was caused but they will need to bring about change in the hearts and minds of emerging generations if a new phase of history is to be established which puts the pain of the past away. Despite the belief that this process would fail, the Irish are now on the path towards working things out together in order to solve their
~~~~~

problems and to establish a peaceful future for their people. This process can act as a model and a source of hope for other trouble spots in our world, even where peace and understanding seem impossible.

Universally, people can forgive; those with religious beliefs and those with none. Forgiveness, it seems to me, is an act of the intellect as well as a spiritual gift. I know that the power of prayer is often dismissed with disbelief; it is regarded as superstitious nonsense. However, I also know from my own experience that I could not have come to my own conclusions about forgiveness without the inspiration I have received through prayer. I have been led through my own searching and have discovered what I needed to find and what I needed to do. I have been given the power to heal painful unexpressed emotions that were buried deep inside me. I came to a point where I knew that I had done everything humanly possible to resolve the problem. I happen to believe in divine intervention but you don't have to. Be patient, be tenacious, be loving and forgiving and reconciliation will come. It isn't easy but it can be achieved.

~~~~~

What's the good of theory without practice? Sometimes, we are called to use our own pain to help others. If we have experienced very deep hurt ourselves we can empathise and express that acceptance, compassion and understanding to others who are in pain. That's what happens in good counselling. And don't forget that counselling is always a work in progress; it takes effort, focus and commitment to achieve a worthwhile outcome. As I've said, a major part of counselling training is the search for self-awareness, self-knowledge and self-development. I remember that during one workshop we were asked to draw a picture of family members, our relationship to one another with
~~~~~

ourselves positioned in the middle. How far away was each member from us in the centre? What was their size in relation to us? What other factors came into the drawing e.g. a house or a tree? Did they symbolise some important issue in our lives? We were then asked to analyse it with our partner and to consider why we had placed all the figures where they were. I found this an overwhelmingly emotional experience. My mother was on the edge of the drawing, the same size as the rest of the adults but her face turning outwards. She was alone. I was surrounded by my husband, my children, they formed a ring around me, Hannah and Simon were a short distance from me just outside the centre circle, Edward and Helen and Daniel and Jane were close by. They were facing towards me. John and Sam were absent from the drawing. When I began to talk through the feelings expressed in the drawing, I broke down uncontrollably. All the hurt flooded out and I cried 'til I could cry no more. I couldn't express myself verbally but I knew without any doubt what it all meant to me. I felt so sad; my greatest loss was the loss of my mother's unconditional love.

I've long accepted that my mother's actions have to be seen in the context of the period in which they occurred. Life then was so different; people didn't express their thoughts and feelings as freely as they do today. They didn't want others to know about their problems. They had what is often described by the British as 'a stiff upper lip' and expected others to show the same resilience. My mother had spent so much time and effort painting her own picture; 'the secure and happy family'; husband and four children, churchgoing Catholic, respectable professional woman, homeowner. She had become the consummate artist and lived inside this representation of her life, secure in its solid frame. The most convincing liars are those who believe their own lies and my mother was determined that nothing would scratch the thick shiny varnish on her picture; it would remain intact for everyone to see and admire. Mum's life was extremely hard and I have always felt compassion for her because of the difficulties she faced. Pride, to her, was a great strength not a failing.

~~~~~

> 'The stupid neither forgive nor forget; the naive forgive and forget; the wise forgive but do not forget.'
>
> Thomas Stephen Szasz

Never claim that you have forgotten how to forgive.

Forgiving and reconciliation can be a complex and lengthy process. Stress caused by family conflict can take time to ease. Over the years, the stress I have suffered has slowly melted away and I am now in a calmer place. I want to convey my forgiveness to my mother beyond the grave and I believe this is possible. My heart and mind can communicate that forgiveness and it can relieve me of the pain of holding it back; I need to pass on to her my acceptance and understanding. I have never stopped loving my mother. I love her soul. To be able to experience this level of love is, perhaps, relatively rare. It is expressed most beautifully by Emily Bronte in her novel 'Wuthering Heights'.

Cathy says:

> '.... I am Heathcliff - he's always, always in my mind - not as a pleasure, any more than I am always a pleasure to myself - but as my own being - so don't talk of our separation again - it is impracticable; and .....'

This heightened awareness of the love we possess for another is brought about by a strong spiritual connection through love. Maybe
~~~~~

there is a sense in which we are all connected to one another by this spiritual bond but, in the majority of relationships, no matter how loving, it is rarely apparent.

> 'Be kind to one another, tender hearted, forgiving one another, as God in Christ forgave you.'
>
> St Paul: Ephesians 4:32

~~~~~

Now it is settled; reconciliation can begin. Reconciliation doesn't just happen; you have to make it happen. It requires conscious effort and the will to fulfill a long-held wish to be reconciled. In conveying my thoughts to my adored mother I can say: 'I may never resolve completely my way of thinking to yours but I accept unconditionally your point of view and I want to re-establish our loving relationship. Our two apparently conflicting perspectives can become coherent with one other. We can be brought together in spirit, our quarrel can be resolved and we can be at peace. I am resigned; I am in harmony with you once more and I believe it is possible to reconcile these opposing views. I understand. I make peace with you. If reconciliation restores harmony and the renewal of a close loving relationship between us then I will reconcile willingly my way of thinking with yours so that we are no longer opposed.'

> 'Happiness is not something ready-made. It comes from your own actions.'
> 'If you want others to be happy, practice compassion -
> if you want to be happy, practice compassion.'
>
> Dalai Lama
~~~~~

Healing restores a diseased or damaged organism to health. It applies equally to the body, the mind and the spirit. It involves repair, regeneration, replacement and renewal.

~~~~~

I can see all around me a lot of deep-seated anger and hatred in people and it takes a small spark to set it alight. There are those who hate politicians for their ideologies; they hate Communism, Marxism, Thatcherism, Conservatism or Socialism. They hate the major religions; Christianity, Judaism and Islam. Others are profound and unmoving in their ideals; they are pro-life, pro-abortion, pro-capital punishment, anti-capital punishment; pro-immigration or anti-immigration and so on. Often, these attitudes are based on personal experiences or what they have been told by others but whatever the basis for these beliefs there appears to be no compromise. It can be both frightening and impressive to be in the company of a fanatic but only rarely is it reassuring.

To me it would seem that in order to settle any dispute there is a need to compromise. Sometimes, it means accepting standards or views which are different to our own. We all have ideals which we feel we cannot compromise and certain principles are non-negotiable but, in the long run, we are left to make our own choices about these and decide whether or not we want to live harmoniously with other people. We are told in the Catechism of the Catholic Church that God loves us at every moment, in every single complicated situation, even in a state of sin. God helps us to seek the whole truth about love and to find ways to live it more and more unambiguously and decisively. By this we learn that every life is a progressive process and that, whatever has happened, we can make a new beginning with God's help.
~~~~~

In writing this memoir, I am communicating my experiences to anyone who has the patience to read about them. I am also conveying to my children my deepest thoughts and feelings so that they may better understand who I am. They are the most precious of all to me and I love them totally and utterly. They are mine but they are not me. They are unique and individual to themselves and they have the right and freedom to hold their own beliefs and to search for their own understanding of why they are here on this earth.

Kahlil Gibran, the great Lebanese-American artist, poet and writer and Maronite Christian writes:

> 'You are the bows from which your children as living
> arrows are sent forth.
> The archer sees the mark upon the path of the infinite,
> and He bends you with His might that His arrows may go
> swift and far.
> Let your bending in the archer's hand be for gladness;
> For even as He loves the arrow that flies,
> so He loves also the bow that is stable.'

Our children, he says, are not our children but '….. the sons and daughters of life's longing for itself.' They don't belong to us but to themselves; with their own thoughts, and their own souls. He talks about 'the archer' 'who sees the mark upon the path of the infinite'. He is the one who guides the arrows set forth from your bow. He loves the bow that is stable.' And so, as parents, we seek to keep our bows stable as we set our children adrift into the world.

Lisa Wingate, the contemporary American author writes,

> 'Your children are the greatest gift God will give to you, and their souls the heaviest responsibility He will place in your hands. Take time with them;

> teach them to have faith in God. Be a person in whom they can have faith. When you are old, nothing else you've done will have mattered as much.'

When I was a child, my faith had a very positive influence on me. At other times, I found it negative and confusing and contradictory, especially in relation to honouring and loving my father; telling the truth and respectful obedience. I would have preferred my own children to have experienced a much deeper religious upbringing but at that time in my life I was battling a lot of conflicting emotions and I chose not to complicate their lives with the same. I believed that they would find their own core beliefs and values through example. In reality, this may have left them confused and unable to understand my deeply held religious beliefs. They know, however, that honesty is the best way of promoting oneself and I would be less than honest if I ignored, or tried to diminish, what I believe.

The Catholic Catechism tells us that in our human state, man's response to God by faith must be free. Nobody should be forced to embrace the faith against their will. (The Freedom of Faith 160)

> 'To be human, 'man's response to God by faith must be free, and. . . therefore nobody is to be forced to embrace the faith against his will. The act of faith is of its very nature a free act.'

> 'God calls men to serve him in spirit and in truth. Consequently they are bound to him in conscience, but not coerced. . . Indeed, Christ invited people to faith and conversion, but never coerced them. 'For he bore witness to the truth but refused to use force to impose it on those who spoke against it. His kingdom. . . grows by the love with which Christ, lifted up on the cross, draws men to himself.'

> 'The act of faith, therefore, is of its very nature a free act.'

We are called by God to serve him in spirit and in truth. We are bound to him in conscience, but not coerced. This quotation illustrates the freedom with which men and women are endowed as seen through the eyes of the Church. The decision to believe is a free choice. The decision to reject its teachings is a free choice.

> 'I believe in Christianity as I believe that the sun has risen: not only because I see it, but because by it I see everything else.'
>
> C. S. Lewis

My faith reflects upon my whole life. Because I believe that love, forgiveness, reconciliation, spirituality, healing and the soul are all bound up together, I need to reconcile this with my religious beliefs and explain how I see they link together and why it is important.

When I was a little girl, the soul was described to me as an imaginary organ, close to the heart. It becomes stained when we commit sin and is brought back to radiant whiteness when we are sorry and we are forgiven. It is at the core or centre of our mystical being and holds our hopes, thoughts, dreams and imagination. It is a reflection of who we are as a person and shows itself in our look – one to another; for 'the eyes are the mirror of the soul'.

Spirituality nourishes the soul. Religion is deeply spiritual and reveals what is sacred. Spiritual awareness arises from an incalculable number of encounters with the wonders of life; the beauty of the natural world, deeply religious experiences, music, art, unconditional love and profound human communication. The soul, I believe, is the deep mystery that is at the centre of each individual. It needs to be nurtured like the body. Given solid foundations, it will thrive.

The family, even allowing for all their faults and weaknesses, pass on traditions and ideals, religious or otherwise, that have been part of their lives for generations. This explains why a loving family is so deeply important and why beliefs and values are held so dear and passed on. In the dysfunctional family these values are splintered; they fail to hold a family together and cause separation and unhappiness.

~~~~~

If anyone asks me 'Why believe? 'Why go to church?' 'Why pray?' I would say: Firstly, it's what I've been taught, it's what I believe to be right, it gives me a sense of soul and purpose. I go to church to practice and consolidate my beliefs. Attending church is an act of obedience and honours the God in whom I believe. Through my attendance at church, I am part of a community of faith which I share with others. I remain focused in my desire to live out the gospel. I am continually reminded of the importance of acknowledging and confessing my faults. I reflect on my own thoughts and actions and I am made aware of God's love.

Prayer can be offered in solitude or with others. Through coming together in prayer, we learn from other Christians how they struggle to live out their faith in various situations, how they deal with challenges and how they experience ways in which God has answered their prayers. Following a religion gives the believer a positive alternative to the messages and moral values which are placed upon us by a secular society which frequently ignores God and denies our society's inherited Judeo/Christian codes and values. This focus on the divine offers me a fresh perspective on life and renews God's message for me through the sermons of the priest; and what God wants of me here in my life at the present time. The Eucharist strengthens our union with Christ and cleanses us. It gives grace and increases our love for God and one another.
~~~~~

'There is a God shaped emptiness in the human heart. Know Christ Jesus is a treasure awaiting discovery'.

C. S. Lewis

The disagreements about the fundamental nature of man will, I'm sure, continue forevermore, but most of us would agree that all living things, including children within the family, need the right environment in which to be happy and healthy. We, like other animals, are programmed by our instincts to live in harmony, although we do not always fulfill this ideal. Human beings are more than animals and we don't merely live in nature, we try to control and direct it. Most people would accept that we possess free will and intellect and are not confined to what nature alone can provide. We need our natural environment to keep us happy and healthy but look continually beyond nature in our quest for solutions to problems, remedies for healing. We also need, and many of us seek, a spiritual and personal setting to teach us the truth and fulfill us in love. In this sense, Christians come to know, love and serve God in our true and natural environment.

'In Him we live and move and have our being' Acts: 17-28

---

[47] Fr Thomas Richstatter, OFM.
Permission granted to use quotation from 'Forgiveness in Our Church Today: Key to Healing'
http://www.tomrichstatter.org/index.htm

[48] Fr James Lloyd, CSP
http://frjameslloyd.blogspot.co.uk/2011/01/meaning-of-forgiveness-from-perspective.html

Chapter Twelve

'Act justly, love tenderly and walk humbly with your God.'
Micah 6:8

Seeking our Irish heritage, Edward and I arranged a three day trip to Newry. We knew from the 1911 census that my birth father's family lived in Charlemont Square North in Camlough, County Armagh. He, at seven years old, was the youngest of six living children. His father, aged forty-seven, was a winding master, his mother, aged forty-two, a housewife. His two older brothers were employed in the linen industry too; one a mechanic, the other an assistant winding master, along with his sister, aged fifteen, who also worked in the Linen mill. The three youngest boys were at school. Their stated religion was Presbyterian. We had also found the 1889 marriage record for his mother and father. A few days before we left for Ireland, we received archive details from Armagh Ancestry of the marriage between Sam Hare (my father) and Mary Jane Jackson. This had taken place at the Church of Ireland in Bessbrook on 6 April 1932. I'd written to about a dozen people by the name of Hare living in Northern Ireland but, although I received a number of responses, none of them proved to be family members. We hoped to trace our heritage and to see if we could confirm the little information that we already knew.

Our early morning flight from Manchester to Belfast International was uneventful. We picked up the hire car at the airport and started our journey south to Newry, armed with the trusty Satnav and the appropriate postcodes. We travelled through beautiful countryside and the sun was shining on a perfect summer's day; we were seeing Northern Ireland at its best. We passed through Camlough, which is about three miles from the centre of Newry and we saw the signs leading to Bessbrook as we drove along the main road.

Camlough is part of the Newry Greenbelt. To the south east of the village, the land rises steeply to Camlough Mountain within the Ring of Gullion. This is an Area of Outstanding Natural Beauty. The Camlough River flows north to south through the countryside into Camlough Lake which is situated to the southwest. The village has grown over recent years and is a popular centre with an important livestock market which serves the area to the south of county Armagh. It has the usual facilities expected in a small community; a primary school, a health centre, a church or two. It is thriving commercially with shops, supermarkets, public houses and other businesses. We didn't stop at this point but headed on to Newry to find our hotel and settle in.

After lunch, we set off on our journey of discovery. We had heard about a well-known pub in the centre of Camlough called 'The Yellow Heifer' or 'Quinn's Bar'. It would be a good place to ask if anyone knew any more Hares. As we walked up to 'The Yellow Heifer', the outside walls of which were painted bright yellow, two men were standing in conversation at the doorway. They beamed a smile at us as we passed by them to go inside. The younger man, who was the owner, explained that the pub was closed on a Tuesday. We smiled and thought he was joking. We stepped inside and in front of us, behind the polished wooden bar was a vast wall, brightly illuminated, lined with countless bottle of wines and spirits and we were sorry to find that, in fact, it really was closed. Returning to the front entrance we chatted again with the owner and his friend. We explained that we were visiting Camlough to try and find out about our family history and wondered whether either of them knew of a family called Hare. They knew plenty of O'Hares but no-one called Hare. They said a man named Bradley would be able to help us as he knew everyone in the area but they didn't know his contact number. We talked about the family house in Camlough and were told that Charlemont Square was in fact in Bessbrook, not in Camlough. Thanking them for their help, we drove on to Bessbrook and coming to a T- junction, with a Catholic church on the left, we turned right towards Charlemont Square.

Around the year 1845, Bessbrook had been chosen by John Grubb Richardson as a suitable site for his linen mill because of its climate and geographical situation and its proximity to abundant water supplies. Charlemont Square was at its centre and had been built as part of the model village provided by Richardson for his workforce. Richardson founded the village on the Quaker philosophy known as the 'Three Ps': no public houses, no pawn shops and, therefore, no need for a police station. He believed that alcohol was the cause of all evil and reasoned that without a public house there would be no need for a pawnshop or a police station. So, for many years Bessbrook was the village without the three Ps. The police did not arrive until the 1890s and, as yet, the other two Ps are still absent although we heard that the local restaurant has recently been granted a license.

The old linen mill, where my father's family had worked so many years ago, was taken over in the 1970s by the British Army and converted into an army base. The Army left in 2007 and the mill, now derelict, has recently been given Listed Building Status.[49]

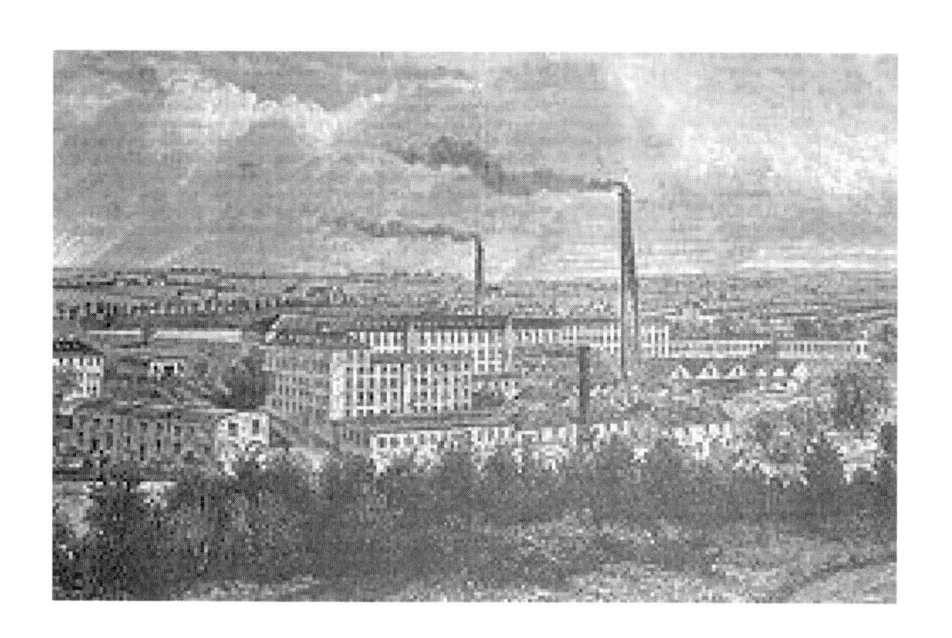

Richardson's Mill, Bessbrook

At the height of the industry, Bessbrook linen was among the finest in the world, and the linen mill provided the majority of the employment in the village. Most of the buildings are built of the local granite, which is in abundant supply. There is a diverse mix of Christian denominations within the village represented by many churches; the Church of Ireland, Methodist, Presbyterian and Roman Catholic. The village also has a Quaker meeting house. We parked on the left hand side of Charlemont Square and considered our next move. The neat little terraced houses we were now standing amongst were constructed for the mill workers and they have survived as good quality housing to the present day.

Bessbrook was at the heart of some of the worst violence in The Troubles.[50] During those years, a helicopter landing area was established to supply other military outposts in the area since road-borne movements of troops and supplies were vulnerable to landmine attack. At one stage, Bessbrook was reportedly the busiest helicopter airport in Europe, even busier than the major heliports supplying the North Sea oil rigs. For several years British Army helicopters would take off and land every few minutes. To avoid the risk of missile attack they would fly at rooftop level over the little village. That alone, would have caused considerable stress to the people living there. For some time, direct access to much of the village was sealed off by security barriers, armed by British troops, to minimise the risk of vehicle-borne bomb attacks on the security forces. Not surprisingly, many have claimed that this contributed to the commercial decline of local businesses. In June 2007, the British Army withdrew their military presence from Bessbrook and closed all their facilities, marking an end to British military presence in the South Armagh region.

Aware of this history and the effect it must have had on the villagers, we made our way to the corner shop which sold newspapers, ice-cream, sweets and groceries. At first, we thought that the shop was on the site of Sam's original house or that it had claimed the house as part of its extension. Then we realised that the square is numbered from one onwards on all three sides, North, East and West and his house was No 1 Charlemont Square North. The house is still there. We spoke to the two ladies in the shop and neither knew of anyone called Hare. Then they remembered that there had been an older couple Billy and Sylvia, who had both died within the last five years or so. They had had children but the women didn't know where they were now. The Christian names sounded familiar and we realised that they were one of the couples we had contacted but of course we had received no reply. We drove back down the main road and parked just past the Catholic church. Two other churches stood on the hill to the right. We passed Bessbrook police station, now awaiting its fate, deserted and defended by a twenty foot high corrugated iron fence.

The next building was the Church of Christ the Redeemer, the Church of Ireland church where my father had married Mary Jane Jackson. The church was locked and there was no-one around to answer our questions so we wandered over to the cemetery which was to the side and rear of the church. We saw graves for Jackson which could have been the same family as Mary Jane. We found two graves bearing the name Hare. One was the grave of William and Irene Sylvia, the other bore the name 'Hare' and the inscription 'A Tribute of Love'. No names or dates were inscribed so we couldn't tell whether this was the grave of Mary Jane and her baby or not. There were several Bradleys in the churchyard and we wished, for a moment, that we were searching for Bradleys instead of Hares; it would have been much easier.

There was a community hall adjacent to the church which was open and was set out for a function that evening but no-one was about so we couldn't ask to see any church records. We moved on a few paces along to the Presbyterian Church. Again, the church building was closed. Walking along the drive, past the newly mowed lawn and blossoming rhododendrons we saw 'The Manse', a fine Victorian house sitting solidly in the bright sunlight. There was a car parked outside and I asked Ed, 'Should we ring the bell and ask if we can see the church records?' 'Why not? We've come a long way and we might as well try.' So, I knocked on the door and it was opened by the minister's wife. 'We're visiting Bessbrook to find out about our family heritage and, if possible, would like to see the church records to check family entries.' She welcomed us in and, directing us to a large comfortable lounge, she heard the main outline of our story and our connection with the village. She fetched several registers of baptisms and marriages; large, hard backed books full of carefully handwritten entries. We discovered all the records of baptisms for the six Hare children. We also discovered the notice of marriage for Sam's brother William Wallace Hare to Agnes Clarke in January 1932, just a few months before his own marriage to Mary in April that year. We saw Sam's signature and that of Mary's on the certificate as witnesses to the marriage. It's a strange feeling when you find something you've lost. I felt a warm sense of satisfaction and achievement. It somehow felt right that we should be making these discoveries. I felt closer to the family emotionally as though I was sharing in their precious moments of birth and baptism and marriage.

The minister of the church returned to the house and joined us. He gave Ed a book he had written on the history of the church over the past one hundred and fifty years. We talked about Bessbrook and its history. He had known Billy Hare well and remembered him with fondness. Billy would have been my first cousin, one of two sons born to my father's brother.

'He was a great character and would have loved to have met you and tell you all he knew about his family but he died a few years ago.'

'Do you know any other family members?' we asked.

'Billy had four children, one is in Australia, the two sons moved away but there is a daughter, Anita, who is married and lives nearby.'

'Do you know her address or phone number?'

'No, but perhaps we can find out for you.'

The minister's wife left the room and telephoned one or two people and came back with a contact number for Anita. We were told that she had a young family and were advised to phone her after seven in the evening as she would be preparing the family meal before that time.

Ed and I returned to the hotel overwhelmed but elated by our discoveries and excited about the prospect of contacting Anita. We were about to go out for our meal when I decided to give Anita a call.

'Hello, Anita? I hope you don't mind my calling you unexpectedly. I hope I'm not disturbing you.'

'No, that's ok' she replied.

'My name's Martha and my brother and I are in Newry for a short visit, while we try to find out more about our family heritage.'

'That's interesting', she said, 'I've been doing some family research myself recently.'

'We looked at the graves by the Presbyterian church today and then we called at the manse to check church records. We're related to the Hare family and we wondered if you might be able to fill in a few blank spaces. Your name was given to us by the minister. '

Anita said, 'O.K. I might be able to help you.'

I read out the names on the 1911 census and asked Anita, 'Do those names mean anything to you?'

'Yes, they do.' She replied.

I explained that we were staying in a hotel in Newry until Thursday. I didn't want to impose upon her but if she was willing I thought it would be a good idea if we met up to exchange information with one another.

'How do you know the family?' she asked.

'We're connected with Samuel Ashwell Hare, the youngest son of William and Martha. After Samuel's wife died, he came over to England and it's from that point on that we are associated with him.' 'It's a complicated story!'

'Can you come to see us this evening?' Anita suggested.

'I'm just serving the meal at the moment but after that …'

'Yes, that would be great', I said. 'We're about to go out for our meal too but we could come over after that. What's your postcode?' The minister had said we would find Anita's house easily with the Satnav.

'No, you won't find it with a Satnav. We'll come to meet you at the church and lead you back to the house.'

We agreed to meet at nine o'clock.

Feelings of intense interest and anticipation raised our expectations to a higher level. Could we possibly hope to find some direct living link with the past? The brilliant evening sun was low on the horizon and, for a time we were blinded by it. Anita and her husband, Davey, drew up beside us in front of the church. Ed and I approached them and introduced ourselves. We then followed them down the narrow country lanes which led eventually to their home. To us city dwellers, it seemed deep in the countryside; it was certainly well outside the Satnav's capabilities. They had built their house on a few acres of land which had originally been farmland. At this point, Anita explained how she had inherited the land from her father. It had passed to him from his uncle who had inherited it from his grandfather. This man was our grandfather and Anita's great-grandfather, born in 1864.

The land had been farmed by my great grandfather but most of his sons had gone their separate ways; my grandfather into the linen mill, another son to Canada, others had married. In the 1901 census, just one son seemed to be at the farm with him – they were described as 'farmer' and 'farmer's son'. Davey explained that the low stone wall adjacent to the garden was all that remained of the original farmhouse. I bent down and touched it, sensing the presence of the spirits of the family who had lived there. We looked across the fields with the hills beyond and imagined our ancestors and how they must have looked at that view so many times; in all seasons, over more than two hundred years of family history. The sun was setting on the horizon and I thought it was beautiful.

Anita's two teenage children were sitting on solid wooden chairs at the garden table, on the raised patio at the rear of the house. They were all very friendly. The boy was home from university and the girl appeared to be working for her A-levels. They had several family documents on the table to show us. Anita brought us tea and we looked over the land maps and photocopies of birth and marriage records. There was so much information to share. It was becoming clearer by the minute that we were from the same family and we felt relaxed and drawn to them as the evening went on.

The night air became chilly and we retreated into the house and continued our long conversation about the family links and our own experiences in England. Davey mentioned that two or three of the men in the family had been ill with sarcoidosis.[51] Edward had suffered from this illness after working in a laboratory for several years and he always thought that it was linked to the chemicals and other substances he was using as a dental mechanic. Now he discovered that this inflammatory lung condition, which had caused him to change his career path, had a genetic link.

As we spoke more intimately of our childhood and our upbringing in Manchester, Davey observed that there was more to this story than first appeared. How was it that Ed's surname was Barkworth and not Hare?

'It's complicated' I said. And then I began to tell the full story.

'A couple of years after Sam's wife and baby died, he came over to England and eventually met my mother. We children were the result of that relationship.'

Anita and Davey were listening with intense concentration.

'There was one major complication; she was already married, in a very unhappy marriage, and she couldn't get out of it. Sam and my mother never lived together as man and wife and we were never able to acknowledge Sam as our father and he couldn't acknowledge us as his children. This whole situation was shrouded in secret. Mum's husband, who we believed to be our father, must have agreed to keep the secret too, perhaps for his own protection or for ours. We don't know.'

'When I was in my early twenties, I started to ask questions. Why was Sam so generous with money? Why was he so interested in us? Why was my mother so upset when he died? '

'I tried to work out the answers and ask the right questions but my mother always steered off track. She wasn't open to divulging the true nature of the relationship. She saw herself as the victim of the decisions she had made and of her disastrous marriage. I put it to the back of my mind but it wouldn't rest. Then, when I was about to get married, I showed David, my future husband, some photographs and he, without hesitation, said that he was sure that Sam was my father because of the strong family resemblance. I confirmed this with one of my mother's oldest friends. She said it was true but that they thought it best for everyone's sake if they kept it a secret.'

I then went on to explain how I had confronted my mother, first by letter and then face to face, how she had reacted; how I'd felt the full force of her anger and how our relationship had changed from that moment. I described how my discovery of the secret had affected me by its negative impact on our once close relationship.

'Both men were dead by this time. What was done was done. There was no point in blaming anyone; no point in making judgements. But I was left with a desolate feeling of loss – the loss of my mother's approval and love.'

'It was all horribly complicated and there were so many conflicting issues that I had to deal with. In fact, I'm writing a book about it.' 'I'm hoping that it will help others to read about the impact of a family secret and perhaps they will be able to identify with some of the issues I talk about.'

'I'd love to read it! I'd be really interested in your story,' said Davey, conveying a sincere sense of acceptance and understanding.

I continued to explain that my mother forbade me to tell my sister and brothers and that, for a long time I carried the secret alone. I respected her wish to remain silent but, eventually, I confided in my sister and then, much more recently in my brothers.

'I've only known for six months!' said Edward with a cheerful smile on his face.

Davey commented that it was often the men who were the last to work things out and he smiled. The family showed great insight and empathy. They were taken by complete surprise, maybe even shocked, yet, their faces showed acceptance of the story and they seemed to relate to my feelings and understand how difficult it had been for me to hold on to the secret for so many years.

'It must have been very hard for you' said Davey. 'You must have been under so much strain'.

'I was, it was very stressful and … there's just one further complication,' I said, with a consciously ironic half-smile on my face. 'My mother was a Catholic and we were all raised as Catholics!'

It then struck me how we're all subject to the accident of birth and I thought about how easy it is to base our judgements on prejudices and assumptions. If I'd been born in Northern Ireland to Sam and his wife, I'd have been a Presbyterian or a member of the Church of Ireland. My Christian faith would have come down to me by another route. The main Christian message would have been the same but the presentation and the practices would have been different. Ed and I felt accepted for who we were despite the complications that came with our story. It was a good feeling.

Anita wrote down details of her family; her grandparents, her mother and father and her sister and brothers and the names of their children and her own children and we did the same. I felt sad that I had never known my grandmother, aunts, uncles, cousins and their children. But, now at last, I had made contact and there was a chance to make some connection. It was now approaching eleven o'clock and Ed and I said we must leave. Anita and Davey invited us for dinner the following evening which we gratefully accepted. We thanked them for all they had done; for all the information they'd given us and for the patience with which they had heard our story. We felt very relieved that we'd got on so well. Exhilarated, we found our way back along the narrow country lanes to the main road and returned to the hotel.

Before I went to sleep, I reflected on an amazing day.

Two thousand years ago St Paul spoke about equality and justice:

> 'All of you are the children of God, through faith, in Christ Jesus, since every one of you that has been baptised has been clothed in Christ. There can be neither Jew nor Greek, there can be neither slave not freeman, there can be neither male nor female - for you are all one in Christ Jesus.'
>
> Letter of St Paul to the Galatians 3:26:28

As Christians, we believe that death is not the end; that our souls will continue in another dimension, whatever that might be. Whatever it is and no matter what you believe, it will be nothing like what we can imagine in this life. In our search for meaning, the Christian religion gives an explanation for why we live and for the sorrows that each of us has to bear. It offers a moral code, a way to live and love, a way to relate to God and to the whole of mankind.

The Christian religion offers forgiveness, consolation and the rites of passage to sustain the soul through its life journey. Its rituals give structure and meaning. Ultimately, it offers a way to die in the belief that we are to meet our creator. Whatever denomination we may follow, we are all Christ's children. I am so happy when I embrace my fellow travellers and listen to their stories. All world faiths have much in common and we all have a duty to share common interests and improve peaceful co-existence, the sanctity of life and the eradication of poverty. My own life experiences have taught me to rise above the differences that separate us and concentrate on what we share in common. One thing I know; the future can only be made secure where there is forgiveness, reconciliation and true acceptance and love.

I know no more than the next person and it may be that when the light of life goes out we are truly dead to everything; destined for a dark and silent eternity. Many people believe that this will be the more likely outcome. All that any on us can do is search for the answers to our questions and accept those answers based on our own understanding, our faith, our reason and our personal experience. Reason alone never seems enough; there are always so many questions left unanswered.

~~~~~

The next morning, still stunned by our experiences of the previous evening, we spent relatively quietly wandering about the little town of Newry. We visited the castle and museum and saw an exhibition devoted to the Brotherhoods and Friendly Societies. This revealed the history of Newry and many organisations such as the Round Table, the Women's Institute, Knights of St Columbanus, the Orange Order, Freemasonry, the Soroptimist International and the development of Trade Unions. On display were regalia and artefacts reflecting common
~~~~~

characteristics of the symbolism and ritual associated with these organisations, some of which date back to the Middle Ages. This long history has entrenched the customs and attitudes of their respective members. They have also provided a very strong sense of identity within the community and have helped many families who have fallen on hard times. Their charitable works continue to support local people with worthy local projects.

The library at Newry had a display devoted to Irish Heritage. The young librarian explained that they had a member of staff specializing in genealogical research, but he wasn't available that day. Nevertheless, we were given useful information pointing us to websites and journals which might be of help to us in our future searches. We then visited the restored mill worker's house in Bessbrook village. Sam Hanna, a well-respected local historian, gave us a fascinating insight into how a family would have lived in this house in the latter part of the nineteenth century. The house, which might have accommodated as many as twelve people, was almost identical to the house where my father lived as a child.

~~~~~

Our second day was winding down to the evening and we looked forward to meeting Anita and her family once more. Anita and Davey had invited another friend for dinner. Graham McAleer had a great knowledge of the local area and the history of the linen mill. He had known Billy, Anita's father, and had worked alongside him at the mill. Before dinner, Graham took us on a history tour of the Bessbrook area – through the village, past mill workers' cottages to where the tramway had run from Bessbrook to Newry and back again. The tram had been an important means of transport for the workers travelling from the
~~~~~

wider region around Newry. We followed the Camlough River and drove down to Camlough Lake. We passed the building which was the home Richardson had provided for those workers who suffered from tuberculosis and another house which was known as the Widows' Home. We saw Derrymore House, a beautiful thatched cottage on the former estate of John Grubb Richardson and now owned by the National Trust. We passed by the remains of Baillies Foundry which, long ago, had provided the wheels and cogs for the mill's machinery.

Graham took us to the foot of Slieve Gullion and showed us the striking landscape of the Ring of Gullion. We gazed up at the eighteen-arch Craigmore Viaduct now carrying the main Belfast to Dublin railway line. Local legend says that one construction worker died for each arch completed. We drove up to The Friends Meeting House Chapel and the graveyard where the Richardsons of Bessbrook are buried and saw many other sites and buildings linked with the linen industry which my father would have known. Returning to Anita's home, our minds overflowing with information, we had a wonderful meal and enjoyed, once again, the hospitality for which the Irish are famous.

On our final day we returned to Camlough Lake and then travelled on to Armagh which for fifteen hundred years has been the spiritual capital of Ireland and the seat of both Church of Ireland and Catholic archbishops. Dating back to pre-reformation times, the Church of Ireland Cathedral is set on a hill in the city of Armagh. Across the valley on another hill sits the French Gothic twin-spired Roman Catholic cathedral. Armagh is the oldest and most venerated of Irish cities and has a long Christian heritage. Both cathedrals are dedicated to St Patrick. Both cathedrals stand on hills. I was sad to remember the bitter conflicts which have been fought in this beautiful country and I hope that increased understanding will develop that will put all religious and political differences aside. With the Good Friday Agreement and subsequent initiatives, I believe that this is possible.

St Patrick's Church of Ireland Cathedral
and St Patrick's Roman Catholic Cathedral
The image is used by permission of Armagh City & District Council.

Our final stop before Belfast was Lisburn and the Irish Linen Centre situated in the quaint seventeenth century market square. Here we saw a fascinating exhibition of the history of the linen industry in Northern Ireland with some amazing exhibits depicting the various processes involved in the production of linen thread and the development of hand looms and weaving machines. The story was linked in to the context of life in Ireland at that time so we saw both the social and economic impact which the industry had on the country. We came away with a better understanding of how life would have been for our ancestors.

I have always felt a great connection with Ireland and have visited the republic several times but this was my first visit to the north. I think of it as a country of great beauty and friendliness, of drinking and laughter and genuine hospitality. I also feel deep nostalgia, for it is an island of enormous sadness. I think of its history; of its poverty, of the Great Famine, of the loss of so many people to emigration, of the troubles, of its famous literary geniuses, of its music and of its humour.

I speak with an English accent but there is a part of me that belongs to Ireland. Two songs in particular demonstrate this longing within the heart of the Irish; 'I'll Take you Home Again Kathleen'**♪26**, which, in spite of being written by an American for his wife, is known and revered as an Irish ballad, and 'Danny Boy'**♪27**, interpreted as the message from a mother to her son who is going off to war or leaving Ireland as part of the Irish diaspora. Both songs are very sentimental but both reach to the heart and demonstrate the longing for Ireland and its connection with its children. A mother's longing for her child must be one of the most compelling emotions we can imagine. How this mother longs for her son to return to her and how well she expresses her undying love.

~~~~~

Despite coming to terms with the secret, I will always have regrets. I wish I'd known my father as my father. I feel I would have had a better relationship with him if I'd known the truth. I also know that the time was not right for that to happen; we lived in a 'don't ask, don't tell' culture. Everything was based on discretion and on outward appearances; be discreet and no-one will bother about what you're doing and you won't be judged. I'm sad to think of my father's loneliness. I'm sad to remember my mother's struggles to bring us up; she was, effectively, a single mother raising four children. I feel sorry when I think about John's difficult life and the tangled emotions which pulled us in so many different directions. I would have loved to have known my Irish family; my grandparents and my aunts and uncles and the numerous cousins. That will never be. But I'm happy to have met Anita and I hope that together we can create a new connection with each other through our shared history.
~~~~~

This book has to end somewhere and although I continue to receive information regarding my ancestry, there is only so much I can relate in this story. I hope that my searching will continue and that, in due time, I'll complete the story for my children and my grandchildren.

---

[49] Bessbrook Mill has recently been given Listed Building status.
http://www.borderlandsireland.com/1800ad.htm

[50] The Troubles The duration of the Troubles is conventionally dated from the late 1960s and considered by many to have ended with the Belfast 'Good Friday' Agreement of 1998. There has been some sporadic violence since then.

[51] Sarcoidosis Despite having been described since the mid-nineteenth century or so, the underlying aetiology remains uncertain. It appears likely that a genetic susceptibility is combined with a triggering infection.
http://www.patient.co.uk/doctor/sarcoidosis

PART FOUR
'Resolution and Reconciliation'

Chapter Thirteen

'Where there is injury let me sow pardon.' 'While you are proclaiming peace with your lips, be careful to have it even more fully in your heart.'

Francis of Assisi

I sometimes wonder where I would be now if I'd taken a different path in my life. I've had many choices. I could have married Harry. I could have continued at Oxford and taken a degree. I could have had an affair with Francis. I could have fallen out entirely with my mother and not spoken to her again. I could have chosen to remain childless. I could have kept the secret and given it no further thought. All these options were possible but I didn't choose them. Sometimes, we are led by certain dreams or aspirations. Sometimes, we feel that choices are made for us due to circumstances outside our control. Whatever choices we make we can put them down to experience. 'Experience: that most brutal of teachers. But you learn, my God do you learn.' wrote C. S. Lewis. If everything happens for a reason, perhaps we should have no regrets. Yet, a life without regret seems a shallow reflection of reality. I certainly have my regrets. I have my doubts and disappointments. I wouldn't feel human if I didn't. I am grateful for all the opportunities life has given me and I hope, for the most part, I've been able to fulfill them.

I can see the sense, now, of earlier trials and challenges; for better or worse, they have made me strong. I can't change anything; it's all in the past. However, I have been able to change the way I think about them. I can make informed choices for the future based on what I know now. This is the most any of us can do. If we can develop the ability to rise above a situation, we can then begin to recognize it more clearly for what it is. Seeing something in this way enables the gathering of more information, analysis and understanding. It offers opportunities for change and a chance for action if this is felt to be necessary. There can be a lot of satisfaction in knowing that you have done everything you can possibly do to resolve a serious situation.

Counselling can facilitate this process of change and can offer support and encouragement whilst working through the stages of problem solving. Eventually, a more peaceful acceptance can be reached in the knowledge that you can do nothing further at this point in time. This realisation brings closure, as far as that is possible. In this way, I have experienced some kind of peace through understanding and forgiving. If a time arrives when further analysis needs to be done, I am prepared for the process by my past experiences. 'To understand all is to forgive all', said Voltaire. But, we never really understand everything.

We are all unique individuals searching for answers to our questions; searching for fulfillment of our hopes and contentment within ourselves. We learn as we go. We learn from every situation; every person communicates something to us. Perhaps this all stems from what we know as 'the human condition' but perhaps there is a higher meaning too. Happiness is not achieved through transitory material possessions; it doesn't arise from luxury holidays in beautiful places or from expensive gifts. Perhaps God has a dream for all of us; one which we must find for ourselves if we are to fulfill it. Dr Anthony Clare, the Irish psychiatrist, once said that happiness is:

'.... a conscious appreciation of the rightness of being'.

Feeling 'right' in ourselves; feeling content with our responses, our relationships, our being with others is a step towards happiness. For me, the most important of these conditions is the state of my relationship with others.

If we make a decision which we believe in our heart and mind to be right, we get a glow of satisfaction, a deeply felt assurance that we have done the right thing. If we can extend this to operate in a higher percentage of our interactions, then, I believe, we are somewhere near to fulfilling Clare's statement. It is never too late to take a different path, or make changes along the way. Determining the true meaning of your life is not easy but once you find the answers you will be eternally grateful. I believe you will be happier and more able to affirm, encourage, inspire and motivate yourself and others. If life is purposeful it is full of meaning and worthy of living.

Celia's secret has had a profound effect on my life. It's always been there in the background and has left its emotional legacy with me. I've tried not to let it dominate my life and if I hadn't been able to share it with Hannah and my husband, David, and other close friends, such as Katie, I think it would have done more psychological damage. It would have been so much better if my mother had told us together as a family. Then, I feel, we would have been able to move away from the negative fallout of the secret at a much earlier stage in our lives. One thing that is remarkable about my family is that none of us have repeated the pattern of marriage presented to us in childhood. We have all, thankfully, made successful marriages which, I hope, indicates that we have learned something from our parents' unhappy lives whether consciously or not.

~~~~~

In this memoir, I have tried to reach the central core of my understanding. I have looked for the things which have transformed me. Art, music, literature, the beauty of nature, all have the ability to take us outside ourselves, out of our ego-centredness and allow us to join with the soul of the artist, the composer, the writer, the creator. Something mysterious happens which lifts our spirit up above ourselves and into the realm of wonderment. That level of appreciation is so joyful that it offers us a taste of momentary happiness. If we want to recognise the complex and paradoxical nature of our relationships, the Transactional Analysis[52] of Berne's Parent, Adult and Child model may provide some degree of self-knowledge. I know it has helped me to understand myself and my interaction with others.

To be mature in acceptance of self, I must be prepared to accept and celebrate what I have achieved; my talents as well as my shortcomings; an overall tolerance and acceptance of who I am and what I have done. As well as self-acceptance and appreciation, our soul, hearts and minds need to learn to forgive and, in doing so, to accept the qualities and the shortcomings of others as we would our own. I never forget the advice of Arnold Bennett, 'It is well, when judgeing a friend, to remember that he is judgeing you with the same godlike and superior impartiality.'

A work of art challenges us to contemplate, to consider, to assess and to arrive at a judgement. Through that process, we experience a deeper relationship with the art form. A piece of artwork, whether it is a painting, a sculpture or a random display of graffiti makes demands on our attention. A song or symphony enters into our consciousness and seeks an emotional response. In this way we are touched by
~~~~~

something beautiful. Something of the spirit of the artist touches our soul. Perhaps we need to look at ourselves as works of art and spare time to allow these feelings to unfold and do their work within us; discernment is one of the most precious elements of the human intellect.

Sometimes, there are no definitive answers to problems. The more we reflect on them, the more we discover new perspectives and new solutions. The same thing seems to be true of art. We can look at a painting many times and continue to make new discoveries. We can gain greater insight into a story by re-reading it. We can appreciate a great piece of music more and more deeply by listening to it again and again. The more we read Shakespeare, the greater our understanding of his characters and themes and his interpretation of human nature. The more we study scripture, the greater our knowledge and identification with the word of God.

If we feel and identify the soul deep within us, we will understand our need to pay attention to it and accept its need for care. Take care of it and nourish it, just as we would nourish our body or stimulate our mind. If we see our soul in a religious context, we will feel drawn to attend a place where we can worship, meet with community, seek guidance through scripture, develop spiritually and become an example of Christianity, because our soul is imprinted with Christ. When something has caused suffering, we might hear the phrase 'What happened was for the good of his or her soul'. Maybe failure could be accepted as 'for the good of the soul' because failure is something we have to come to terms with, accept and overcome. We cannot fail without trying in the first place; failure is borne out of a positive initial attempt to succeed. Failure is not a negative thing if it teaches us lessons from which we can learn. I believe that no-one gains in experience without some significant failures.

As I look back, I realise that there has been no major cathartic moment when suddenly all my problems were solved. Everything we do leaves a trail behind us; Celia's secret left its trail. I'm sorry that Daniel was so upset when he heard that John was not his father, as he had believed him to be. He loved him as a father and has lived with that feeling all his life. I'm sorry that my mother did not tell her secret whilst she was alive. I can now see how her side of the story polarised my view of her situation and John's story polarised Daniel's view. Neither of us realised this at the time. We were open to different interpretations and made our judgements based on those interpretations. I'm sorry for many things left behind in the trail of my own actions, but, we can only act as we think right and then accept the consequences.

This story is only *my own limited* interpretation of the facts; I'm not saying that I know everything or that I know the meaning of life any better than anyone else. I've been exploring the themes in order to make sense of it all. If I can work out some of these questions in my lifetime, I stand a better chance of putting things right. I can attempt to repair relationships and experience the benefits arising from forgiveness. Not forgiving locks me into resentment and pain. Not forgiving is perpetuating my misery. I wasn't able to achieve this forgiveness during my mother's lifetime but I hope that I have succeeded beyond the grave. It's easier to forgive when time has passed and the pain has eased. One person's secret is another person's chaos; this was certainly the case in my life.

~~~~~
~~~~~

There were no photographs on display in my home, except one of my mother with her parents. The above photograph is the only picture I possess of my father with his complete family. My mother saw her secret as belonging to herself alone and she protected and defended it. No-one need know about it; no-one should know about it. Her little secret, closed and hidden away, allowed her to deny her situation and to present a totally different story to the outside world. She was used to making her own decisions and didn't feel the need to be answerable to anyone but herself.

Secrets can cause havoc in people's lives. I would ban them - but, of course, I can't. Do you remember the family circle that I made during one of my counselling exercises? My mother was on the edge of the drawing, the same size as the rest of the adults but her face was turning outwards. She was alone. I was surrounded by my husband and my children and other family members. They formed a ring around me. Facing towards me, they provided a wall of protection. John and Sam were absent from the drawing. I want to approach my mother now, I would like to see her smile and walk towards me. I will hug her and cry tears of regret and take her by the hand. I will lead her back into the family circle. I want her to know that she is forgiven and accepted. I want her to know that I seek her forgiveness. I will draw her close to her family and show her how much she is loved. I also want John and Sam to know that I don't blame them for their part in withholding the secret. I believe they were acting to protect themselves and the children; they were doing what they felt to be right. I don't think they had any idea that this mangling of relationships would have such a profound psychological and emotional impact as the years passed by. They made their judgements based on the knowledge they possessed at the time.

'All will be well, and all will be well, and all manner of things will be well.' wrote Julian of Norwich. There are Christians who believe this and who trust in God to the ultimate degree. In order to do this they have to commit themselves to God, surrender in humility and trust him, believing that, in the end, all will be well. I've always struggled with this sense of absolute trust. My little problems count for nothing in the vast universe. We are tiny specs on earth and look up to the billions of specs in the heavens. How can we understand such things? And yet, if we place ourselves in the hands of God, who is Love, we are told that anything is possible.

> 'Love is patient and kind; love does not envy or boast; it is not arrogant or rude. It does not insist on its own way; it is not irritable or resentful; it does not rejoice at wrongdoing, but rejoices with the truth. Love bears all things, believes all things, hopes all things, endures all things.'
>
> St Paul's 1st Letter to the Corinthians 13:4-7

God knows all things and forgives all things. It was only when I realised that I had done everything humanly possible that I placed my problem in God's hands and prayed for resolution.

In the film 'The Best Exotic Marigold Hotel', based on the novel 'These Foolish Things' by Deborah Moggach, the character Sonny Kapoor says, 'Everything will be alright in the end. If it's not alright it's because it's not yet the end.' He always says this with a beaming smile on his face and as a sign of reassurance that indeed all will be well in the end. I want to believe that he is right.

~~~~~

I have gained so much from writing this memoir. I have learnt about compassion and forgiveness and what it means to search for reconciliation with another human being. Uncountable millions of words have been written about Christ and his message. It's so easy to criticise others and to blame others for the difficulties in our own lives. When we develop understanding through knowledge, it is not difficult to recognise our own weaknesses, failures and distorted beliefs and it is a humbling experience. Humility is perhaps the greatest of all virtues and is essential to humanity. It seems to me that you cannot heal or be healed unless you experience the hurt from both sides and truly acknowledge your own failings.
~~~~~

Clearly, every generation affects the next. We all have a duty to remember this and to act so that the generation following us is not borne down by our acts or by our mistakes. If we are to set our children free, we must give them truth and emotional freedom as well as the physical freedom to live their lives and follow their dreams.

~~~~~

I am almost at the end of my story. As you will see, I have needed to draw on the inspiration and wisdom of many writers to communicate my message, hence the numerous quotations and references. I am not very wise in myself; I have tried to express my own ideas based on what I have read and what I have discovered.

> 'Who can ever learn the will of God?
> Human reason is not adequate for the task, and our philosophies tend to mislead us, because our mortal bodies weigh our souls down.
> The body is but a temporary structure, and a burden to the active mind.
> All we can do is make guesses about things on earth; we struggle to learn about things that are close to us.
> Who, then, can ever hope to understand heavenly things?
> No one has ever learned your will, unless you first gave him Wisdom, and sent your holy spirit down to him.
> In this way people on earth have been set on the right path and have learned what pleases you, and they have been kept safe by Wisdom.'

Book of Wisdom 9:13-18

~~~~~

The songs and music noted at the end of this book have also contributed a great deal to my emotional experiences and are a valuable source of recollection, enabling me to remember the way I was thinking and feeling at certain times in my life. The carols which we sang so long ago shaped my view and love of Christmas which I now re-live every year with my children and grandchildren. My education and upbringing set down the foundations of my life. Counselling has taught me that change is always possible.

The writing of this memoir has not only enabled me to reflect on and analyse my life story, it has also provided the process by which I and my sister have been able to divulge the secret to our brothers. In doing so, we came to the point when it could at last be revealed. I have freed myself of the burden of the secret. I hope I haven't forced that burden on others; that was not my intention. I hope the truth, even though uneasy, has met with a degree of acceptance that, in the long run, will be positive.

This is my memoir and I haven't tried to speak for anyone else. It has been an interesting exercise. It has helped me to review my judgements, to consider where I have laid the blame and to reassess my perspective as I look back over my life. I have tried to replace suffering and anger with forgiveness. I have communicated my love to my mother and to all those affected by my family situation. I have done everything in my power to understand the differing views of those involved and I have sought reconciliation from the deepest place in my heart. I have done all that it is possible to do; I can do no more. It has brought me a sense of closure and a peace that I did not have before. For this I am thankful.

~~~~~

Looking back and reflecting helps us to understand what has happened in our lives. Sometimes, it provides answers we would rather not hear. It does, however, satisfy our longing to know, to accept and
~~~~~

to forgive. We can then be free to live our lives facing forward. The writing of this memoir has enabled me to engage more closely with my own identity. There's a sense in which I feel refreshed and revitalized; my eyes can see more clearly now and my spirit feels free to explore wherever I want to go in the future. I will continue to learn about my Irish heritage and I feel comfortable with my history, free from judgement and recrimination.

With the love of my family anything is possible. I feel that many issues have been resolved and I know which strategies to use in the future. I continue to gain strength from my Catholic faith and from my belief in a higher power, a loving and reforming presence in my life. Reconciliation is possible; it brings peace and a new beginning. However, reconciliation is not the end; the little girl inside me is still searching for the man who stood beneath the lamp-post so long ago waiting for his packet of sandwiches. He didn't stay around long enough for me to get to know him.

~~~~~

52

Transactional Analysis was first developed by Canadian-born US psychiatrist Eric Berne in the late 1950s. It is described as an integrative theory because it has elements of psychoanalytic, humanist and cognitive approaches. Transactional Analysis has wide applications encompassing communications, management, personality, relationships and behavior and personal development. See Eric Berne's 1964 book 'Games People Play'.
~~~~~

Epilogue

More than a year has passed since our visit to Northern Ireland. I have kept in contact with Anita by email and telephone. Edward and I will visit in a few days' time and meet her family once more.

The redevelopment of Bessbrook's historic mill is being considered by town planners and developers. The plan is to transform the derelict army base and mill complex into a modern residential facility. It promises to deliver vital regeneration in a careful and sensitive manner and to rekindle the industrial heritage of the site and re-establish the mill's historic connection with Bessbrook village. The developers now await an improved economic climate before their plans can be fulfilled.

From the time it was built so long ago, the mill has provided work for many thousands of people and, originally, formed the key element of Richardson's model village. These proposals represent the first opportunity to bring the buildings back into beneficial use for the village. The Architect Director responsible for the project comments: 'After a varied and chequered past the proposed redevelopment of the site aims to reinstate the mill to its rightful place in the heart of the village.' The dominating presence of the mill will be brought into scale with the creation of tree-lined avenues and landscaped pedestrian squares. These will aim to create communities and spaces of more human scale. In addition, hard landscaped areas will form a large proportion of the site and will remain as usable parkland. It is the architects' intention to retain the site's heritage by reusing existing structures. This process gives hope for the future and will offer innovation and rejuvenation to Bessbrook.

~~~~~
~~~~~

♪ Catalogue of Music and Song ♪

All performances are available on: https://www.youtube.com/music at the time of publication.

Chapter 1

1. 'Now is the hour' Vera Lynn
https://www.youtube.com/watch?v=3-jz54Mf1Ok

Chapter 2

2. Bach's Toccata and Fugue in D minor Stephen Hough
http://www.youtube.com/watch?v=20RhLjJNcEg

3. 'Love me Tender' Elvis Presley
http://www.youtube.com/watch?v=-Y-bd3aDMGA

Chapter 3

4. 'What is Life to me without Thee?' Kathleen Ferrier - Orpheus and Eurydice by C W Gluck
http://www.youtube.com/watch?v=ypePP1ENcmw

Chapter 4

5. 'It Doesn't Matter Anymore' Buddy Holly
https://www.youtube.com/watch?v=KOTv9jY4X5E

6. 'Raining in my Heart' Buddy Holly Songwriters: Bouleaux Bryant, Felice Bryant
http://www.youtube.com/watch?v=WNf7Y7Z5Jq8

7. 'The Mountains of Mourne' Jim Bannigan
https://www.youtube.com/watch?v=kGp3kexsIg8

8. 'Let's Twist again like we did last Summer' Chubby Checker http://www.youtube.com/watch?v=VjQwfkQj6e4

9. 'Twist and Shout' The Beatles
http://www.youtube.com/watch?v=pVlr4g5-r18

10. **Beethoven Violin Concerto 3rd movement** Itzhak Perlman
https://www.youtube.com/watch?v=fh0eMXNSPKo
11. **Brahms - Violin Concerto in D major - II. Adagio**
Perlman/Giulini https://www.youtube.com/watch?v=v4s_laQS3Vo

Chapter 5

12. **Beethoven - Symphony No. 6 in F 'Pastoral' Op 68**
(V. Allegretto - Shepherds Hymn)
https://www.youtube.com/watch?v=Do3tL7oEAt8
13. **'For Unto us a Child is Born'** Handel's Messiah
From a recording of Handel's Messiah in the 1742 Dublin version, performed by the Dunedin Consort and Players under director John Butt. http://www.youtube.com/watch?v=GfZqZlUN1qE
14. **Pearl Fishers duet** Jussi Bjorling and Robert Merrill
http://www.youtube.com/watch?v=5PYt2HlBuyI

Chapter 6

15. **Mozart's 21st Piano Concerto** K 467 Andante
http://www.youtube.com/watch?v=UB1lXO31nVE
16. **'In Dreams'** Roy Orbison
http://www.youtube.com/watch?v=ZOTPKWNj0xU
17. **Tchaikovsky - Symphony No 6 'Pathétique' 4th Movement**
http://www.youtube.com/watch?v=3ebQYH6EpJ8
18. **Bruch's Violin Concerto Final Movement**
http://www.youtube.com/watch?v=-MjGpsy_vCU
19. **'And I love You so'** Nana Mouskouri Words and music by Don Mclean http://www.youtube.com/watch?v=6vhWhWvDrIQ

Chapter 7

20. **'You are the Sunshine of My Life'** Ani Curtis
http://www.youtube.com/watch?v=6qIIRM1FA0g
21. **'In the Morning' ('Tis the Morning of My Life)** Bee Gees Lulu https://www.youtube.com/watch?v=S_EGgiDjH2E
22. **'There Ain't no Cure for Love'** Leonard Cohen
https://www.youtube.com/watch?v=ksRl6yZSLDw

23. Mary Stuart's Prayer: Father in Heaven Above - Donizetti opera The Manchester Boys' Choir arr. Boustead 1986
http://www.youtube.com/watch?v=-1mdjx-qs6E&list=PL8597EF660196C4FD

Chapter 8

24. 'Sweet Heart of Jesus' Maureen Hegarty
(recorded on CD 'A Quiet Heart'
https://www.youtube.com/watch?v=9MdYg62EtD0

Chapter 11

25. The Rose' Bette Midler
http://www.youtube.com/watch?v=l3SVXz3TFr8

Chapter 12

26. 'I'll Take you Home Again Kathleen' Elvis Presley
https://www.youtube.com/watch?v=wFotS2PbV44
27. 'Danny Boy' Jackie Evancho
https://www.youtube.com/watch?v=8s_jleJFR_M